KIDNAP, HIJACK AND EXTORTION: THE RESPONSE

Also by Richard Clutterbuck

ACROSS THE RIVER (*as Richard Jocelyn*)
BRITAIN IN AGONY
CONFLICT AND VIOLENCE IN SINGAPORE AND MALAYSIA
GUERRILLAS AND TERRORISTS
INDUSTRIAL CONFLICT AND DEMOCRACY
KIDNAP AND RANSOM
LIVING WITH TERRORISM
PROTEST AND THE URBAN GUERRILLA
RIOT AND REVOLUTION IN SINGAPORE AND MALAYSIA
THE FUTURE OF POLITICAL VIOLENCE
THE LONG LONG WAR
THE MEDIA AND POLITICAL VIOLENCE

Kidnap, Hijack and Extortion: The Response

Richard Clutterbuck

Foreword by Sir Robert Mark

St. Martin's Press   New York

First published in the United States of America in 1987

Printed in Great Britain

ISBN 0-312-00906-2

Library of Congress Cataloging-in-Publication Data
Clutterbuck, Richard L.
Kidnap, hijack, and extortion.
Bibliography: p.
Includes index
1. Terrorism—Case studies. 2. Kidnapping—Case
studies. 3. Hijacking of aircraft—Case studies.
4. Extortion—Case studies. I. Title.
HV6431.C549 1987 364.1'54   87-4809
ISBN 0-312-00906-2

To my friends in Control Risks who don't know what it means to have a quiet life; who are prepared without notice to take the next flight to places facing the highest risks in the world, and to work there under intense pressure until the job is done; who have thereby saved many lives and helped the police catch dangerous criminals and terrorists who, but for that, would have deprived more people of their right to life and liberty.

Contents

Foreword
Sir Robert Mark, GBE, QPM

Eight years have passed since Richard Clutterbuck published his book *Kidnap and Ransom: The Response*. It was my privilege then to contribute a foreword and I do so again for two reasons, pleasure and obligation. The first book was an informative, workmanlike treatise on a subject of growing interest. It sold out, became difficult to obtain and was unlikely to be republished unless expanded and brought up to date. I found it particularly useful as a convenient reference book and have repeatedly urged the author to return to the subject, knowing well his impressive qualifications for the task. The result gives one pleasure, but perhaps more relevant, a sense of satisfaction that a book so well-informed and so useful should appear at a moment of such obvious need.

A number of books on terrorism have appeared in recent times. They cover a wide spectrum, geographically, historically and politically and will undoubtedly be of interest to the researcher. This book, however, is rather different. It reflects the author's experience as a senior army officer involved in counter-terrorist activities as the Chief Army Instructor at the Royal College of Defence Studies, as a Senior Lecturer in Politics at Exeter University and, most important of all, as a director of Control Risks Ltd, a British company which has in recent years probably had more actual experience of countering kidnap, ransom and extortion worldwide than any other organization, public or private. It is interesting that a company established in a country in which kidnap, ransom and extortion are comparatively rare should have acquired a worldwide reputation for countering that activity and should have gained the respect and confidence of law-enforcement agencies and governments to such a remarkable extent.

I must make it clear that I, too, have been a director of Control Risks Ltd since 1981 when the company accepted my invitation to help in countering a difficult problem of extortion in Australia. My continued association with it is a direct result of that experience and reflects my admiration for the motivation and dedication of its staff, many of whom are drawn from public service of one kind or another.

The author deals at length with kidnapping for political reasons and for extortion. The uninformed reader, particularly in mainland Britain, will be astonished by its frequency and extent. It emerges clearly that, for political kidnapping in particular, there is no likelihood of an effective response capable of universal application. The demands of the criminals can sometimes only be met by governments other than that of the country in which the victims are being held. One country's terrorist, it is often said, is another's freedom fighter. Add to that the natural unwillingness of any government to show weakness under pressure and the complexity of the problem becomes positively disheartening. A curious tendency by many governments to regard politically motivated crimes as less reprehensible than conventional wrongdoing affords the terrorist encouragement and occasionally even sanctuary. Sadly, the greatest strength of the political terrorist lies in the fragmentation and variable response of those authorities whose cooperation is necessary to counter it.

Simple extortion by kidnap, bombing, product contamination or threats may involve more than one government but does not impose quite the same pressures, at least on those responsible for countering it. The likelihood of defeating it or lessening its impact is considerable, as the book clearly shows. Moreover, it could be increased by wider knowledge of the problem.

The reader interested in countering political terrorism will learn a great deal from this book, but will not find it comforting. The threat will not go away. Criminal extortion, however, has been kept at a low level in Great Britain because, during the past 15 years, crimes of that kind have been dealt with very effectively. But they will remain a rarity only so long as the response to them remains a professional one, ensuring a low rate of success and a high prospect of arrest and conviction. The book will contribute to this prospect by its clear distillation of how the successful response has been achieved.

The likelihood of kidnap for extortion is created by an obvious ability to pay. Those who work for multinationals, banks, other major companies, wealthy familes, are all at risk in jurisdictions in which crime of this kind is common. Much can be done to prevent it, counter it or lessen its effect. The first requirement is to be well-enough informed to avoid being picked as a target and this applies to middle management and travelling representatives as much as to senior executives.

This book should find a place in the libraries of all commercial institutions with employees who work or travel overseas. They would be well advised to read it now rather than when faced with a crisis for which a management policy has never been contemplated.

I hope, too, that the book will be read by politicians and journalists. It will help both to avoid mistaken assumptions and impractical recommendations. Indeed, that may prove the most valuable of its several purposes.

Robert Mark

Preface

I first became involved in terrorism 40 years ago as a young man in Jerusalem, then again 30 years ago in Malaya. For the last 15 years I have been writing, broadcasting, lecturing and advising people about it – mainly police and businessmen – in the course of which I have visited about 25 countries facing terrorist problems. I have talked to many victims of kidnap, hijack and extortion, their families and colleagues, police, army and other security force officers, prison officers, diplomats, government officials, security consultants, businessmen and journalists. Most of these people have for obvious reasons preferred not to be quoted by name so I have attributed nothing unless I am quoting things they have said or written publicly.

Since 1977 I have been a non-executive director of Control Risks Ltd and this book is my own interpretation of their practical experience in advising many hundreds of clients all over the world on threat assessment and prevention, and in advising on the handling of 200 such crimes. Of the case studies which make up a major part of this book, CR were involved in some but not others and, though the book is based on their collective practical experience, CR's abiding principle of protecting client experience has been adhered to. I have only recorded names, places and events where these have been published in the press or elsewhere. CR's research department, headed by Sheila Latham, maintains records of most known cases worldwide, whether they were involved or not, and I am immensely grateful both to her and to the many others who have given up so much time for me. They are not, however, in any way responsible for what I have written.

For readers in a hurry or using the book for reference, I have tried to make each chapter as self-contained as possible within Part I (The Threat) and Part II (The Response). This has inevitably meant striking a balance between occasional repetition and cross-referencing. Within the framework of a few pages of Prologue and Conclusions, the reader who wants to refer quickly to, say, the Organization of a Kidnap or International Travel or Hostage Survival or Crisis Management should be able to do so, pursuing if he wishes any connected cross reference (e.g. to case studies) aided by the table of contents.

As in my previous books, I have faced the dilemma of deciding whether anything I say might help criminals or terrorists as well as their potential victims or the police. In reaching my decision I have taken account of the material already available to them in the bookshops in revolutionary manuals, etc. Before any major operation I know that they spend many hours, spread over weeks and months, in planning and preparation – they have all the time in the world and nothing else to do. On the other hand, their potential targets are usually busy people, with all too little time to study criminal and terrorist organizations, motivation, tactics and techniques, how to reduce the risk of being a target and how to handle a crisis if it occurs. If this book helps them to fill that gap it will have achieved its purpose.

March 1987   *Richard Clutterbuck*
                                                          Exeter

Abbreviations

Note: For foreign acronyms, and in other cases where it is judged to be more helpful to the reader, an English description (in parenthesis) is given instead of spelling out the words.

AD	(Direct Action) (left-wing movement in France).
ALF	Animal Liberation Front (UK).
ANC	African National Congress (South Africa).
ARM	Animal Rights Militia (UK).
ASU	Active Service Unit (IRA unit in Ireland and UK).
BR	(Red Brigades) (left-wing movement in Italy).
CCTV	Closed circuit television.
CMC	Crisis Management Committee.
CNG	(National Guerrilla Coordination) (group of revolutionary movements in Colombia).
CR	Control Risks.
CSPPA	(Committee in Solidarity with Arab and Middle Eastern Political Prisoners) (Arab/Iranian terrorist movement responsible for many bombings in France; a front organized by FARL, q.v.).
DEA	Drug Enforcement Agency (USA).
DNA	Deoxyribonucleic acids (molecules carrying hereditary instructions unique to each individual and detectable in the blood, skin fluids and saliva).
EGP	(Guerrilla Army of the Poor) (left-wing movement in Guatemala).
ELN	(National Liberation Army) (Castroite movement in Colombia).
EPL	(People's Liberation Army) (Maoist movement in Colombia).
ERP	(People's Revolution Army) (Trotskyist movement in Argentina; also Castroite movement in El Salvador).
ETA	(Basque terrorist movement in Spain).
FALN	(Armed Forces of National Liberation) (Puerto Rican nationalist movement in USA).
FAR	(Rebel Armed Forces) (Castroite movement in Guatemala).
FARL	(Lebanese Armed Revolutionary Factions) (Arab

	Christian–Marxist terrorist movement active in France and Lebanon, see also CSPPA).
FARN	(Armed Forces of National Resistance) (Castroíte movement in El Salvador).
FARC	(Armed Revolutionary Forces of Colombia) (pro-Soviet).
FMLN	(Farabundo Marti National Liberation Front) (guerrilla grouping to fight government in El Salvador).
GRAPO	(October First Anti-Fascist Resistance Group) (extreme Marxist movement in Spain).
IATA	International Air Transport Association.
IMT	Incident Management Team.
INF	Islamic National Front (Sudan).
INLA	Irish National Liberation Army (Northern Ireland).
IRA	Irish Republican Army (also PIRA).
KDP	Kurdish Democratic Party (in Iran, Iraq and Syria).
KSPI	Kurdish Socialist Party of Iraq (Kurdistan).
M19	(April 19 Movement) (left-wing movement in Colombia).
MNLF	Moro National Liberation Front (Muslim secessionist group in the Philippines).
MPLA	Party which forms government of Angola.
MRTA	(Tupac Amaru Revolutionary Movement) (Peru).
NORAID	Northern Aid (Irish–American group supporting IRA).
NPA	New People's Army (guerrilla wing of Communist Party of the Philippines).
OPEC	Organization of Petroleum Exporting Countries.
PIRA	Provisional Irish Republican Army (also IRA).
PUK	Patriotic Union of Kurdistan (left-wing grouping supported by Syria).
RAF	Red Army Faction (left-wing movement in West Germany).
RFF	Ricardo Franco Front (dissident FARC faction in Colombia).
RNM	(Mozambique National Resistance) (right-wing movement in Mozambique).
SAS	Special Air Service (provides British army anti-terrorist force).
SL	Sendero Luminoso (Shining Path) (ultra-Maoist movement in Peru).
SPLA	Sudan People's Liberation Army (black African resistance movement in Southern Sudan).

UNITA   (National Union for the Total Independence of Angola) (resistance movement in south-west half of Angola).

ZANU   Zimbabwe African National Union (party in power, based mainly on majority Shona tribe in the north).

ZAPU   Zimbabwe African People's Union (opposition party based mainly on minority Ndbele tribe in the south).

ZIPRA   Zimbabwe People's Revolutionary Army (guerrilla movement based on ZAPU).

Prologue

The largest known ransom, $60 million, was paid by the president of an Argentine firm, Bunge Born, for the release of his two sons kidnapped by political terrorists in 1974. The longest recorded kidnap was 1219 days stoically endured by William Niehous, kidnapped in Venezuela in 1976 and rescued by the police in 1979.

Few kidnap victims have been killed and many rescued or released without payment of ransom, or for a much reduced proportion of the original ransom demand. A number of kidnappers have been arrested, usually as a result of skilful negotiation in cooperation with the police, which has provided the time and information needed for detection and arrest.

In December 1983, Freddy Heineken, head of the Dutch brewing firm, and his chauffeur were kidnapped by a group of professional criminals. The corporation, his family and the police cooperated in three weeks of shrewd negotiation, enabling the police to monitor the payment of a ransom, rescue the hostages, arrest the kidnappers and recover nearly all the money.

In February 1981, Leon Don Richardson, head of a multinational firm based in Australia, was kidnapped while on a sales visit in Guatemala. His partner Tom Dundon, kept the business running while negotiating from Sydney and Mexico city. Richardson quickly detected that his kidnappers did not really intend to 'destroy their merchandise' by killing him and both he and Dundon managed to seize the initiative. After 100 days the kidnappers cut their losses and let him go when the police began to close in on them. No ransom was paid.

On 8 April 1986, Mrs Jennifer Guinness was kidnapped in Ireland. As a result of close cooperation between the family and the police and her own coolness, she was rescued unharmed and the kidnappers were arrested. No ransom was paid.

Brigadier General James Dozier, US army, was kidnapped by the Red Brigades in Italy in December 1981. Thanks to the Italian government's new policy of leniency to terrorists who give information, the hideout was discovered and he was rescued, leading to a further flow of information and the arrest of several hundred more terrorists.

There have been many other examples of successful rescue

operations resulting from negotiation providing the time and information required to mount them, notably the rescue of the passengers and crew of the Lufthansa aircraft hijacked to Mogadishu in 1977 and of the hostages in the Iranian Embassy in London in 1980.

Typical of a new kind of kidnap to strike at development in Third World countries was the kidnapping in May 1982 of two managers of the Atco corporation by Kurdish dissidents in Iraq. By skilful crisis management, the company, in cooperation with all the governments concerned, secured their release without payment or concessions.

Woolworths in Australia were plagued by bombs and various forms of extortion in 1980–81. They developed an effective crisis management organization which enabled them to continue trading while they cooperated with the police in securing the arrest and conviction of the extortioners. And a major oil company, with 10 bombs set to explode in one of its major installations unless it paid a large ransom, handled the crisis coolly and enabled the police to arrest all those involved.

Product contamination for extortion or to do malicious damage cost a Japanese confectionery company $24 million in sales in a month; the manufacturers of Tylenol in USA about $500 million; and a confectionery company in the UK £2.8 million ($4.2 million) in a few days. A multinational food corporation, however, handled such an extortion attempt with great skill, paying no ransom, losing virtually no sales or stock, and cooperating with the police in the arrest of the poisoners whose leader had scientific qualifications.

All of these are amongst the 60 cases, studied in Part III, which form the main basis of the analysis of the threat and the response to it in Parts I and II.

Computer fraud and drug-related crimes have grown alarmingly in recent years and now account for a significant share of the illegal money at large in many industrialized and developing countries. Abduction and extortion, though not comparable in scale, have remained continuously high since the late 1960s, though fashions rise and fall; they are likely to increase as technological developments make theft and robbery more difficult (see Chapter 1).

Politically motivated abduction, for publicity, political blackmail and ransom, takes many forms. Abduction of expatriate businessmen to drive out foreign investment and trade, and to disrupt economic development, has been endemic for over 15 years, and anti-development abductions for this purpose burgeoned in the early 1980s. International support for political terrorism and sometimes state sponsorship (e.g. of hijacking) is now a much-used tool of foreign policy. In guarding against and handling all these types of threat, it is important to detect who the perpetrators are, what are their motives and organization, and what are likely to be their tactics and techniques. That is the purpose of Part I of this book.

Part II deals with response, with risk management, prevention and crisis management. It examines the actual and potential restraints, legal and otherwise, under which this response must be conducted, and the contingency planning and crisis management organization on which success is likely to depend. It brings out the paramount need for cooperation with the police. Since this type of crime strikes suddenly and hard, and usually hits a target which has not been hit before, Part II also discusses where to turn for experienced advice, both to prepare for it and to handle it.

Negotiation is an art and the art lies in looking through the eyes of the adversary. The kidnapper and extortioner knows that his adversary aims to save, first, life and, secondly, financial loss. The political terrorist will ask for more than he hopes to get; he knows, for example, that few governments will now release convicted killers to kill again. His minimum aim may be publicity for his cause; and if he feels that this has been achieved, and the pressure is high, he may settle for that rather than lose everything.

The criminal extortioner's equation, however, is a financial one. He is less lavish with manpower because each member of the gang has to be paid or to have a share of the booty. Bully as he may, he will in fact be reluctant to destroy his bargaining lever (e.g. to kill his hostage or to blow the threat of publicity in a product extortion by allowing the poisoned product to reach a member of the public) before a ransom has been paid. His absolute minimum will be to cover the costs he has already committed to the operation and he will fight hard for that. But if skilled negotiation is coupled with relentless police investigation, he may cut his losses and settle for his minimum. He will continue negotiating so long as he believes that there will be eventual financial benefit from doing so. And it is negotiation which provides the time and the information which the police require to build up the pressure and, in the end, to arrest and convict the extortioner. The likelihood of being caught is the best deterrent.

Part I
The Threat

1 Sources and Forms of Attack

KIDNAP AND EXTORTION IN PERSPECTIVE

Kidnapping is amongst the most loathsome of crimes because the victims are held under suspended sentence of death, sometimes for months or years, at the whim of the kidnapper, either to extort money for himself or to impose a political aim on the public which he cannot accomplish by legitimate means.

Abduction is a crime as old as civilization – and no doubt older in its commonest forms – for amorous purposes or to take the victim away to a place where he or she could be used as a slave or maltreated with impunity. As soon as men began to live as communities, first as hunting tribes, then in agricultural villages and later in city states, they had a deep longing for security and the rule of law. The rule of law meant that leaders and hierarchies were given (or took unto themselves) the necessary powers to enforce it. Rivals or dissidents who wished to oust them learned very quickly that pressure could be put on the leader by abducting his son or daughter. The origin of the word 'kidnap' (nab a kid) was to seize a child. It could be used to extort money as well as political concessions and the seizure of princes and their dependants for hostages was regularly used for both purposes in Europe, North Africa and Asia Minor in Roman times and the Middle Ages, and no doubt also in the earlier civilizations in South Asia and China. So there is nothing new about criminal, political and state-sponsored kidnapping and extortion.

Such crimes include various forms of abduction and kidnap: hostage seizure including hijacking; contamination of food, drinks, pharmaceutical products, etc., and extortion by threat to do so; and extortion by bomb threats or threats of personal assault. These take their place in the spectrum of other kinds of criminal and political violence, including malicious damage to property by arson, bombing, and sabotage; malicious disruption of lawful activities by hoax calls, by interferences with the processing, storage and communication of data and by blocking access by violence or mass demonstrations; contamination or interruption of public utilities; contamination of consumer products; assassination; and personal attack.

3

TYPES OF ABDUCTION, EXTORTION AND INTIMIDATION

Abduction can be defined as the forcible and illegal carrying off or detention of a person for any purpose, criminal, political or domestic. Domestic abductions (e.g. by parents in custody disputes) or psychopathic abductions (i.e. for reasons other than extortionary or political aims) are outside the scope of this book.

Short-term abduction is a growing form of crime in Europe and in some Latin American countries. A common pattern is the seizure of an executive and/or his family to extort immediate handover of cash from the safe. The commonest targets are branch managers of banks, building societies, etc. The techniques and responses are discussed further in Chapters 5, 12 and 17.

Kidnapping is the abduction of a hostage or hostages to an unknown location to be held there for as long as may be necessary to extort concessions which may be financial or political and are usually considerably larger than those demanded in a short-term abduction. Kidnappings occur equally in urban and rural areas, though the hostage may be abducted in an urban area and held in a rural area or vice versa. Kidnapping and the response to it are discussed in Chapters 2 to 4, and Parts II and III.

Anti-development abduction, a recent variant, is the abduction of expatriate workers or industrial, mining or agricultural staff, usually from remote workplaces, by dissidents seeking recognition or publicity or wanting to put pressure on their own governments by disrupting development projects. This differs from other forms of kidnap, whether urban or rural, in that search and negotiation usually have to take place in countries, or areas of countries, which lack a developed infrastructure. Anti-development abduction, and the response to it, is discussed in Chapters 5, 11, 12 and 16.

Hostage-seizure and barricade differs from kidnap in that the victims are held in a known location, usually government premises or residences, and held there under threat of violence, not for criminal gain, but to extort political concessions such as release of prisoners (sometimes with ransom) the publication of revolutionary manifestos or, most commonly, to obtain worldwide media publicity for their cause. This is discussed in Chapters 2, 5, 7, 12 and 18.

Hijacking of aircraft, ships, trains, etc., is a form of hostage-seizure with similar aims. The threat is to the lives of the passengers and crew rather than to the transport vehicle itself. This is discussed in Chapters 2, 5, 7 and 18.

Product contamination is the malicious contamination of a consumer product, normally in such a way as to arouse fear of danger to life or health (e.g. contamination of food, drink, pharmaceuticals, toiletries or cosmetics). This may be done to harass, damage, intimidate or coerce the manufacturers or distributor, or to obtain publicity for a cause (e.g. animal rights). Though the damage to physical assets and profits may be very large indeed, the essence of the threat is to the lives and health of the consumers and it is this which is used to secure the concessions. It may take the form of **product extortion**, i.e. the contamination of a product, or the claim to have contaminated it, or the threat to do so, in order to extort money or other concessions. These are discussed in Chapters 2, 6, 10 to 12 and 19.

Bomb extortion and other forms of **extortion by threat** are related directly to violence, whether used against property or people. The extortion may occur before any action has been taken at all, i.e. by the threat that if the money or concession is not given, there *will* be an attack by arson, sabotage, bombing, contamination, disruption, personal attack, kidnapping or hijacking. There are many recorded cases, and no doubt many more unrecorded, of corporations or small operators (e.g. hotel and taxi owners) paying 'protection money' to avert such attacks. This is the prime source of funds for the IRA. In some countries the demands and sometimes the payments have reached seven-figure sums in dollars. These forms of extortion, and responses to them, are discussed in Chapters 2, 6, 12 and 19.

Personal attack, and **intimidation** of executives, staff and families by the threat of such attacks, are sometimes aimed at diplomatic and other foreign government personnel, but more often it has the aim of making it difficult for expatriate companies to continue operating through their subsidiaries and, if possible, to drive them out of the host country altogether. This has been very effective in some Latin American countries. It may be used increasingly by Islamic terrorists in the Middle East and Europe, by anti-US movements in NATO countries and by African terrorists in Southern Africa. A variant of this technique is the intimidation of locally-recruited nationals to deter them from working for an expatriate government or company. Methods of intimidation other than killing and wounding may be used: for example, harassment of families or malicious damage to cars or homes.

More insidious methods may be used to intimidate locally-recruited staff, not just to deter them from working for the expatriate organization but to suborn them into sabotage or the betrayal of confidential information. Such intimidation may be hard to detect because a staff member of apparently proven loyalty and integrity may be placed under intolerable pressure by threats to his family, to whom his loyalty will ultimately be greater. He may be persuaded that to reveal that he is under coercion at all could put them at risk.

CRIMINAL GANGS

The greatest threat of kidnap and abduction is from criminal gangs for monetary gain rather than from political terrorists. There is, however, some overlap. Individual political terrorists may be unable to resist the temptation to embezzle some of the proceeds of extortion and robbery (Eddie Gallagher, kidnapper of Dr Herrema, was accused of this by the IRA) and they sometimes hire professional abduction gangs or guards. On the other side, few Italian or American readers will need reminding of the political power wielded by the Mafia, built upon money as much as upon violence. Some smaller criminal kidnap gangs (e.g. in Colombia and the Philippines) have pretended to be political terrorists to give an impression of having wider backing and resources, in order to increase the pressure on the victim's family, to deter members of the public from giving information and to confuse the police.

The organization of criminal gangs ranges across a spectrum almost as wide as that between a multinational corporation and a corner shop. There are major international criminal networks (such as the Mafia); there are sophisticated independent criminal organizations, large or small, with or without international contacts and often led by rich 'respectable' men leading double lives; there are powerful strong-arm gangs, which terrorise their own localities and offer their skills for hire by bigger fish; and there are the loners, whose lack of resources and back-up may make them dangerously unpredictable.

POLITICAL TERRORISTS

The philosophy of terrorism was best expressed by an ancient Chinese philosopher over 2000 years ago: 'Kill one, frighten 10 000'. For every kidnap, hijack or assassination, huge resources are devoted to the protection of other potential targets, and the threat can drive corporations to abandon operations in countries where the risk is perceived to be high.

Though most kidnaps are by criminals, a percentage of them – substantial in Latin America, the Middle East and in some West European countries – comes from political terrorists, who may have a much wider range of aims: to extort money like the criminals; to extort political concessions such as release of convicted terrorists; to obtain publicity; to make the law unworkable by intimidating witnesses and juries; or to erode the economy of a target country by driving away trade and investment or frustrating development. These in turn may be intended to lead to destabilization of the existing society to the brink of chaos or civil war so that public confidence in the government and its law-enforcement agencies is eroded, possibly to such an extent that the people rally in desperation to whatever alternative seems to offer the best hope of averting a collapse of order and the means of livelihood for their families. The most likely of these alternatives is a right-wing takeover, usually military, as happened in Turkey in 1980; sometimes by a political or religious leader like Hitler or Khomeini; or by a highly organized revolutionary party which knows what it wants to do and has credibility, like the Bolsheviks in 1917, Castro in 1959 or the Sandinistas in 1978.

Of the more immediate dividends from political terrorist actions, their potential for attracting publicity is beyond compare. The kidnap and murder of 11 Israeli athletes at the 1972 Munich Olympics, with access to every television channel in the world, ensured that few people remained unaware of the Palestinian cause. The South Moluccans can fairly argue that the world neither knew nor cared about their cause until they seized two trainloads of Dutch hostages in 1975 and 1977. The kidnap and murder of Aldo Moro in 1978 forcibly focused the world's attention on the Italian Red Brigades. The fact that all of these incidents proved counter-productive in the long run has not reduced the short-term appeal of 'armed propaganda'. The holding of more than 50 American diplomatic hostages (endorsed by Khomeini) in Tehran in 1979–81, and of 39 American airline passengers in Beirut in 1985, all brought massive publicity and (in the eyes of their own supporters) prestige to Khomeini and the Shia Muslims.

Political blackmail by terrorism is equally effective, at least in the short term. Five convicted terrorists were released to save the life of

Peter Lorenz in Berlin in 1975, one of whom is known to have taken two more lives with her own hand at the OPEC kidnapping in Vienna a few months later. Virtually every convicted Palestinian hijacker has been freed, usually very soon, and often as a direct result of a further terrorist incident or the threat of one. And, rightly or not, the Arab world will always believe that some 700 Shia prisoners held by Israel were released as a result of the hijack of the American TWA aircraft to Beirut in June 1985.

Ransoms, too, can be of a size almost beyond comprehension; the largest on record ($60 million for the release of the Born brothers in Argentina in 1974) was extorted by a political terrorist movement – the Peronist Montoneros.

INTERNATIONAL EXPLOITATION AND SUPPORT

Since 1945, the fostering of guerrilla warfare or terrorism in other countries, including attacks on international travellers or visitors, has become the prevalent, and generally the most effective, means of the pursuit of foreign policy by violence, largely supplanting conventional military force (invasion and bombardment). Conventional wars such as the Korean, Indo–Pakistan, Arab–Israeli, Falklands and Iran–Iraq wars, have sometimes been bloody and technologically sophisticated, but have remained limited by the fear of escalation into nuclear war if both superpowers were to become directly involved. Sometimes terrorism and guerrilla war have escalated into conventional war (e.g. the invasion by North Vietnam of South Vietnam in 1972 and 1975, and subsequently of Laos and Kampuchea). More often however, the foreign powers concerned have tried to bring about changes of government in the target country by exploiting and supporting internal conflicts, overtly, or covertly. This method has succeeded frequently in sub-Saharan Africa and Latin America, sometimes in the Middle East, but less often in South and East Asia. Terrorism is also supported by foreign countries to drive other foreign influences out of areas in which they compete, e.g. Iran, Syria and Libya trying to drive out US influence from Lebanon and from the Islamic world generally.

These last examples could fairly be described as state-sponsored terrorism. In most other cases, however, sponsorship is too strong a word. The traditional Marxist philosophy (as practised by the USSR and, up to the 1970s, by China) is to exploit and support revolutionary terrorist movements which are self-generated by internal or regional tensions and rivalries. This support generally comprises arms, money, propaganda, intelligence and training (inside or outside the target country). The KGB maintains a lavish network for providing such support worldwide under the cover of diplomatic staffs, trade delegations, press bureaux, etc., but they do not normally use this network to take part in or direct actual operations. The Cuban intelligence service maintains a similar network in countries in which their involvement and interest makes this possible and they sometimes participate or advise more actively and overtly than the KGB does, especially in Latin America and Africa.

As well as covert or overt support from foreign governments, some terrorist organizations receive support from sympathetic non-government communities (e.g. amongst Palestinians in Arab countries for the Palestinian terrorists or amongst the Irish–American community for the IRA).

Popular sympathy for internal conflicts comes sometimes from a majority of the people where they are denied constitutional means of changing or influencing their government (especially in some African and Latin American countries); sometimes from a substantial minority (e.g. of up to 10 per cent of Basques for ETA and 10 per cent of the Northern Irish population for the IRA); and sometimes from only a minute proportion of the people (e.g. for terrorist movements of the extreme right and left in France, Germany and Italy).

For the expatriate conducting business in countries where such conflicts may affect him, it is important to assess where the politically violent movements stand in these two spectrums of foreign support and internal popular sympathy.

TECHNOLOGICAL DEVELOPMENTS

Technological developments, especially in the fields microelectronics, weapons, sights, surveillance and other security equipment, will affect target selection, terrorist tactics and techniques, and protection measures used against them.

Target selection

Target selection in the future by criminals and terrorists will be influenced by the growing interdependence of all kinds of administrative, industrial and commercial activities on a small number of key points concerned with data processing, storage (software) and communication. This will be to some extent mitigated by the use of more intelligent terminals and grid systems but these may do no more than limit the trend rather than reverse it. The spread of robotics will also make industry more vulnerable. In all these spheres, machines are less flexible and less adaptable than human beings and one key machine or communication channel seriously disrupted can be more damaging than putting even the most skilled staff member out of action.

On the other hand, rising standards of living and the magnification of events by the media make modern societies more susceptible to threats on the lives of human beings, the more so if those human beings are personally identified and pictured in the press and television. A corporation can write-off a material asset worth millions of dollars at its face value but if it is perceived to be callous about a single human life the effect on staff morale and its public image can be catastrophic – and in the long run even more expensive. The rapid expansion of public information direct to the home – through cable and satellite television and visual display units – makes the use of people as pawns in the criminal or terrorist game still more effective.

Technological progress and commercial competition also make the knowledge retained in a person's memory a fast-growing target for criminals (notably in industrial espionage) and political operators to exploit. The suborning, intimidation and coercion of key personnel – either personally or through their families – will become increasingly attractive. Moreover, as working hours decrease and electronic technology enables more people to work at home, their security will pass out of the hands of their employers in business or government for many more hours of the week, if not entirely.

The rapid replacement of cash by electronic credit transfer is having a marked influence on theft, robbery, fraud and extortion. Within a few years, even payment for a basket of groceries in cash will be rare, and so will the payment of wages in cash. This in turn will mean that the holding and movement of cash in tills, safes, vaults and security vans will rapidly decline. The most effective way (with high yield and low risk) of extracting money will be to apply pressure on an individual who has the means of initiating its electronic transfer and, in view of the relative ease with which such transfers can already be made across international borders, a sophisticated criminal or terrorist will have a good chance of receiving the money untraced. In 1985 the revolutionary M19 movement in Colombia succeeded in the fraudulent transfer of more than $12 million to a foreign bank to which they have access and which has never been traced.

Weapons

Development of weapons will also affect terrorist and counter-terrorist tactics. Trends are towards smaller weapons with higher rates of fire, greater accuracy and more sophisticated day and night sights. There is already a machine pistol which can be concealed in a briefcase, linked to a laser sight which will project an orange dot on to the target at the short ranges used by terrorists. This dot is unlikely to attract the attention of anyone but the firer who can then squeeze a trigger on the handle of the briefcase putting three rounds in one-eighth of a second through the dot without anyone else being aware of his having a gun. The potential of this weapon for assassination in, say a crowded airport lounge is obvious.

Hand-held guided-missiles with an effective range of more than two kilometres, capable of penetrating any armoured limousine of practicable weight, are already available in both NATO and Soviet armies. Given a firing point from which the moving target will be in view for about 12 seconds, a terrorist of reasonable competence, having brought his weapon in his car or on a mule, should have a good chance of a hit.

The bomb with a precisely-timed delay fuse, which can be set to fire at a particular minute several weeks in advance, uses the same technology as the time-selection system on the ordinary household video recorder. This was used in the IRA attempt to kill the British prime minister and her cabinet at the Grand Hotel, Brighton, in October 1984. Remote-control devices capable of initiating the firing mechanism of a bomb can equally easily be obtained from any shop selling radio-controlled model aircraft.

Radio-controlled firing is already used on the car and truck bombs driven to their targets by suicidal drivers. A likely development is radio-control of the driving of the vehicle itself, at least for its final approach, to avoid depleting the limited number of volunteers willing to commit suicide. The technology for this is already familiar in unmanned target aircraft, ships and vehicles, and in the remote-controlled bomb disposal vehicle used in Northern Ireland; but further development would be needed to drive vehicles fast through narrow streets, gates and barriers, especially through road-blocks with staggered bollards.

The use of nuclear, biological and chemical weapons by terrorists has been technically feasible for many years. Though there have been a number of hoax calls (over 60) none has been convincing enough to cause serious disruption. There are probably two main reasons why this technology has not been used by terrorists: first, because the organization and logistics are much more complicated than for guns and bombs, carrying greater risks of failure and of detection; secondly, because the political consequences of carrying out a threat of mass murder, if challenged, are so great that the bluff would probably be called. Though the stereotype 'mad anarchist' who cares nothing for consequences might, in theory, carry out the threat, he will, by his nature, be less likely to be able to overcome the logistic problems. In fact, a thinking terrorist will probably realize that a pistol pointed at the head of an identifiable human hostage has greater credibility and coercive value than a less personal threat of mass destruction.

Security equipment

Technological development of security equipment is clearly also having an effect on criminal and terrorist tactics and techniques. Perimeter security and surveillance, alarm systems, access control and identification have improved and will continue to do so. The most urgent need for research in this field is to detect impersonation – i.e. to prove that the person presenting or inserting an identification card or card key is the person to whom it was issued. The best hope lies in instant matching of digital data on the card with such personal characteristics as finger-prints, including DNA 'finger-printing' voice-prints, the dynamics of the signature, eyeball retina reading or a group of precise facial measurements. If the threat becomes more intense, companies will make fuller use of the security technology available. The psychological or political restraints (e.g. on the erosion of civil liberties or staff morale) are likely to prove greater than the limitations of technololgy and expense.

Detection of weapons and bombs at present depends largely on the presence of metal or explosive vapour, but the continuing development of plastic weapons and firing mechanisms and the hermetic sealing of explosives can currently defeat both methods of detection. The impetus of the threat may stimulate research to solve these problems, and legislation for registration of weapons and tagging of explosives may be tightened in some countries.

Security of data processing, storage and communication is already a lively area of competitive development because of the enormous scope for fraud presented by the galloping development and use of microelectronics. Despite tighter password control, monitoring, burst transmissions and fibre-optics, the growing mass and centralization of data and its communication have so far given the criminal and fraudster the edge in this competition, but this in itself may stimulate the development of better defences.

2 The Growth of Kidnap and Extortion

COST EFFECTIVENESS: HIGH YIELD, LOW RISK

Almost all of the factors discussed in Chapter 1 have contributed to a growth in the crimes of kidnap and extortion of all kinds, for political or pecuniary gain. This growth has been a part of two other trends: a general growth of violent crime; and a general growth in political violence since 1968. There have been about 2500 recorded kidnaps since 1976 and there have undoubtedly been many more which were never reported.

The growth in violent crime is a recognizable and paradoxical phenomenon linked to growing affluence. The growth in political violence seems to have its roots in three world events of 1967–68: Arab exasperation with the loss of their last areas of Palestine in the 1967 war; the exasperation of Latin American revolutionaries with the failure of rural guerrilla activities epitomised by Che Guevara's failure and death in Bolivia in 1967; and the student revolts in the USA against the war in Vietnam which spread like a forest fire to students worldwide, especially in Europe in 1968. This gave rise to a plethora of Palestinian, Latin American and European terrorist movements. More recently the growth has been accelerated by the emergence of Islamic fundamentalism, emanating from Libya and Iran.

The increasing expression of this violence in the form of hostage-seizure and extortion, including kidnap, hijack and product contamination, has occurred because these techniques have proved most cost-effective in achieving their aims.

DIPLOMATIC KIDNAPPINGS 1968–73

The explosion in kidnapping began in January 1968 with a rash of abductions and murders of diplomats by left-wing political groups in Latin America – making the switch from rural to urban guerrilla techniques following the death of Che Guevara in Bolivia. Most of the victims were US ambassadors or officials with diplomatic status. In Guatemala on 16 January 1968, two US military advisers were shot

14

dead and, on 28 August, the US ambassador himself was killed – all in kidnap attempts. On 31 March 1970, the West German ambassador, Count von Spreti, was kidnapped and, when the Guatemalan government refused the kidnappers' demand to release prisoners, he was murdered on 4 April. The effect of this was a backlash, the liberal President Mendez being replaced by the right-wing Colonel Arana Osorio.

Meanwhile in Brazil, four diplomatic kidnappings occurred between September 1969 and January 1971, of the US ambassador, the Japanese consul-general in Sao Paulo, the US consul-general in Porto Allegro and, finally, the Swiss ambassador. The Brazilian government secured their release by releasing in turn 15, 5, 40 and 70 prisoners into exile. Further escalation was widely predicted, but the government was in fact playing for time, conscious of what was happening in Guatemala and, when the time was ripe, they too cracked down ruthlessly on the terrorists and the kidnapping ceased abruptly.

A similar pattern emerged in 1968–71 in Uruguay, where the Tupamaros began by kidnapping a close friend of the president and then, simultaneously on 31 July 1970, the Brazilian consul and two US officials, one of whom (Dan Mitrione) was murdered. A week later another US official was kidnapped and then, on 8 January 1971, the British ambassador, Sir Geoffrey Jackson who was held for eight months, amid considerable publicity orchestrated by the Tupamaros, which rebounded on them. Public revulsion at the murder of Mitrione (father of nine children) and admiration for the dignity and courage of Jackson, led to a strong swing to the right in the Uruguayan election three months after Jackson's release, resulting in the return of a president with a mandate to suppress terrorism and wide powers for the military. The military later supplanted the president, with a suspension of democracy for the next 12 years in what had traditionally been the most liberal country in Latin America.

Thus, in Guatemala, Brazil and Uruguay, these diplomatic kidnappings achieved virtually nothing apart from the release of 130 Brazilian prisoners into exile; they resulted in a right-wing backlash in all three countries, echoed in many other Latin American countries, often helped by government connivance with right-wing guerrilla groups. Canada, Mexico and Turkey also had their share of political kidnappings during these years all of which (excepting one in Mexico) were handled firmly with no concessions.

Meanwhile the Palestinians, reflecting their own frustrations with their inability to get into Israel after losing Sinai and the West Bank in the 1967 war, started their campaign to sieze the world's attention by international terrorism. From 1968–72 they concentrated on hijacking and hostage-seizure, including the dramatic triple hijack to Dawson's Field in Jordan in 1970 (initially with 400 passengers held as hostages), and the abduction and murder of 11 Israeli athletes at the Munich Olympics in 1972. In March 1973, eight Palestinian terrorists seized the Saudi Arabian Embassy in Khartoum, taking one Belgian and two US diplomats as hostages, murdering them in cold blood when the governments concerned refused to agree to their demands. They then surrendered and were tried and imprisoned by the Sudanese, but were in fact, released about a year later. Whether this was a secret agreement in the surrender terms or whether the Sudanese government feared retribution if they were not released is not known.

There was widespread revulsion with the cold-bloodedness of these murders of defenceless hostages, even in the Arab countries to whom the odium attached itself because of their sympathy with the Palestinians. Several of the more moderate Palestinian leaders disowned such activities – as they still do, though with little effect, 15 years later.

During the years 1968–73, some 50 diplomats had been kidnapped and several murdered, mainly, as described, in Latin America. Generally, however, the feeling by 1973 was that political kidnapping had proved to be a weapon which tended to backfire, and governments were learning to stand firm against it.

CHANGING PATTERN OF ATTACKS ON DIPLOMATIC TARGETS

In fact, as the statistics in Tables 2.1 and 2.2 indicate, the peak of diplomatic kidnappings was in 1970, mainly in Latin America. Thereafter the terrorist groups realized that kidnapping of businessmen for ransom was a more cost-effective technique and since 1973, year by year, more businessmen have been kidnapped than diplomats or other government officials. Meanwhile, however, bombing and assassination attempts against diplomatic targets continued to rise.

In 1979–81 there was a brief but sharp surge in the fashion of seizing embassies with diplomatic hostages (see Table 2.3). The seizure of the US Embassy in Tehran with more than 50 hostages of diplomatic status was the most spectacular example and it was at once condoned by the

Table 2.1 International Terrorist Incidents Against Foreign Diplomats, January 1968 to June 1981

	1968	1969	1970	1971	1972	1973	1974	1975	1976	1977	1978	1979	1980	Jan–June 1981	Total	Percent
Kidnapping	1	3	30	16	4	8	5	12	6	4	12	8	4	7	120	4.5
Hostage barricade	1	0	4	1	3	7	7	9	3	6	15	9	25	13	103	3.8
Incendiaries	12	20	31	14	15	16	17	16	28	41	44	14	20	7	295	11.0
Letter bombs	0	1	3	1	64	20	8	1	2	6	8	5	3	2	124	4.6
Other bombs	51	33	64	56	37	42	67	54	60	45	60	82	100	33	784	29.2
Assassination	2	6	10	8	3	6	5	6	16	13	12	17	29	12	145	5.4
Armed attack	0	4	3	3	8	4	7	8	6	8	9	14	33	18	125	4.6
Sniping	2	2	5	3	4	3	1	7	13	6	10	24	20	8	108	4.0
Theft, break-in	0	2	11	6	2	1	1	3	1	1	2	1	12	4	47	1.8
Conspiracy	0	0	4	2	0	4	4	3	4	4	9	2	9	6	51	1.9
Threat	11	10	45	39	67	75	17	16	41	31	98	64	97	34	645	24.0
Hoax	0	0	2	0	3	0	0	0	1	0	0	3	42	36	84	3.1
Other	0	0	1	4	3	1	2	4	3	2	2	9	15	11	57	2.1
Total	80	81	213	153	210	187	141	139	184	167	281	252	409	191	2688	100
Percent	3.0	3.0	7.9	5.7	7.8	7.0	5.2	5.2	6.8	6.2	10.5	9.4	15.2	7.1	100	

SOURCE: US State Department, *Terrorist Attacks Against Diplomats* (Washington DC, December 1981).

Table 2.2 Locations of Terrorist Attacks on Foreign Diplomats, January 1968 to June 1981

	North America	Latin America	West Europe	East Europe	Africa	Middle East	Asia	Pacific	Other	Total	Percent
Kidnapping	2	59	15	0	13	21	8	0	2	120	4.5
Hostage barricade	5	49	23	2	1	19	3	0	1	103	3.8
Incendiaries	43	55	122	3	5	30	24	5	8	295	11.0
Letter bombs	6	10	92	0	4	6	3	0	3	124	4.6
Other bombs	117	209	225	11	8	154	49	8	3	784	29.2
Assassination	10	23	51	2	4	40	13	1	1	145	5.4
Armed attacks	1	33	19	0	9	53	9	0	1	125	4.6
Sniping	15	54	5	1	0	25	7	1	0	108	4.0
Theft, break-in	2	20	9	1	7	5	3	0	0	47	1.8
Conspiracy	6	11	12	0	1	11	7	0	3	51	1.9
Threat	71	166	171	28	22	107	52	25	3	645	24.0
Hoax	39	12	9	2	2	7	11	1	1	84	3.1
Other	13	8	17	2	4	8	5	0	0	57	2.1
Total	330	709	770	52	80	486	194	41	26	2688	100
Percent	12.3	26.4	28.6	1.9	3.0	18.1	7.2	1.5	1.0	100	

SOURCE: US State Department, *Terrorist Attacks Against Diplomats* (Washington DC, December 1981).

Table 2.3 Embassy Seizures, 1979–81

	Embassy seizures	Number of ambassadors included	Total killed
1979			
Latin America	18	4	—
Europe	8	1	—
Elsewhere	9	2	3
Total	35	7	3
1980			
Latin America	20	21	45
Europe	15	1	7
Elsewhere	7	—	3
Total	42	22	55
1981			
Latin America	8	1	—
Europe	12	2	1
Elsewhere	5	—	—
Total	25	3	1

head of state, Khomeini who thereafter used his army and police force to sustain the detention of the hostages for 444 days. By contrast, Khomeini's own embassy in London was seized by anti-Khomeini dissidents in April 1980 and the British used their army and police to contain the siege and rescue the hostages.

The aim of these embassy seizures was publicity and this was undoubtedly achieved, but it tended to backfire. Moreover, except in very few cases (e.g. the seizure of the Dominican Embassy by M19 terrorists in Bogota in 1980 as described in Part III), the terrorists ended up in custody. The fashion therefore declined as rapidly as it had grown and since 1982 the seizure of embassies has been rare though bomb attacks on them (e.g. in Beirut in 1983) have become more violent than ever.

HIJACKING

Hijacking is a form of hostage seizure in which the aircraft is a mobile extension of the urban environment which is considerably more vulnerable to the threat of destruction than a static building; it is also a more hazardous target for a rescue operation and, if the hijackers suspect that a rescue is being planned, they may force the aircraft to fly somewhere else.

From 1945–52, hijacking was used mainly as a means of escape for refugees from Stalin's Eastern Europe and, in the 1960s, to and from Cuba. In 1968 – in parallel with political kidnapping – political hijacking suddenly exploded on to the world reaching a peak of 91 in 1969, no less than 63 of them to Castro's Cuba. From 1968–72 there was also a steady stream of Palestinian hijacks.

In January 1973, after two years of experimenting, with limited success, with armed guards in aircraft ('skymarshals') the USA pioneered the 100 per cent search of passengers and baggage at the boarding gates. This had a quite remarkable effect and was rapidly copied by most other airports in the world. Since then the rate of hijacks – despite some spectacular individual cases – has been kept

Table 2.4 Aircraft Hijacking

1968	38	
1969	91	80% achieved aim (40 to fly to Cuba)
1970	88	
1971	65	Armed skymarshals reduced success rate to 40%
1972	75	
1973	35	US introduced 100% search at boarding gates, 5 Jan. 1973*
1974	33	
1975	31	
1976	25	
1977	35	
1978	31	
1979	28	
1980	33	
1981	29	
1982	18	
1983	23	
1984	17	
1985	16	
1986	19	

* More than 2000 guns have been taken from would-be passengers at US airports every year since January 1973.
SOURCE: IATA.

down to an average of less than 30 a year, and under 20 since 1982 (see Table 2.4).

Nevertheless, there have been, in all, more than 700 hijacks since 1968. Though the number in 1985 was down to 16, the lowest for 18 years, the results in that year were both spectacular and bloody; the hijack of TWA flight 847 to Beirut in June 1985 dominated the world's headlines, and 68 people were killed in hijacks during the year. Fifty-seven of these died in a single incident in Malta in November when, after the hijackers had shot eight passengers (killing two) in cold blood, the aircraft caught fire during a rescue operation by Egyptian commandoes (see Chapter 18). Both of these, and the great majority of all the hijacks, were carried out by Arabs.

Piracy at sea, which may take the form of hijacking a ship, or armed robbery, rape and murder, has also been showing an alarming increase, especially in South-east Asian waters where the Vietnamese boat people have, since 1975, offered easy pickings for pirates (see Chapter 3). In a book published in 1985, *Piracy Today*, Captain R. G. Villar records some 400 cases of piracy in 1980–84 and believes that there may be as many more unreported. Most attacks now occur when the ship is close to shore or in harbour, in the waters of Third World countries which lack resources to combat them. Hijacking of large passenger ships is rare and seldom successful, e.g. of the *Santa Maria* off Brazil in 1961 and the *Achille Lauro* off Egypt in 1985 (see Chapter 18). There were, however, a total of 47 recorded terrorist attacks on ships during 1975–85, 8 of them hijacks, and 11 seagoing ships were destroyed.*

KIDNAP AND EXTORTION IN THE BUSINESS WORLD

The decline in diplomatic kidnappings after 1973 was matched by a growth in the kidnapping of businessmen for ransom which proved extremely lucrative for criminal gangs, especially in Italy, and more cost-effective than diplomatic kidnappings for political movements in Latin America, where the new fashion was initiated by the two very large left-wing terrorist movements in Argentina, the ERP and the Montoneros. The ERP's first kidnap was on 23 May 1971, of an executive of the Swift Meat Packing Company, Stanley Sylvester, who was also the honorary British consul. From the start, both movements

* 'Piracy', in *Navy International* (March 1986) pp. 181–2.

selected executives from multinational companies as their victims, with the dual aim of driving the corporations out of the country and of obtaining money to finance their operations. During the years 1971–74, the ERP extracted $30 million in ransoms and the Montoneros did even better, with $240 million before they were suppressed after the military coup in 1976; $60 million of this was in a single ransom for the Born brothers (see Chapter 14).

By 1977 kidnapping for ransom had reached an horrific level, especially in Italy. Table 2.5 shows the major kidnaps recorded in the world from 1977–86. The statistics exclude the large number of domestic kidnaps and short-term abductions, mainly for small ransoms, and there have undoubtedly been other major kidnaps which were kept secret by all those concerned. Of the recorded major kidnaps in 1977–80 it will be noted that less than 5 per cent were politically motivated, over 95 per cent being for criminal pecuniary gain. Since then, the proportion of political kidnaps has risen slightly but has still averaged only around 10 per cent, distorted by a sudden surge of political kidnaps in Lebanon and Peru in 1985 when the proportion was 20 per cent. It will be seen that the total number of major kidnaps grew from an average of 173 per year in 1977–81 to almost double at 323 per year in 1982–85, largely accounted for by the dramatic growth of criminal kidnappings in Colombia.

Parallel with this there has been a growth in almost every other kind of extortion. Short-term abductions doubled from an average of 12.5 in 1971–81 to over 25 per year in 1982–85. Anti-development abductions (see Chapters 5 and 16) were a phenomenon virtually unknown before 1980, since when there have been 66 recorded cases (some by large guerrilla armies like UNITA in Angola and others by small independent groups in remote areas of central Africa), involving 495 hostages.

Extortion by bombing or other threats have increased two and a half times from 26 per year in 1979–81 to 65 per year in 1982–85. Recorded cases of extortion by product contamination have also increased more than three-fold from 8 per year in 1979–82 to 27 per year in 1982–85, and there are almost certainly a much larger number of unreported cases (see Chapter 6). Of the recorded cases, most have occurred in Germany, the Netherlands, Spain, UK, USA and Australia.

The rise in long-term kidnap for ransom, both in numbers and scale of demand has, however, been the most dramatic. In 1971, the sudden burgeoning in the kidnapping of bankers and their families in the USA and of expatriate executives in Argentina (as described above) led to a

Table 2.5 Recorded Major Kidnaps, 1977–86

	1977	1978	1979	1980	1981	1982	1983	1984	1985	1986	Total 1977–86
Colombia	56	83	5	21	59	148	167	237	136	99	1011
Italy	78	46	75	42	46	50	42	22	14	18	433
Guatemala	5	2	13	24	22	40	39	14	—	2	161
Peru	—	—	—	—	—	—	4	4	66	62	136
El Salvador	5	15	16	21	7	6	4	5	4	2	85
Lebanon	—	—	—	1	1	6	3	12	39	19	81
Spain	2	6	10	6	9	7	5	6	3	6	60
Philippines	—	5	5	2	4	2	—	1	9	20	48
USA	5	9	9	4	—	2	7	6	1	1	44
Argentina	16	4	3	2	2	—	1	2	10	3	43
West Germany	4	3	2	4	11	8	5	2	1	—	40
Venezuela	2	—	1	—	1	6	6	2	4	7	29
Iraq	—	—	—	—	5	13	2	3	4	—	27
France	4	2	1	9	1	1	1	3	—	1	23
UK	—	2	—	4	3	2	6	2	2	2	23
Mexico	6	3	1	2	1	1	1	1	4	1	21
Other countries	12	9	9	7	11	16	27	46	33	33	203
Total	195	189	150	149	183	308	320	368	330	276	2468
Political kidnaps	7	8	7	2	18	28	34	43	60	28	235
Percentage of total	3.6	4.2	4.7	1.3	9.8	9.1	10.6	11.7	18.2	10.1	9.5

SOURCE: Control Risks Ltd.

rapid growth in kidnap and ransom insurance by Lloyd's of London; premium income rose from $150 000 in 1970 to $70 million in 1976, of which $50 million was placed with Lloyd's. Thereafter, the totals of ransom payments varied as certain countries took effective measures to curb kidnapping, e.g. in Argentina where there was a military coup in 1976, and in Italy where the kidnap and murder of Aldo Moro in 1978 led to the introduction of an effective package of laws in 1979 which gave greater powers to the police and intelligence services. These successes, however, have been balanced by growths in the crime elsewhere. Recorded ransom payments in Colombia, for example, have increased five-fold from less than $3 million per year in 1977–81 to more than $15 million per year in the next three years reaching a peak of over $21 million in 1984.

The changes arising from the electronics revolution and other technological development (see Chapter 1) suggest that this increase in crimes of kidnap and extortion will continue. Changes in society and life-style, in the flow of money (electronic transfer, less cash), in scope for instant and dramatic publicity, in public attitudes to violence, improved physical security, and more efficient access control and identification, will all contribute to this further growth in extorting both money and political demands by the threat of damage and disruption – but most of all by the threat to human life.

3 Kidnap and Extortion Around the World

THE VARYING PATTERN

The patterns of criminal and political kidnap and extortion vary greatly from country to country and from year to year, though trends can be discerned and analysed. Of the three centres of greatest political turmoil in the world – Latin America, southern Africa and the Middle East – only in one (Latin America) has kidnap and extortion been a major ingredient of this turmoil. Colombia has, for several years, had the highest kidnap rate in the world, followed (a long way behind) by Guatemala and Italy, but in 1985–86 it looked as if Peru might overtake all of them. In Latin America a high proportion of kidnaps have in the past been politically motivated, though the trend is now towards more of a criminal motivation. In Italy the great majority of kidnaps have always been by criminal gangs and of Italians rather than expatriate businessmen. Other forms of extortion, notably product extortion, have occurred predominantly in the industrial countries of Western Europe, and in the USA, Australia and Japan.

In politically-inspired international terrorism, Islamic fanaticism of various kinds has probably outstripped Marxism and anti-capitalism as the prime source of motivation, except in Latin America.

In political kidnappings the trend is away from politicians and government officials towards Western businessmen as victims. The risk to expatriate workers on development projects in Third World countries (usually to embarrass and frustrate their own governments' development plans) and to journalists have also increased.

WESTERN EUROPE AND TURKEY

Western Europe has long been plagued by political terrorism and violent crime. Italy has been the worst hit, by both right- and left-wing terrorists and by large and small criminal gangs, who specialize in kidnap and ransom. Spain, UK and France, with their Basque, Northern Irish and Corsican secessionists, have also experienced much political violence, including considerable kidnapping, especially in

Spain. The 'anti-NATO alliance' of German, French and Belgian terrorists, announced in 1985, focused for its first year on the bombing of defence targets and murder of people involved in the defence industry rather than kidnapping or political blackmail. Turkey, despite an horrific scale of political violence before the military coup in 1980, has experienced little kidnapping or extortion. The UK, Germany and the Netherlands have been the countries worst hit by product contamination by criminal extortioners and animal rights activists.

Italy

In Italy the rate of kidnapping, though still high, has been substantially cut since 1980 by more efficient police and intelligence work backed by legislation. These have included measures aimed, for example, at curbing the intimidation of witnesses and juries, facilitating rapid tapping of telephones in the event of kidnap and offering leniency to 'repentant' terrorists or criminals willing to give information to the police or evidence for the prosecution. Criminal kidnappings, however, remain higher than anywhere else in Europe and there are probably many which go unreported due to fear of the criminal gangs. Kidnapping, in fact has been an established and lucrative industry in Italy for many years.

The criminal gangs, large and small, are frequently part of, or linked with, the major criminal networks – the Mafia, Camorra (based in Naples) and 'Ndrangheta (based in Calabria). These gangs are highly organized, benefiting from their networks and being well funded, as is proved by their ability to hold their victims undetected for long periods (the average has been 77 days). Another independent group are the Sardinians, of whom some 18 000 settled during the 1960s in depopulated farms in Tuscany, some bringing their customs and techniques of kidnapping with them. They began operating around Florence and Pisa, treating their hostages barbarically and often killing them after receiving a ransom. This engendered hostility as well as fear and the police, acting on information, were able to break up several gangs in the late 1970s. Since 1980 they have turned to more sophisticated methods.

Nearly all the victims of Italian criminal gangs are Italians. In the islands and in Calabria, these are often the children of relatively small farmers, and it has been the custom for their village neighbours to rally round to help raise the ransom money, but this has been in the range of tens of thousands rather than millions of dollars. In recent years the gangs, even those remaining in their traditional bases, have established representatives in the prosperous northern cities, where wealthy businessmen or their families are kidnapped and then taken south to be held more securely in the heartlands during negotiation for ransoms running into millions. Examples of these types of kidnapping are described in Chapter 15.

The kidnapping of expatriate businessmen or officials in Italy remains rare. Exceptions include the kidnapping of the British businessman, Rolf Schild, and his family by a gang in Sardinia in 1979 and of US Brigadier-General Dozier by the Red Brigades in Verona in December 1981 (see Chapter 15). Resulting partly from the police and intelligence measures introduced in the late 1970s, and particularly from the successful application of these measures in 1982–83 following the kidnap and rescue of General Dozier, political kidnapping in Italy had largely ceased by 1984 – but criminal kidnap continues.

Spain

In Spain, by contrast, the majority of kidnappings have been politically motivated and carried out by various factions of the Basque separatist movement, ETA, who have taken about 40 hostages since the 1960s. Most of these have been prominent men in public life or local businessmen or their families. Ransom demands (for ETA funds) have been as high as $10 million and a payment of $2.5 million has been recorded. Thus far, foreign businessmen have not been targeted.

Another aspect of ETA operations in the Basque country is closely related to kidnap and ransom: the extortion of money or other concessions by the threat of kidnap or bombing, i.e. as protection money. There have also been examples, on occasions, of the anti-development abduction in which kidnap, murder and bombing have been used to force the abandonment of economic development projects. Bombing and assassination (though rarely abduction so far) have also been used to disrupt the tourist industry and deter visitors going to Spanish holiday areas. In view of the economic value of tourism to Spain this has, not surprisingly, made ETA extremely unpopular in Spain as a whole including their own Basque country. Opinion polls in 1985–86 suggested that sympathy for ETA may have fallen from 10 per cent to as low as 2 per cent of the Basque people, but the General Election in June 1986 suggested that it had risen again.

Ireland

In Ireland, North and South, kidnapping and short-term abduction have been regular tactics of the Provisional Irish Republican Army (PIRA) and the Irish National Liberation Army (INLA) to extort money to finance their campaigns. In 1981, PIRA allegedly extorted $500 000 by kidnapping Ben Dunne of Dunnes stores chain, and $2 million in August 1983 by kidnapping the chairman of another stores chain, Don Tidey, from his home in County Wicklow in the Republic. Tidey, for whom PIRA had originally demanded a ransom of $7 million, was rescued by Irish security forces after three weeks in captivity. Later, the Irish government seized a bank balance of about $2 million which was believed to be the money obtained from that or some other extortion by the PIRA.

As a result of a number of well-publicised trials for gun-running in the USA in 1983–84, the flow of US dollars to the PIRA declined, when a number of previous Irish–American subscribers to the Northern Aid Committee (NORAID) who had until then believed that their contributions would be used solely for welfare purposes, stopped subscribing.

This forced the PIRA to rely more on their other main sources of funds – robberies from banks and liquor stores, extortion in the form of demanding protection money from hotels, shops, taxi drivers, etc., as the alternative to being bombed; also by short-term abduction, typically of a bank manager's family to force him to hand over money from his bank. The protection money is extorted mainly in the North, while more of the robberies and abductions occur in the Republic of Ireland.

Great Britain

In Great Britain, operations by PIRA and INLA have thus far all occurred in England, not in Scotland or Wales. They mostly comprise major bomb attacks, such as that in October 1984 on the Grand Hotel in Brighton where the prime minister and most of her cabinet were staying for the Conservative Party conference. Such operations typically take at least six months to prepare (planning for Brighton began more than two years in advance). The main reason for this is that the British public (unlike the 'sea' in which Mao's 'fish' operated in China) are overwhelmingly hostile to the actions of PIRA and INLA, so anything suspicious, however small, will quickly be reported to the police. There has seldom been more than one PIRA Active Service Unit (ASU) operating in England at a time, and occasionally two but never (so far as can be deduced from the evidence) more than that. Only the hardcore of such an ASU, (typically five or six strong: the cell leader, bomb-makers, etc.) come across from Ireland, spending as little time as possible in England; they recruit and train unskilled auxiliaries (drivers, lookouts, bomb-placers, etc.) from their few trusted sympathizers among the large Irish community working in Britain.

At the time of writing, PIRA and INLA have not attempted abduction or extortion in Britain. These are much more complex operations than bombing and the hostile popular environment would cause them greater problems, but they could certainly try.

Kidnapping in Britain has been wholly for criminal gain and has had a poor record of success. A number of cases are discussed in Part III. Other forms of extortion have largely been based on product contamination or the threat of it, again by criminals. Animal rights activists have contaminated products of food and pharmaceutical companies but this has been to inflict economic damage (see Chapter 19) and not to extort ransoms.

Germany, France and the Netherlands

In Germany there were a number of well-publicised political kidnappings, assassinations and hijackings in 1976–77 but, thereafter, improved police and intelligence methods have kept the more sophisticated terrorist units, such as the Red Army Faction (RAF), under such pressure that they have been deterred from attempting anything so complex; also, like the PIRA in England, the RAF faces overwhelming hostility from the majority of Germans. They have, however, carried out a number of assassinations and bombings, sometimes in conjunction with the *Action Directe* (AD) in France. AD has similarly concentrated on assassination and bombing rather than political abduction and extortion, of which there is also very little in other West European countries. French people, both in France and in Lebanon, have been a particular target of both Muslim and Christian Arab terrorists. During two weeks in September 1986, six bombs were set off without warning in Paris, killing eight people and injuring more than 160 others. These were believed to be the work of the Christian–Marxist Lebanese Armed Revolutionary Factions (FARL) (usually operating under the title CSPPA, see list of Abbreviations) whose leader Georges Ibrahim Abdallah was in prison awaiting trial for other offences. He was later given a life sentence.

Criminally-motivated abduction and extortion, however, has occurred quite often in Germany and the Netherlands and some cases are examined in Chapter 15. Most, however, have been unsuccessful; few ransoms have been paid and the perpetrators frequently arrested. Product contamination by the animal rights movement has also occurred in both the Netherlands and Germany, where animal rights activists avowedly follow their British comrades in this field.

THE MIDDLE EAST AND NORTH AFRICA

Kidnapping for ransom is generally low in the Middle East and North Africa but political kidnapping and hostage-taking have been rife in Lebanon and by Kurds in Iraq. Iran and Libya have introduced a new dimension of overt terrorism using government security forces to abduct and detain diplomats and other expatriates to apply political pressure.

Lebanon

In Lebanon, Shia extremists backed by Iran, such as Islamic Jihad and Hezbollah, massacred large numbers of French and American victims using suicide bombers in 1983. They turned in 1984–86 to kidnapping American, British, French and Soviet expatriates – journalists, teachers, priests, diplomats, aid officials, etc. – some of the hostages having been murdered with calculated bestiality, sometimes in front of a video camera. This is terrorism in its most literal sense of 'killing one to frighten ten thousand'. In March 1986, while negotiations for the release of four such French hostages were still in progress, the Hezbollah kidnapped a complete French television team of four, probably hoping that the French government would be susceptible to pressure in the final weeks before their general election. Other victims in 1986 included Spanish and South Korean diplomats and there has been an increase in abduction of Lebanese businessmen and their children for ransom. Abduction (which could be called capture) of militiamen by rival militias has become commonplace in the general lawlessness of Beirut.

Iran

Iran, as well as sponsoring Shia terrorism in Lebanon, must have a place in history for the most flagrant of all breaches of the Vienna Convention (and of Islamic traditions of hospitality). They first condoned, and then used government forces to support, the seizure of the US Embassy and 50 diplomats whom they held hostage for 444 days in 1979–81. Though expatriate businessmen have not otherwise been at particular risk in Iran, the absence of normal civilized standards in the philosophy of Khomeini's government must demand constant vigilance.

Iraq

In Iraq there have been a substantial number of abductions of expatriates to discourage development projects such as water supply and construction; also to force the Iraqi government to release Kurdish prisoners. Most of these abductions have been by the Kurdish Socialist Party of Iraq (KSPI) which has about 1500 of the 15 000 guerrillas operating in Kurdistan. The largest of the Kurdish movements is the KDP, with some 10 000 combatants supported by Iran, Syria and Libya, and then the PUK with 4000 (see list of abbreviations) but neither of these have so far used this abduction technique. An example of a KSPI anti-development abduction is described in Chapter 16.

Kuwait

Of the Gulf States Kuwait must be regarded as having the highest risk of kidnap and extortion, both by criminal gangs connected with drug trafficking, and possibly also by political groups sponsored by Iran, which carried out the bomb attacks in 1983 for which a number of terrorists are held in Kuwait prisons. More than half of Kuwait's population are foreigners, including a large number of Palestinians, and there are many Shia nationals and immigrants.

Libya

Following the shooting down of anti-Gadafi demonstrators by Libyan diplomats firing from the windows of their embassy ('people's bureau') in London in 1984 and the killing of a British policewoman, the Libyan government detained six British citizens in Tripoli, a technique they had earlier used against West Germany. These and other incidents must place Libya, with Iran, in the lowest place of civilized standards of behaviour in the world and expatriates working there must recognize the risks of such behaviour at any time.

Gadafi's openly avowed encouragement and support for the murder of US citizens 'anywhere in the world' led to the US bombing raid on Libya in April 1986, some of the bombers flying from NATO bases in UK. Gadafi did not take retaliatory action against US and British expatriates in Libya, probably because he did not want to lose their services, but also because this would invite further retaliation. But his actions are often irrational and Libya will remain a risky place for US citizens and citizens of their NATO allies, especially Britain, and Gadafi is unlikely to abandon his policy of supporting terrorism in other countries.

Egypt

Egypt is under threat from its own Islamic fundamentalists encouraged and supported by Libya, and from various Palestinians including the Abu Nidal group. Until early 1986 this risk was contained by strong security forces but the sudden rebellion of part of the security police and its crushing by the army must increase the risk of terrorism, including abduction of expatriates. A combination of unrest arising from Egypt's severe economic problems and more radical action by the Muslim Brotherhood could conceivably lead to the overthrow of the Mubarak government by Islamic fundamentalists which would, of course, have a dramatic effect both inside and outside Egypt.

SUB-SAHARAN AFRICA

Sudan

In Sudan, the military coup which ousted President Nimeiri in April 1985 did not end the rebellion by the Sudanese People's Liberation Army (SPLA) in the south which, after a brief ceasefire, resumed operations in October 1985. They had already, in 1983 and 1984, brought two major development projects to a halt by kidnapping 15 expatriate workers and killing a number of local workers – the Jonglei Canal and Bentiu oil refinery projects (see Chapter 16). Both projects were still in suspension in 1986.

Late in 1985 the SPLA kidnapped the West German captain of a Nile river steamer and released him on 10 February 1986 with a warning to other foreign nationals to stay out of the areas of rebel operations.

Meanwhile in the north and west of the country the Islamic National Front (INF), a political front of the Muslim Brotherhood, is prepared to fight leftist and other rival political groups and there have been more Libyans in Khartoum than before the coup.

All round, the risk to foreign companies and expatriate staff, especially those on aid and development projects in remote areas, remains high.

Ethiopia, Nigeria and Zaire

Ethiopia also remains torn by guerrillas in Eritrea and the Tigré province, where in 1983 eight charity fieldworkers were kidnapped and held for seven weeks to be shown conditions in Tigré as a propaganda exercise.

Many East and West African governments continue to be subject to instability and overthrow and, though abduction of expatriates has been rare, the possibility of this being done either by dissidents (anti-development abductions) or by governments must be borne in mind. The previous Nigerian government of General Buhari, which was ousted in July 1985, was widely suspected of involvement in the attempt to abduct a former minister, Umaru Dikko, from England and, when the perpetrators were arrested, the crew and passengers of a British Caledonian flight were detained for two days in Lagos.

In Zaire, insurgents in Shaba, the southern province bordering Tanzania and Angola, include kidnapping as one of their techniques of political violence, but the victims are seldom expatriates. Here, and in the rest of the country, corruption is rife and refusal to pay bribes may result at least in inconvenience and at worst in assault or abduction.

Angola

In Angola, expatriates probably face one of the highest risks of abduction (though not of death), paradoxically from an insurgent organization fighting a communist government and enjoying some sympathy and support from the West – UNITA, led by Dr Jonas Savimbi, who has carried out a number of spectacular anti-development abductions to try to scare off foreign support for the

MPLA government. Thus far, UNITA has not succeeded in seriously disrupting the oil industry in the Cabinda enclave, which provides 90 per cent of the nation's export earnings. The enclave is protected by 25–30 thousand Cuban troops, whose payment consumes some 60 per cent of the oil revenue. Next in importance is the diamond industry which UNITA attempted to disrupt by abducting 77 expatriate workers from the diamond-mining centre of Cafunfo in February 1984 (see Chapter 16). This and other incidents (including well-publicised South African support and more discreet support from some African countries hostile to the MPLA government) have resulted in what amounts to *de facto* recognition of UNITA as the government of the south-eastern half of Angola – including, it is claimed, more than half its population.

UNITA has staged several other abductions, including the capture of two Soviet airmen supporting the Cubans in 1981–82 and 20 Czechoslovaks in 1983–84, all of whom were held for more than a year. In March 1986 they abducted another 197 expatriate workers from the diamond-mining town of Andrada close to the northern border with Zaire, but they were released a few days later, presumably because the aims had been achieved – to deter these and other expatriates from working in Angola.

The Cubans are likely to continue to devote whatever resources are needed to protect the Cabinda enclave because the collapse of the oil industry would lead quickly to the collapse of the economy and of the MPLA government. UNITA, for the same reason, are likely to continue their efforts. To complete the paradox, the US and other expatriate companies involved in the oil and diamond industries are doing their best to help the MPLA government to protect those industries while their governments are urging the withdrawal of the Cuban troops.

Zimbabwe

In Zimbabwe, six tourists were kidnapped in Matabeleland in July 1982 and their bodies were eventually found in 1985, though they appear to have been killed within a few days of their abduction (see Chapter 16). There have also, since 1983, been a number of abductions of white residents in the same area, where the Ndebele tribe are in a majority though they are in a minority in Zimbabwe as a whole. Mugabe wants and needs a one-party state to strengthen his hand in the growing confrontation with South Africa to which he is committed;

he is therefore likely to try to bring the Ndebele back into the mainstream by accommodating their party, ZAPU, in this one-party state, and ZAPU may be ready to do a deal accordingly. Whether this solves the problem of armed dissidence and banditry in Matabeleland remains to be seen. South Africa will do its best to destabilize Zimbabwe by fomenting this tribal rivalry and by economic pressure, and also possibly by military raids and covert action, including the use of proxies. Overall, however, the effect of the South African confrontation is likely to be a force for unity rather than disruption in Zimbabwe.

Mozambique

In Mozambique, as in Angola, the threat comes from an anti-Marxist guerrilla movement, RNM, originally formed by Rhodesians, with involvement of ex-Rhodesian and Portuguese officers. RNM was openly supported by South Africa until March 1984, when it signed the Nkomati Accord with the Mozambican government withdrawing this support in exchange for an agreement by Mozambique not to provide the ANC with bases. Since then, though Mozambique has generally honoured its side of the bargain, South Africa has continued to give clandestine support to RNM, whose efforts to disrupt the economy and deter investment have so far been mainly by sabotage, bombing and assassination. There have been a number of abductions but not on the scale of those in Angola.

South Africa

South Africa has been in turmoil since 1984 in the wake of President Botha's attempt to liberalize the constitution and dismantle, or at least modernize, apartheid in the face of bitter opposition from the white Conservative right-wing and organized violence by the radical black ANC. It offers a classic parallel to Alexis de Tocqueville's analysis of the French Revolution which began not when the *ancien regime* was at its most repressive, but when it accepted the necessity of change; whereupon the radicals demanded more change more quickly while the conservatives feared the gathering slide and tried to block reforms of any kind. Such situations invariably lead to violence, usually prolonged, which ends eventually in repression by a totalitarian government of the revolutionary left (the Terror in France) or of the right (the Thermidorean reaction, when an alarmed and exasperated majority settle with relief for a 'Napoleon' who offers the best hope of restoring order). Very occasionally such a situation has resulted in a liberal democratic government. It is still too early to say which of the three solutions is most likely in South Africa, but the turmoil will continue for some time until there is a radical change in constitutional power in the country, which is now inevitable.

In such circumstances, the prime target of the revolutionaries are their own people who collaborate with the government. The majority of those killed by rioters in South Africa in 1985–86 were blacks (many of whom served in the police, local councils, administrative offices, etc.), with the aim of making the country ungovernable and specifically to turn the black townships into 'no-go areas' under *de facto* control of the ANC. Intimidation of blacks was the order of the day, though a small but growing number of whites were killed. There has also been some sabotage of utilities, especially oil and power installations, and the ANC may increasingly turn to tactics designed to drive out foreign investment. This could include abduction of both South African and expatriate managers. Unless the general security situation deteriorates badly, however, the police, army and intelligence services will probably make it difficult for dissidents to hold hostages for prolonged periods, and the economic dependence of the neighbouring African states on South Africa may deter them from providing safe havens for the holding of hostages from South Africa in their countries.

ASIA AND AUSTRALASIA

South-east Asia

Criminal kidnapping for ransom has a long tradition amongst the Chinese communities in East and South-east Asia. Victims are nearly always resident Chinese citizens and very seldom expatriates. The style is of short-term abductions, and ransoms are often paid quickly without the press or the police being told. The incidence of this kind of kidnapping has been much reduced by the introduction of the death penalty for convicted kidnappers in Singapore and Malaysia, but it was prevalent in the Philippines during the Marcos era, and it remains to be seen how successful President Aquino proves to be in suppressing this and other forms of crime. There have also been some political kidnappings in the Philippines by the two main insurgent groups, the

MNLF in Mindanao and the NPA elsewhere. Most of the victims have been Filipinos but a number of expatriates were included in 1985–86. NPA officially disapproves of kidnap for ransom but a number of timber workers have been held hostage and one Australian was held for five months, though this may have been the work of local renegades. There has, however, been much less political kidnapping in South-east Asia than in Latin America, Africa or the Middle East.

Piracy has been part of the way of life in the China seas for 1500 years and South-east Asian waters remain the most dangerous in the world. The worst area is the Gulf of Thailand, especially against the defenceless boat people from Vietnam. In 1984, for example, about 35 000 people left Vietnam under the UN 'orderly departure programme' but another 17 000 fled independently in small boats. About half of their boats were attacked, some several times, at least 61 people were killed, 110 women raped and many hundreds kidnapped. In the Straits of Singapore the government has kept piracy under control in Singaporean waters but the Indonesian side remains extremely hazardous, especially amongst the Riau Islands and in the eastbound lane of the Philip Channel. Much of the piracy is robbery by armed boarding parties. All recorded attacks have thus far been at night, so ships have been advised to navigate the straits by day. Piracy has also been rife off the Philippines, in Manila Bay and the Sulu Sea. In 1981, for example, off the Tawi Tam Islands, the 135-ton *Nuria 767* was held up by pirates who shot 11 people and forced the other 48 to jump overboard, 25 of them being drowned.*

The Indian sub-continent

There is a lot of criminal kidnapping for ransom by bandits in remote areas of India and Bangladesh, and by professional criminal gangs in Pakistan. Relatively few expatriates have been taken, though two Shell executives were kidnapped in Bangladesh in January 1984, and Baluch dissidents took an Australian couple from Pakistan in May 1985 and held them in Afghanistan. A French couple were held hostage in Burma in October/November 1983. In Sri Lanka, Tamil separatists kidnapped two US citizens doing development work in the Jaffna district in May 1984, demanding a $2 million ransom and the release of 20 Tamil prisoners. The Indian government, however, on whose goodwill the Tamils depend for sanctuaries in southern India,

---

* 'Piracy', in *Navy International* (March 1986) pp. 181–2.

applied strong pressure and the hostages were released without concessions within a few days. In January 1986 the Eelam Revolutionary Organization of Students kidnapped Penelope Willis/ Tremayne but otherwise up till now there have been no attempts to kidnap foreigners, though the lure of abductions to drive out foreign investment and development could conceivably take hold. If it did, however, the Indian government would almost certainly again apply pressure on the Tamils to desist.

Japan

In Japan there have been an average of 10 reported kidnaps per year, mainly by amateurs trying to extort money to escape from the stigma of debt, most of whom have been caught by the police. There may, of course, be other cases which never come to light. The most significant kidnap was that of Katsuhira Ezaki, head of the confectionery firm, who managed to escape after three days, but this was followed by a notorious series of product extortions in which the criminals (some probably copy-cats) used the title of 'the man with 21 faces', who claimed to have injected cyanide into sweets. These cases are examined in Chapter 19.

Australia and New Zealand

In Australia and New Zealand the kidnap risk is low, though there have been some criminal attempts in both countries. In Australia the crime rate is growing fast and there have been a substantial number of product and bomb-threat extortion cases (see Chapter 19). These and short-term abductions of businessmen, especially store-owners and bank officials, are the likeliest forms of extortion.

NORTH AMERICA AND THE CARIBBEAN

The USA

Inside the USA political kidnapping is rare but criminal kidnapping has always been rife. It reached a peak of 279 recorded cases in 1931 during Prohibition and it was made a capital offence after the kidnap and murder of the Lindbergh baby in 1933. During the next 40 years (1934–74) the average was much lower – 647 cases over the whole period. The FBI kept it low by a well-known policy of giving priority to the safe release of the hostage rather than to detection and arrest. Paradoxically – as is described more fully in Chapter 9 – this policy resulted in a much *higher* level of detection and arrest because of greater cooperation by the hostage's family or colleagues who are really the only source of information whereby the FBI can arrest and convict the kidnappers.

Nevertheless, abductions do continue in the USA. If all kinds of abductions (e.g. short-term abductions and seizures of children, etc., in family disputes) are included as well as kidnaps to secret hideouts, the average was nearly 200 each year from 1974–81, though the number of major kidnaps remained low (see Table 2.5). Since 1981, the robust stance of the Reagan administration regarding crime against the person has reduced the number of kidnaps quite significantly. The average duration of recorded kidnaps in the 1980s has been seven days – again very low by world standards.

Attempts at political kidnapping in the USA have been very rare and most of them have either been detected in the planning stage and snuffed out, or have failed. Members of the Iranian Students' Organization targeted the governor of Minnesota in 1979; 11 members of the FALN (Puerto Rican) were arrested in 1980 revealing plans to abduct a leading businessman; and in October 1981 police investigations revealed the existence of 20 safe houses and dossiers of businessmen for future targeting, some based on physical surveillance. The terrorists of the 1960s and 1970s, white (Weather Underground) black (Liberation Army) and Puerto Rican (FALN), may now have merged and further attempts may be expected but it is hoped that the past successes of the police in countering political terrorism will continue. Threats from international terrorists (e.g. the Palestinians and Armenians) must remain but they too have probably been deterred so far by their fear of intelligence and police effectiveness.

Domestic political terrorism has been very low since the student-inspired terrorism of the late 1960s and early 1970s shot its bolt, and has declined still more in recent years, again because of FBI efficiency and because of lack of popular support.

The main threat to US citizens is from Middle Eastern terrorists when they are outside their own country. In 1985 for example, out of about 450 incidents of international terrorism worldwide, a quarter (111) were against American targets – over four times as many as there were inside the USA (24).*

* Bruce Hoffman, *Terrorism in the United States during 1985* (Santa Monica, Rand Corporation, 1986).

Canada

In Canada, as in the USA, there have been large numbers of minor kidnappings and abductions, many of them domestic and mostly by amateurs working alone. None have been politically motivated and few have sought high ransoms. Kidnapping of rich businessmen (presumably with high ransoms in mind but where the attempts were quashed before reaching that stage) included: the abduction in April 1982 in Edmonton of Peter Pocklington who escaped with minor gunshot wounds; that of a member of the prosperous Irving family in May 1982 in New Brunswick, whose captor was quickly overcome by the police; and, in Calgary in December 1982, that of Hyman Belzberg who was rescued by the police on the day of his abduction.

Terrorism by Quebec separatists exploded briefly in the 1960s and early 1970s and included the kidnap of British diplomat James Cross, and the kidnap and murder of Quebec Provincial Minister Pierre Laporte. The present political climate in Quebec and in Canada as a whole, however, makes it unlikely that this form of terrorism will reappear.

The Quebec terrorists of 1970 were led by extreme Marxists and anarchists, which may have contributed to their failure to attract any significant popular sympathy. People of this philosophy have now been drawn into a new anarchist group, Direct Action, which has carried out some bombings and tries to infiltrate issue groups concerned, for example, with environmentalism, peace and animal rights. Such groups, especially the last, have resorted to extortion in other parts of the world and could do so in Canada, though this is unlikely at present.

Armenian terrorists attacked the Turkish Embassy in Ottawa on 12 March 1985, intent on killing the ambassador who escaped by jumping from a window. A guard was killed and the terrorists took 12 hostages but surrendered after four hours. The terrorists were Armenians resident in Canada and the considerable Armenian community in the country showed some sympathy for them, though most of them disowned the use of violence.

The greatest potential threat, however, comes from militants in the 250 000 Sikh community based mainly in Vancouver and Toronto. Two members were arrested in connection with the crash, believed to have been caused by a bomb, of an Air India flight from Montreal to London in June 1985, and an explosion amongst baggage from a Canadian flight in Tokyo airport on the same day. This and other violence and intimidation by Sikh militants has angered the Canadian population, and the Canadian government is negotiating a treaty to facilitate the extradition of Sikh suspects to India. This, coupled with growing anti-Sikh feeling, could trigger personal attacks and abductions by frustrated Sikh militants against both moderate fellow-Sikhs and against white Canadians. The Sikhs, when aroused, have shown themselves to be violent and ruthless, both in India and elsewhere. Developments in the Punjab could contribute to the tension.

The Caribbean

In the Caribbean, the risk of political kidnapping is largely confined to Martinique and Guadeloupe, where there is active terrorism to further independence. Puerto Rico is also subject to bomb attacks by the small separatist movement, and the crime rate is high but, thus far, abduction and extortion have been rare. Nor is there any significant threat to expatriates in the Dominican Republic or Haiti, though conceivably frustration with unfulfilled expectations aroused by the fall of President Duvalier coupled with less ruthless policing could affect this. In Jamaica the crime rate, though still high, has receded and the government has clamped down hard on anything likely to damage the tourist trade on which the island's economy largely depends; so foreign residents and visitors are probably less at risk than might be expected in such a violent and disparate society. Similar considerations apply to most of the other islands, where police forces organized and trained on British lines are generally effective, but economic and social tensions throughout the Caribbean could lead bitter and frustrated criminals to turn to extortion by abduction or other forms of threat.

Expatriates may be most at risk in the expanding tourist sailing industry amongst the Caribbean islands. Those owning or chartering yachts are assumed to be rich and are vulnerable to piracy in the form of robbery and possibly abduction by criminal gangs, including those involved in the thriving and throat-cutting activity of smuggling drugs from Colombia and neighbouring countries.

LATIN AMERICA

Latin America contains the most hazardous countries in which businesses can operate with the single exception of Lebanon, though the threat to their own nationals remains far greater than the threat to expatriates. The most dangerous countries are Colombia and Peru and in many others the crime rate in the cities is alarmingly high. On the credit side, whereas 12 years ago the majority of Latin American countries were under dictatorships, usually military, the majority do now have elected presidents and/or legislatures. While the return to elected government may sometimes result in more, not less violence (as in Peru) the long-term effects of the growth of democracy must give grounds for optimism. It is also worth noting that Latin America, while historically plagued by internal conflict, from urban terrorism to rural insurgency, *coup d'état* and revolution, has been and remains largely free from the inter-state wars from which Western Europe and the Middle East have suffered at enormous cost to both lives and wealth. Nevertheless, many of the Latin American economies, too reliant on primary products and borne down by corruption and debts to foreign banks and governments, are very unhealthy and therefore a source of instability. Latin America will remain a high risk area.

Guatemala

In Guatemala, democratic rule was restored in January 1986, after more than 30 years of almost continuous military dictatorship, when Christian Democratic President Vinicio Cerezo took office with 68 per cent of the vote. He quickly dismantled the secret police with the cooperation of the army. Though rural guerrilla activity continues, Guatemala city remains relatively peaceful.

Since 1981, in fact, the guerrilla groups have suffered heavy reverses, and political kidnappings have declined sharply. Criminal kidnappings continue but ransom demands are much smaller – seldom more than $100 000. President Cerezo's proven determination to restore human rights is backed by this being a condition of continued US military aid, so he has a good chance of maintaining the loyalty of the army on whom his survival will depend.

El Salvador, Honduras and Nicaragua

In El Salvador, the launching of the current guerrilla war was financed by a concerted campaign in 1978–80 of kidnapping expatriates from the richest multinational corporations. Senior executives from several countries at once were kidnapped and their parent governments and corporations were cleverly played off against each other to extort huge ransoms (see Chapter 14 for one example). This is a pattern which well-organized revolutionary movements might attempt in other countries. It certainly gave the FMLN a sound financial base for their war in a small country and, although the government of President Duarte has made great progress both militarily and socially, continued Nicaraguan and Cuban support is ensuring that the civil war continues with little likelihood of outright victory for either side.

The kidnapping of President Duarte's daughter in September 1985 and his concessions for her release six weeks later (she was released along with 24 abducted mayors in exchange for the release of 22 prisoners and safe conduct for 96 wounded guerrillas) damaged his prestige and provided ammunition for his right-wing rivals. The public, however, seemed both to sympathize and to approve his action.

The risk of abduction or involvement in the civil war remains high in rural areas but most of the victims are now local people abducted in pursuit of the war, and businesses are operating with reasonable confidence in San Salvador.

Honduras has remained relatively peaceful, though there were some transnational kidnappings with Salvadoran connections in 1980–82 and another of an 80-year-old widow in December 1985 (she was released next day, presumably for ransom). The main risk lies on the borders with El Salvador and Nicaragua due to Honduras's involvement, however unwillingly, in the civil wars in those countries. In Nicaragua, the Sandinist regime, supported by Cuba, is likely to contain the challenge of the US-backed Contras, but anyone visiting the border areas risks being caught up in the ambushes and raids which this comprises.

Colombia

Colombia has long been the Mecca of kidnapping and extortion. Most of the victims are Colombian businessmen (especially Jews) in the cities, and ranchers and oil technicians in rural areas (including two US oil engineers on 10 December 1985). Statistically, the average duration of detention in the 1980s has been 47 days; the holding of Richard Starr for over three years in 1977–80 (see Chapter 14) was not typical. Ransom demands in urban kidnaps have averaged $5 million and payments less than $1 million; in rural kidnaps, demands have averaged $720 000 and payments $300 000.

The police have been limited in their effectiveness. Of 359 people taken between January 1984 and April 1985, only 31 were rescued by the authorities and 151 people imprisoned on kidnapping charges. A further 34 were killed in clashes with security forces. In the continuing guerrilla warfare, casualties on both sides have been considerable.

Most of this kidnapping has been for ransom rather than for intimidation or political concessions, though some of it has been by the revolutionary political groups (see below). Crime (including abduction and the extortion of protection money) is, however, high and is particularly violent in connection with the massive production and smuggling of cocaine to the USA. Following the assassination of the Minister of Justice, Rodrigo Lara, by drug traffickers in 1984, the government of President Betancur launched a campaign against the industry. This included some extraditions to the USA, retaliation for which is likely to continue to pose a threat to US business and diplomatic interests. Early in 1985 drug smugglers offered a price of $350 000 for the kidnapping of a member of the US Drug Enforcement Agency (DEA) and in Mexico a DEA agent was abducted and murdered.

In parallel with this, President Betancur in 1984 opened a promising peace initiative with the guerrillas and three of the four main guerrilla movements signed a truce. This, however, only lasted a year and by the middle of 1985 only one of these continued to observe the truce – the Soviet-aligned Armed Revolutionary Forces of Colombia (FARC). The two which abandoned the truce were the April 19 Movement (M19) and the People's Liberation Army (EPL, Maoist). The fourth movement – the National Liberation Army (ELN, Castroite) never joined the peace process at all. ELN is ideologically hostile to all multinational activities, especially by US corporations, and it particularly targets the operations of the oil companies in the Llanos which interfere with its activities on the Venezuelan border.

M19 staged a spectacular incident in November 1985 when they seized the Palace of Justice in Bogota, taking several judges and civilians as hostages. After a few hours the army stormed the palace in an attempt to rescue the hostages. The result was a bloodbath in which more than 100 people were killed, including all the guerrillas (41), plus 12 judges, 17 soldiers and more than 30 civilians.

When the FARC decided to continue the truce, a dissident group broke away, the Ricardo Franco Front (RFF), and in December 1985 the bodies of 111 guerrillas were found, massacred by the RFF for 'cooperation with the army'.

In 1986 the three other 'rejectionist' groups – M19, EPL and ELN – formed an alliance, the National Guerrilla Coordination (CNG) from which they excluded the RFF because of its massacres of dissidents in December 1985. The CNG has claimed responsibility for sporadic urban attacks and for heavy fighting in the south-west of Colombia, where it is also reported to be cooperating with Ecuadorean and Peruvian guerrillas.

Despite the scale of rural violence, rural and urban kidnapping, the drug trafficking and the massive crime rate in Bogota, President Betancur succeeded in preserving the fabric of orderly administration and elective civilian government which has continued without interruption since 1958, a rare achievement in Latin America. While his predecessor was more pro-American Betancur's non-aligned stance has led to at least the beginnings of a decline in violence and a reasonable prospect of survival for democratic rule, but he was not eligible for re-election in May 1986. A new liberal President, Virgilio Barco Vargas was elected with a clear majority over all others; but the election of a parliament in which the Liberals are the largest party but do not have an overall majority, must leave the future rather more uncertain, and there is every reason to expect that the political violence, the corruption, the drug trafficking, the high crime rate and the kidnapping and extortion will continue.

Peru

In Peru a sudden surge of kidnapping by criminal gangs struck the business community in Lima, growing rapidly in 1985. About 15 gangs were believed to be operating in 1986 and some were extremely vicious, mutilating or threatening to mutilate their victims. On one occasion, for example, they sent the ear of a 17-year-old hostage to his parents with a video recording which they made while it was being cut off. There is a real possibility of Peru supplanting Colombia as the country with the highest rate of kidnapping in the world, mostly by the criminal gangs.

There are two extremely violent revolutionary terrorist movements operating in Peru, the SL ('Shining Path') and the MRTA (Tupac Amaru). Soon after democratic government was restored in 1980, SL emerged in the rural areas, dedicated to revolutionary seizure of power by the Indians, many of whom have been inspired to support it. They provide enough funds and infrastructure to maintain its operations so it has not needed to resort to kidnap and ransom. SL has mounted large-scale ambushes and sabotage operations both in the provinces and in Lima, where public services have frequently been interrupted, and hotels and restaurants attacked. Violence escalated in June 1986 after troops stormed three jails to suppress rebellions by SL prisoners. Several hundred SL prisoners were killed, some allegedly after they had surrendered. President Garcia condemned the killings and a number of republican guards were arrested – which was clearly resented by the army. SL appeared to be doing their best to provoke a military coup which will always be a likely outcome of this kind of situation.

The MRTA has close ideological links with M19 in Colombia and may also have operational links. It attacks prestige targets (hotels, restaurants and multinational companies) mainly in Lima, and may well – like M19 – carry out spectacular kidnaps as armed propaganda.

Some 10 000 people were killed in political violence in Peru in 1980–86.

Venezuela

Venezuela is relatively free of terrorism. The Red Flag movement (which again has links with the Colombian M19 movement) has suspended its armed struggle to concentrate on trade union infiltration. There is, however, a serious crime hazard, both in Caracas and near the Colombian border due to the activities of drug traffickers. There have been an average of four or five abductions each year, mainly short-term ones, since 1982. In the rest of Latin America – Brazil, Bolivia, Paraguay and the Southern Cone, the risk of abduction and extortion is currently low, although opposition to General Pinochet's dictatorship and economic frustration could explode in Chile, and the high crime rate and economic frustration in Brazil could lead to extortion by short-term abduction in the big cities.

4 Organization of a Long-term Kidnap

SCALE AND PATTERN OF A KIDNAP

A kidnap can be conducted by a lone criminal and, because of his lack of resources and support, he may be driven to the greatest brutality of all when he feels himself being cornered, as was illustrated by the chilling story of the kidnap and murder of Lesley Whittle by Donald Neilson in 1975 (see Chapter 15). More often, however, an urban kidnap is carried out by a group consisting of between 5 and 50 individuals. The larger groups are usually politically motivated since professional criminals keep their numbers down both to avoid risk of betrayal and to reduce the wage bill or the share-out of the ransom.

In almost every case, large or small, there will be seven identifiable phases in an urban kidnap plan:

target selection,
reconnaissance and surveillance,
abduction,
detention in one or more hideouts,
negotiations,
ransom collection,
hostage release.

Though some of these tasks may be carried out by the same people, others are carried out by separate cells, e.g. an expert abduction group may be employed, and highly paid, for that task alone. At the other end of the scale there will be a group of guards for detention, who are the least skilled, probably the lowest paid and the most expendable in the event of the hideout being discovered and raided.

Large revolutionary groups, which may have plenty of student volunteers to call upon, often deploy auxiliary cells (sometimes unarmed) for such tasks as staging 'accidents' to block the traffic from feeder roads to the gateway route for the abduction, providing logistic services to the hideout, running transport, communications, publicity and intelligence networks, and carrying out robberies and extortions for operational funds. There may also be more open political cells (e.g. in the universities) to recruit and test probationers for graduation later to more active cells, and to carry out overt fund-raising, run the party newspaper, organize demonstrations and prepare and distribute propaganda. Low-risk probationary work of this kind is an important part of building and maintaining the security of a revolutionary movement.

Political terrorist groups often devote a quite astonishing amount of time to planning future operations. One of the reasons for this is that they have plenty of time to spare. The number of operations they can do is limited by their financial and material resources, and they are obsessed with the need that these must succeed, not least because a botched operation is likely to set the police on their tails. In between these operations they have little to do but subsist (with minimum essential exposure to acquire money and supplies and carry out surveillance and reconnaissance), and to discuss politics and the next operation. They read journals, local directories, etc. avidly to seek ideas for targets. They discuss endless plans and put them on paper with details of the habits and life-styles of potential targets, alternative strategems for abducting and holding them and for coercing their corporations or families or governments to get what they want. When terrorist hideouts have been discovered, they have frequently contained large numbers of such plans, some discarded, some still under consideration, but few actually carried out. Those that do come to fruition have, therefore, usually been planned in more detail, albeit sometimes with less professional expertise, than criminal operations.

TARGET SELECTION

For a political kidnap, publicity will usually be a primary aim, though on occasions the bargaining value of the victim to bring about the release of prisoners may be equally or more important. In either case his public image will be a major factor. Sometimes, even in a political kidnap, his perceived market value for ransom may be the decisive consideration.

For a criminal kidnap for ransom, the wealth of the individual or of his corporation will be the principal consideration, coupled with his accessibility and the predictability of his movements. For these reasons, in an overseas subsidiary, the resident manager whose life-style can be monitored is more commonly selected than a visiting chief executive from the head office (though there have been exceptions). The selection of a resident executive as a target will best be made by someone who moves in the same social circle, e.g. who plays golf at the same club. The leader or godfather of a major criminal gang may well move in such circles, or at least will have friends who do.

RECONNAISSANCE AND SURVEILLANCE

Once the target has been selected he is placed under surveillance. This task will be combined with reconnaissance, including dummy runs, to select the best time and place for abduction. Political groups often use students to do the surveillance, and both political and criminal groups will use people whose presence in the environment will attract the least attention. The abduction is most commonly carried out when the victim is on a regular journey, e.g. between home and office or dropping children at school, so much of this surveillance may be done from small nondescript vehicles, motorcycles or mopeds, but a potential target who is alert to the risk may well spot it. For an example, see the case of Sir Geoffrey Jackson, the British Ambassador to Uruguay kidnapped in 1971, described in Chapter 15.

Surveillance and reconnaissance may also be carried out by apparently casual visitors, salesmen, delivery men, etc. at the office or residence of the target or (if his family is targeted) in the vicinity of his children's school. Telephone calls may be used to discern the pattern of his movements and life-style and those of his family. Potential victims alert to the danger may detect sgns of this and will be wary of giving information. An experienced political group or professional criminal gang may spend several weeks over this reconnaissance phase. The leader will be closely involved in the planning and the decisions but will probably avoid exposing himself except at a discreet distance in the actual reconnaissance. Some groups are better at decentralizing than others. Sharp-eyed victims have sometimes retained valuable recollections of faces which appear again.

ABDUCTION

Reconnaissance and planning will lead a kidnap gang to select the time, place and method which offer the highest prospect of a successful abduction and getaway. A major factor in this will be the degree of confidence provided by the surveillance for predicting that the victim will be at a certain suitable place within fairly narrow time limits. More than half the recorded kidnaps of executives and their families have taken place between office and residence (most often close to one or other end of the journey) between 8 and 9 a.m. or between 5 and 7 p.m. About a quarter have been from inside the home (mainly of wives and children) and less than 10 per cent within the victim's workplace. A substantial number (about one in eight) have been on the way to or (more often) from social visits, usually between 10.30 p.m. and midnight, when the victims can be expected to be at their least alert.

Kidnappers will almost always use or be prepared to use force for the abduction. They must be assumed to be armed, though they may have no intention of using their weapons. A dead hostage will be of no value to them, either commercially or politically, unless they can trick his corporation or his family into believing that he is still alive. (There have been only a small number of known attempts to do this, but see Chapter 12 regarding proof of life.) Kidnappers will seldom have any intention of killing him while abducting him, though they may well do so if he resists violently and especially if he himself draws a gun. Few hostages have in fact been killed during abduction, statistically less than 1 per cent with 4 per cent injured. Resistance, however, will always be risky, because the kidnappers will be in a particularly high state of excitement and instability at the moment of abduction. Defensive or offensive driving to evade ambush probably offers the best chance, but this requires considerable skill and instant judgement.

The size of the actual snatch squad will depend upon the force that reconnaissance and planning has led the kidnappers to believe will be needed to be sure of overpowering the victim and or bodyguards. If any of the bodyguards are armed, it is likely that at least four or five armed kidnappers will be deployed, and more if they expect there to be an escort vehicle, even though they will have the advantage of surprise.

This surprise is often enhanced by deception or disguise. The commonest disguise is as policemen manning a roadblock (see, for example, the Herrema case in Chapter 15). In another city-centre kidnap, in Latin America, the kidnappers were disguised as shoppers or street vendors and produced guns from their baskets.

As described above, an abduction in a city centre may involve complex operations to block feeder roads to keep the getaway clear. The victim may be driven away initially in his own car or in a kidnapper's car, but it is quite common for him to be transferred, somewhere in a quiet suburb, to another 'switch' vehicle – usually a closed van – in case bystanders have given the police a description of the getaway car. This also has the advantage that the abduction gang can be kept in ignorance of the location of the hideout in case any of them are caught and interrogated.

DETENTION IN A HIDEOUT

The abduction will not have been attempted unless a safe place for detention has been prepared in advance. It will usually be in or under a house, workshop, etc., where there is a closed garage into which a vehicle can be driven and unloaded out of sight from the street. The victim may well have been blindfolded or incapacitated by drugs or by a blow to the head to remove any risk of his gaining clues to the location. His 'cell' is most often a cellar or locked room, but some have been imprisoned in caves or dugouts, sometimes in very bad conditions, e.g. with seepage of water or even sewage into the dugout. In a number of cases, the cell has been a tent inside the living room of a house, in which the hostage has been chained to a bed, to ensure that after his release he cannot report details of wallpaper, carpets, etc.

The kidnappers will often have an alternative safe house in readiness in case police pressure forces an emergency move but most often they will, if they can, hold the hostage in the same place until his release.

The guards face the highest risk of death or capture if the safe house is detected, so commitment and discipline may be bought by a promise of a percentage of the ransom. The leader will probably ensure that the guards know as little as possible about the rest of the gang and other aspects of the operation. It is comparatively rare for guards to abuse or maltreat their hostage (though there have been some unpleasant exceptions) and sometimes they establish a rapport with him (the 'Stockholm syndrome') in the face of shared discomfort and danger. They will, however usually protect their identity with masks or keep the hostage permanently hooded.

Mutilation, though frequently threatened in negotiation, is in fact rare, and has occurred in less than 1 per cent of known cases.

NEGOTIATION AND RELEASE

Over 90 per cent of recorded kidnaps are for a cash ransom; in 5 per cent there was a demand for publicity (e.g. for a manifesto); and in 3 per cent a demand for release of prisoners or other political concessions. Kidnappers almost always demand more cash than they hope to receive. They expect to have to negotiate though they obviously try not to give this impression in their first aggressive demands.

Sophisticated or experienced kidnappers make good psychological use of time, particularly of long periods of silence (since the victim's firm or family have no way of getting in touch with them), to create anxiety and doubt and to break down resistance. The average duration of recorded major kidnaps has been longest in Latin America and southern Europe (ten weeks) and shortest in North America and the Far East (average four days). Two cases lasting over three years have been recorded, both in Latin America (see Chapter 14).

Means of communication vary and kidnappers often ask the hostage whom he thinks they should contact and by what means. Frequently several methods are used, so the following figures add up to more than 100 per cent. The commonest means is by telephone (61 per cent) and calls are brief and brusque to reduce the risk of being traced. Kidnappers increasingly use or direct the use of coded newpaper advertisements (54 per cent) especially for acknowledgement and agreement to their demands. Letters (32 per cent may come through the post or by hand, or left where they can easily be found, sometimes in conjunction with a telephone call. Face-to-face contacts with negotiators or an intermediary have occurred but are very rare (1 per cent).

Negotiation is a two-way process so it will be discussed in the context of crisis management in Chapter 12. So, too, will the various ways in which a hostage may be released or rescued.

A statistical study of about 300 cases has indicated that 10 per cent of hostages died (from natural causes, killed in rescue attempts, or killed by the kidnappers – often unintentionally during or soon after abduction). The few who have been deliberately murdered have usually been prestigious figures kidnapped by political groups or, very occasionally, hostages who are believed to have acquired knowledge which might put the kidnappers in danger of arrest of conviction.

Ninety per cent of the hostages survived: 61 per cent were released after payment of a ransom averaging about a quarter of the sum originally demanded; 6 per cent were released without concession; 2 per cent escaped; and 21 per cent were rescued by police.

5 Other Forms of Abduction and Hostage-taking

ANTI-DEVELOPMENT ABDUCTION

Anti-development abduction (usually rural) is largely a new phenomenon since 1980, and accounted for nearly 500 hostages in the 66 cases during its first six years. The pattern was usually (not always) of large numbers of hostages taken from isolated construction, mining or development projects and held in areas where remoteness was a bigger factor than concealment. The aim was to disrupt such projects, deter people from working on them and apply pressure to the host government. Because of the isolation and vulnerability of the targets, there was often little or no planning. The abductors varied from small dissident groups to large guerrilla forces such as UNITA in Angola (see Chapter 16).

Victims are not usually selected for their personal wealth or influence. Typically they have been junior engineers and technicians rather than top management, and expatriates rather than local people. They are chosen because they are accessible, and because their disappearance is likely to bring world publicity and recognition to the rebels and cause maximum embarrassment to the host government.

Such planning as there is will often consist only of reconnaissance. The victims are usually recognizable because of their race or their jobs; on the other hand, they are not likely to spot those observing their movements, who will appear as casual labourers or mingle with the ordinary inquisitive inhabitants who find such projects interesting to watch. Having identified and selected a suitable time and place, the guerrillas may then either ambush the victims en route to an outlying site or seize them in the course of a larger-scale attack on government security forces protecting the project. Though a few victims have been killed, this has seldom been deliberate. On the other hand, they may suffer severely from long marches to a remote place of detention in jungle, mountain or bush, under primitive conditions. Conditions in the camps are often fairly relaxed and the victims allowed to take exercise within the camp area provided that they observe the necessary

53

rural guerrilla disciplines of camouflage, silence and concealment.

Demands are usually made for political concessions. In an analysis of 66 cases in 1980–85, demands were as follows:

	percentage
release of prisoners or return of property	22
cessation of trade	7
publication of political manifestos	10
material resupply	9
ransom	12
status recognition	21
manipulation of governments (aid, etc.)	12
withdrawal of foreign presence (non-trade)	7

Time is often of little concern and, in contrast to urban kidnaps, is seldom used to apply pressure in negotiation. In the 66 cases the hostages were held for periods ranging from 44 to 521 days.

Negotiation usually involves written communications and intermediaries. This can be a cause of many problems and frustrations. Several people may approach the company claiming to represent the guerrillas. There may be cultural as well as language barriers: for example, a tribesman from a remote area will not be accustomed to cut-and-dried questions and answers nor have the sense of urgency which an expatriate executive may expect in negotiations. Further complications will arise if the guerrillas, to establish recognition, refuse to negotiate other than with governments, which in turn may be reluctant to get involved. Moreover, if a large number of expatriates have been captured, there may be many parent governments as well as the host government concerned.

Most of the 66 cases analysed resulted in demands being met or the hostages being released without concession. Where a ransom was involved this sometimes presented considerable logistic problems, since it was often demanded in forms other than money (e.g. medicine, food supplies or, in one case, gold) and was delivered in convoys to remote areas by complicated routes. The same problems arose over release of the hostages.

The conclusions of the 66 cases analysed were:

	percentage
ransom paid	32
no concessions	20
rescue	8
death	3

escape   1
still unresolved   36

SHORT-TERM ABDUCTIONS

Short-term abductions sometimes have purely domestic motives, e.g. arising from conflicts over custody of children or by people distracted by failure of a love affair or perceived persecution.

There are a large and probably growing number of short-term abductions for criminal extortion of money. Recorded figures are misleading, because both extortioners and victims often do their best to settle the matter secretly, so there are probably many unreported cases for every one recorded – some policemen think as many as ten to one. It is also likely that, for the reasons given in Chaper 1, this crime will increase as technological developments make it likely to yield higher gains at lower risk than other forms of extortion and robbery, and the volume of money involved may in time be exceeded only by forgery (including counterfeit money and goods) and fraud, which also show every sign of increasing.

Many short-term abductions are attempted by loners and amateurs and may be successful if the sums demanded are not too large. Larger-scale abductions for extortion usually involve several people and are most commonly carried out by small professional criminal gangs.

Typically, the manager of a bank, building society (or, less often, of a supermarket or other establishment handling large amounts of cash) receives an apparently bona fide visitor, e.g. to open an account or arrange credit. His telephone rings and his wife tells him that two armed men have broken into the house and are threatening to abduct or shoot her and the children unless the manager at once pays a named sum of money to the visitor in the office. The sum is usually based on the anticipated contents of the safe at the immediate disposal of the manager – or in some cases the demand has simply been to 'open the safe'. The aim of the criminals is to complete the whole operation before it is practical for the police to respond to an alarm so the demands are usually made very aggressively, sometimes supported by physical brutality at one or both places involved (home and office). A variant is to abduct a member of staff or to abduct the manager himself. On occasions the operation is an aggravated form of armed hold-up.

If, as he should, the manager has a time or delay lock on his safe, he is able to plead that he cannot obtain the money quickly even if he wants to. Though there is a risk of this provoking the criminal to violence this is in fact rare because, if he is a professional, he understands this system and knows that violence will not open the safe. If there are prominent notices in the public part of the establishment that all safes are fitted with delay locks, a professional gang is likely to observe this in its reconnaissance and may turn away to seek an easier target. Other overt aids such as alarm systems and automatic cameras and a high-profile liaison with the police are also valuable deterrents.

There are, of course, many other ways in which short-term abductions may be conducted and they may merge into long-term kidnaps. Some examples are given in Chapter 17.

HOSTAGE SEIZURE IN THE HOME OR WORKPLACE

Hostage seizure differs from short-term abduction in that the place of seizure is quickly besieged, either because the abductors are surrounded before they get their hostages away or because (as in an embassy seizure or the occupation of key commercial or industrial premises) the hostage-taker wishes to use the incident to obtain publicity or extort political concessions. It is very rare for criminals to get into a siege situation except by mishandling a robbery or kidnap attempt. Abductions for psychopathic or domestic reasons are outside the scope of this book.

Since it is usually a complicated operation, often against guarded premises, a thorough reconnaissance may be expected and alert security staff may detect that they are being targeted. Political terrorist groups, as was pointed out earlier, usually spend many weeks or months in surveillance and planning, and are not short of people to do it – often nondescript or personable people, and frequently young. Victims of the German RAF (Baader–Meinhof) operations were afterwards sometimes surprised to learn that the attractive, well-dressed, well-spoken girl who had made apparently bona fide enquiries was in fact already a murderer. Arab terrorists operating in a Western environment (e.g. some of those who seized the Iranian Embassy in London in 1980) have often received higher education and had considerable sophistication and charm.

If, as is usually the case, the hostage-takers know that there will be a quick response to the seizure and that they will be surrounded by armed police, they will attack in large enough numbers (sometimes in more than one phase) not only to overpower the guards, but also to deploy rapidly to block and guard all the doors and windows likely to be used by police attempting to recapture the premises. This will take priority over dealing with the hostages, who will be herded aggressively into a small room to minimise the task of guarding them. The charm which may have been beguiling during the reconnaissance (and which may reappear later) will certainly not be apparent in these early stages. This will be the most dangerous period when terrorists in a high state of excitement are most likely to react violently.

When the situation stabilizes there may be a honeymoon period during which the terrorists to try to persuade their hostages of the justice of their cause. This is a time when it is worth the hostages endeavouring to develop a working relationship with their captors without sacrificing their dignity or allowing the terrorists to become too confident that their demands will be conceded. The more they come to regard their hostages as human beings the less likely they are to kill them, though some politically-motivated terrorists may have been ideologically or religiously indoctrinated to regard life and death as of no consequence.

HIJACKING

In an aircraft hijack, the threat which is used to achieve the aim is against the lives of the passengers and crew, not against the aircraft, train or ship. The aim is most commonly political blackmail (e.g. release of prisoners), sometimes combined with gaining publicity; or of transport to a stated destination, often with a ransom. There is sometimes an aim to frighten passengers away from a particular airline (e.g. El Al) or to drive airlines off particular routes (e.g. TWA from certain Mediterranean airports). There is sometimes an element of blind hatred (e.g. of Arabs for Jews or Americans), and hijacks have also been staged by exhibitionists seeking attention, and by criminals or crackpots.

There have been very few hijacks of trains, coaches or ships and these have had a very poor record of success. An aircraft is more compact, more easily controlled and provides an enclosed environment for the highly-charged emotional blackmail inherent in a threat to cause it to crash or to blow it up in the air or on the ground.

Surface transport is much more difficult to destroy or to move to another country.

The vital line of defence against aircraft hijack lies at the point of boarding, whether by a terrorist passenger or by one masquerading as a cleaner or baggage-handler on the tarmac. Once a hijacker has produced a gun or grenade (or even a convincing replica of one) the captain of an aircraft with passengers on board has little option but to do as he is told, though he can sometimes persuade the hijacker that his aircraft lacks the fuel or the specification to reach or land at the nominated airport. Second in priority to saving the lives of his passengers, the captain should try to handle things so as to land in a country which offers a good hope of successful resolution of the crisis.

The greatest problem arises if there is reason to believe that a hijacker is so indoctrinated (usually by a perversion of religious fervour) that he will kill himself and everyone else in the plane rather than fail to reach his objective. A hijacker will often claim that this is his position and hold a grenade with the safety pin out and the firing lever held so that it will fire if released from his hand (e.g. if he is shot or knocked unconscious); but such claims are seldom fact, and it may be hard to tell whether the grenade is armed. The aircrew must, if in doubt, assume that it is armed, and the hijacker relies on this.

As with any other hostage seizure or abduction, the terrorists in this early stage are at their most unstable so the crew and passengers should do their best to avoid exciting them. Armed skymarshals posing as passengers have had some successes where they have been quick, ruthless and lucky, but if not their actions may increase the hazards. Individual passengers should try to be as inconspicuous as possible and restrain themselves from showing either anxiety or hostility to the hijackers (see Chapter 7).

After the aircraft has landed, much will depend on the attitude of the host government. The problem of negotiation and rescue are discussed in Chapters 12 and 18.

6 Product Contamination and Extortion by Bomb Threat

THE NATURE OF THE CRIMINALS AND THE CRIME

Extortion by product contamination and bomb threat has occurred mainly in the USA, the UK, the Netherlands, Germany, Italy, Spain and Australia, and a number of case studies are included in Chapter 19. Product extortion attempts have thus far been carried out by criminals rather than political terrorists, usually operating in small numbers or even alone. Bomb extortion attempts have occasionally been linked to political groups but most again, have been by criminals. A large proportion of both product and bomb extortions have been by hoaxers or by individuals who did not possess the capability of carrying out the threat.

Statistics of product extortions, however, can be misleading since there are a large number (perhaps as many as ten) which go unreported for every one which becomes public knowledge. The kind of corporations picked as targets, which make or sell products for consumption by the public, are reluctant to publicise any product extortion attempt, whether successful or not, since this is likely to have an adverse effect on sales. They will generally only do so if there would be a genuine risk to public health if no warning of the possible contamination were given. Since the extortioner's primary weapon is the *threat* to publicise the incident he will not usually publicise it himself since he would then throw away his means of coercion to extort money. If he receives a ransom or (as more often happens) he takes fright and abandons the attempt, publicity would make his detection and arrest more likely. That is why so many extortion attempts never reach the knowledge of either the police or the public. Of those which do, the great majority (between 85 per cent and 90 per cent) end in failure – either by the arrest of the extortioner or the abandonment of the attempt.

An associated, but in fact very different, crime is malicious product contamination to 'punish' a corporation or to coerce it into changing its policy. This is most commonly done by animal rights activists against

59

companies which use or support animal experiments (e.g. pharmaceutical, cosmetic or confectionery companies) or which use intensive farming methods (turkeys, chickens and calves have been particularly targeted). It has also been done for pure malice by people whose reasons have not been identified, e.g. the poisoning of the analgesic Tylenol in 1982 and 1986 in the USA, resulting in eight deaths, and the poisoning of confectionery in Japan by the person or gang using the title 'the man with 21 faces' (see Chapter 19). In the case of contamination by animal rights activists, the activists usually announce it first to the media, since their aim is not extortion but to do the maximum economic damage to the company.

The product or bomb extortioner may, however, also have other motives besides the extortion of a ransom, e.g. a political motive (normally only in bomb extortions), to apply commercial pressure, to exert vengeance, to pay off a grudge, or simply for excitement or as a 'copycat' operation by individuals whose lives are unsatisfactory or frustrating.

As was described for kidnapping in Chapter 4, there are recognizable phases in a bomb or product extortion: target selection; reconnaissance; the actual bomb attack or contamination; negotiation; and collection of a ransom.

TARGET SELECTION AND RECONNAISSANCE

Product extortion may be aimed at the producer, distributor or retailer. The effectiveness of the threat will depend on the prospect of a large number of innocent members of the public being affected if it is carried out, and this is a major factor in selecting the target. Other factors are its accessibility, its vulnerability to contamination or disruption and the likely cost of resistance to the demand, e.g. the recall, withdrawal and destruction of stocks and a lasting effect on sales and market share. The aim of a skilled extortioner will be to pitch his demand high enough to make him personally (or his gang) rich, but low enough to tempt a large corporation to pay rather than face the possibly much greater cost of refusing to do so. Thus, large supermarkets, other retail chains and the manufacturers of widely distributed consumer products which would kill or seriously damage people if contaminated (e.g. food, drink or drugs) are usually chosen.

Many of the criteria for selecting targets for bomb extortion are similar: that a large number of innocent people will be put at risk;

accessibility; vulnerability to disruption; and the prospect of heavy financial loss if the threat is carried out (or if the belief takes root amongst the public that the target is likely to be bombed). As well as stores and supermarkets, other common targets for bomb extortion have been airlines, banks, oil companies, public utilities, hotels and places of mass entertainment.

Because operations of this type have so far been carried out by smaller and less sophisticated groups or individuals, reconnaissance and planning have often not been so detailed and prolonged as those described in Chapter 4 for kidnapping. Nevertheless, there will almost always have been a study of the layout and of the security arrangements. Bomb extortioners will have selected suitable places and means for insertion and concealment of their bomb. Product contaminators will have selected suitable products and purchased (rather than stolen) a stockpile for contamination, possibly of several different items if they plan a series of mounting threats to break down any initial resistance (see below).

PATTERN OF BOMB EXTORTIONS

Bombs have generally been small for easy concealment – typically ½ lb to 2 lbs of high explosives in an unobtrusive package or container. Petrol bombs, letter bombs, other incendiary devices and dummy explosives have also been used. They are usually planted in one of two places: where they would do maximum technical damage to installations (e.g. to critical machines or fuel or chemical storage tanks or pipes); or randomly placed in areas where they would inflict maximum casualties on the public (e.g. in a busy supermarket). There have been a few cases in which the extortioner has recruited an accomplice within the target company but this has been rare.

Initiation is usually by a timing device. Many extortioners have claimed that they are using radio-controlled firing and this has sometimes been so, but, once again, it is rare – probably because bomb extortioners so far have mostly been fairly unsophisticated criminals; their intention, also, is usually to get money without setting off the bomb. A particularly large proportion of bomb threats are hoaxes with a view either to extorting money by the threat or, more commonly, simply to get the satisfaction of watching a building being evacuated, i.e. by a small-minded person wishing to make a lot of people dance to his tune so he can gloat from along the street. In the latter cases, of course, the ransom demand (if there is one) in the initial message is not pursued.

Sometimes the operation will begin with real bombs which do (after warning to evacuate the building at once) go off, to show that the criminal is to be reckoned with. Subsequent threats (real or hoax) will then be accompanied by aggressive extortion demands.

Examples of bomb extortion are included in the long-running series of attacks on Woolworths (by bomb and product contamination threats) in Australia during 1979–81 (see Chapter 19).

PATTERN OF EXTORTION BY PRODUCT CONTAMINATION

A typical pattern of product extortion is illustrated by the form of a demand (paraphrased) received at the head office of a large supermarket chain:

On the shelves displaying tomato ketchup in your branches at A, B and C you will find a bottle on which a blue label with a cross is pasted on the bottom. Analyse the contents and you will find a lethal dose of paraquat. You may choose one of three courses of action:

Course A. Be ready to pay $500,000 on Wednesday, 15 May, in used notes of $20 or less, with non-consecutive numbers, packed in a suitcase. To indicate your willingness to do this place an advertisement in the *Argus* on Monday worded 'Jane. See you at the barbecue. Jack'. You will then receive instructions for payment. Do not tell the police. Carry out these instructions and that will be the end of the matter.

Course B. Act as in A but tell the police. If you do this we have our sources of information and we will at once inform the media that there are contaminated products on your shelves.

Course C. Refuse to cooperate. If you do this we will distribute a large range of contaminated products on to your shelves. We have these products already in our possession. We will tell the media what we have done but we will not say which products we have contaminated nor where we have put them.

You had better choose Course A.

The temptation for the board to buy the extortioners off with Course A must have been intense. With branches all over the country they stood to lose vastly more than $500 000 if the story reached the press. In fact they chose Course B. They prepared the money, put in the advertisement and carried out the instructions precisely, in full cooperation with the police, who behaved with discretion and skill. The extortioners were caught in the process of collecting the ransom.

This example illustrates, first, that one of the arts of extortion lies in not pitching the demand too high; and secondly that, given police cooperation and discretion, there is a strong probability of handling the crisis successfully. In the great majority of *reported* cases in which the target company cooperated with the police, the extortioners were either caught or faded away without pursuing either the extortion or further contamination. As stated earlier, however, there are known to be a large number of unreported cases; in many of these a ransom will have been paid – also unreported – and the police will have had no means of detecting or arresting the extortioners.

In the great majority of cases, the extortioner does not really intend the contaminated product to reach the consumer. In only about 25 per cent of the reported cases was the contamination such as would have killed or seriously injured anyone; in the other cases the product either contained something which merely befouled or discoloured it, or there was no contamination at all. In about 50 per cent of cases the extortioner stated where the contaminated product was placed (as in the example quoted above) and in 50 per cent he did not. Overall, it is estimated that only in about 10 per cent of the reported cases did the extortioner intend that the contaminated product should reach the consumer if his demands were not met. Indeed, in some of the other cases, he was almost frantic in his efforts to prevent this happening where the product really was contaminated and the company was resisting the demand.

NEGOTIATION BY THE EXTORTIONER

Techniques of contingency planning, crisis management and negotiation for all types of extortion are discussed in more depth in Part II. In this chapter, they will be considered briefly in the context only of the nature and the threat of the product and bomb extortion crime.

Communication has been by letter in about two-thirds of recorded cases and by telephone in about one-third. A very small number of extortioners have used newspaper advertisement and other means.

The duration of these incidents is generally very much shorter than for kidnap cases – the average being 14 days. Whereas in kidnap cases the psychological use of delay and silence is a common technique of coercion, this is seldom the case in bomb and product extortions.

The prime basis of coercion by the product extortioner, as indicated in the example described earlier, is the threat of publicity, coupled with the immediate threat to sales and long-term damage to the target company's image and market share. Other techniques of coercion, common to both bomb and product extortion, are the threat of indiscriminate casualties, the threat to a key product, and the simultaneous threat to multiple locations or multiple company targets. Although long delays are seldom used, aggressive pressure to act quickly or take the consequences is often applied in the hope of bouncing the victim to precipitate action or to a quick settlement. While using the threat of publicity in a product extortion, a skilled extortioner will use every means to encourage the victim not to report the existence of the threat and to settle without bringing in the police. In bomb extortions, considerations of public safety will usually necessitate either evacuation or at least a search; this will probably involve calling in police experts – and the damage done by publicity will be less than in a product extortion.

Other matters involved in the crisis management of these incidents are discussed further in Part II. These include such questions as evaluation of the reality of the threat and of the intention or ability to carry it out; whether to refuse to pay or to negotiate with the real or apparent intention of paying a ransom; the morality, legality and commercial implications of making such payments and of concealing the threat from the public; relations with the police and the media and conflicts of interest with and between them; and, as with all crisis management, minimizing the disruption and diversion of management and the continuation of commercial operations throughout the crisis.

MALICIOUS CONTAMINATION

Malicious contamination with no apparent aim other than to do maximum economic damage to the target company does not involve extortion of money but it may be used to blackmail the company into changing its policy – e.g. not to sell a certain product line or to cease carrying out or financing animal experimentation.

The world's worst recorded case was the injection of the analgesic

Tylenol with cyanide resulting in seven deaths around Chicago in October 1982. No demands for ransom or anything else were received except one from a person believed to have no connection with the contamination but pretending he had in order to extort money. He was arrested and imprisoned. This incident is believed to have cost the manufacturers, who are part of Johnson and Johnson, about $500 million (see Chapter 19).

Another case of contamination with no apparent motive other than malice was the series of poisonings and claims of poisonings of Japanese confectionery during 1984–85. Ransoms were paid but seemed to have little effect and they may have been extorted by criminals other than the contaminators. This series is also examined in Chapter 19.

ANIMAL RIGHTS ACTIVISM

Much more common is product contamination by animal rights activists. There have been some damaging cases in Britain and less damaging ones (with a copycat element) in Germany and the Netherlands. The worst incident in Britain was the contamination of Mars bars in 1984, which is believed to have cost the company several million pounds in destroyed stock and lost sales. This is examined as a case study in Chapter 19. Another case was the contamination of Christmas turkeys in 1984.

The Animal Liberation Front (ALF) who admitted guilt for both of these crimes – a more appropriate phrase than their own of 'claiming responsibility' – is a name rather than an organization, which means that there are no individuals or funds who can be prosecuted or sued unless those actually committing the crime are caught with evidence for conviction. As stated in one of their journals:

> The ALF is not a small group of elitists with a formal membership. It is a name people go under if the particular action is outside our immoral laws. Anyone can do an ALF action, but people who feel the same usually work together in small groups because of safety reasons, transport costs etc. (*Animal Liberation*, no. 2, April 1984)

Ronnie Lee, described as press officer of the ALF, regularly gives interviews to the press, radio and TV, and claims justification not only for contamination of consumer products but also for other kinds of violence against members of the public. He is editor of the *ALF Supporters' Group Bulletin* in which an article signed RL in the issue of October 1984 stated:

> There are times when violence has to be used to prevent a greater evil . . . Pacifism attempts to appeal to the 'better nature' of the opposition. But what happens when those who oppose us have no 'better natures'? . . . Violence is the only language many of these people understand . . . There will be injuries and possibly deaths on both sides before our ultimate victory for animal liberation is achieved.

And to quote 'RL' again, from December 1984: 'The main aim of ALF action is the destruction of animal abuse industries through the causing of economic loss and disruption' and adds that 'the ALF is about sabotage, *not* symbolism'.

The form of product contamination practised under the ALF name is easy to do and difficult to prevent. The purchase of 20 or 30 packages of food from any of the thousands of shops and kiosks in which they are sold, the injection of poison (or the insertion of a leaflet claiming to have injected poison, as was done in a number of these cases) and the return of the packages to the display shelves are not easy to detect. The best deterrents are arrest and conviction and, as in the Mars case, an outburst of public revulsion against people who contaminate a product most likely to be eaten by children (at least one child spent an evening in terror, thinking she had eaten poison – see Chapter 19). The same applies to the contamination of turkeys before Christmas.

There are signs that this public revulsion did alarm the activists because there were no similar incidents on that scale during the subsequent eighteen months, during which their main activity was smashing the windows of butchers' shops and daubing the homes of butchers, scientists and research workers with Nazi-style slogans (with 'animal torturer' in place of 'Jew'). 'RL' has claimed in the *ALFSG Bulletin* that it is 'a perfectly attainable aim to drive thousands of researchers out of their jobs' by direct action such as attacking their homes and cars and 'the smashing of windows, slashing of tyres and arson'.

Some animal rights campaigners may be motivated only by love of animals. That might seem to justify activities which do not involve breaches of the law. However, some people may regard even illegal activities as justified means to serve what is felt to be a moral end.

When, however, the activists placed potentially lethal bombs in the cars and homes of research staff in January 1986, they used a different name – the 'Animal Rights Militia' (ARM) – but some of the activists have admitted that they use whichever name best indicates the type of operation they are doing, (e.g. ALF for poisoning food, slashing tyres or breaking windows and ARM for using bombs) 'for the benefit of the media', i.e. to establish a public image.

Most of the established animal rights groups officially disown the violence used under the ALF or ARM labels, though some of their members, including paid staff, have also taken part in illegal operations under these or other similar names.

One of the most militant animal rights campaigners, who has had many public order convictions but condemns violence has commented that activists who contaminate food are motivated 'not by love of animals but by hatred of people'. That seems also to be the view of the public and perhaps the best counter of all is to encourage this view – because poisoning or arousing fear of poisoning *is* an attack on ordinary people.

In February 1987, ten animal rights activists were convicted in Sheffield on charges including conspiracy to commit arson and cause criminal damage following incendiary and other attacks on stores selling meat, furs, etc. Ronnie Lee, founder of the ALF, was sentenced to ten years' imprisonment, and six other people to four years each. Much of the damage was done by incendiary devices to activate sprinkler systems and during 1985–86 damage from this cause and fires themselves amounted to hundreds of thousands of pounds. This was in line with the ALF declared objective of inflicting maximum economic damage on businesses of whose activities they disapproved. A booklet describing in detail how to make incendiary and explosive devices was circulated to ALF cells throughout the country in 1986.

The copycat syndrome is a regular hazard in the product contamination field, especially when an incident receives wide media coverage. After the ALF contamination of Mars bars, a man attempted to extort £50 000 by a threat of further contamination and was caught and sentenced to two years' imprisonment. And after the second contamination of Tylenol capsules in the USA in 1986, there were further deaths from malicious contamination of other pharmaceutical products. All of these are described more fully in the case studies in Chapter 19.

Part II
The Response

7 Risk Management and Security

RISK MANAGEMENT

Risks can be prevented, reduced, transferred or ignored. There are very few terrorist risks that can safely be ignored, and it is unrealistic to depend on 100 per cent prevention, so this leaves the other two: to reduce risks by good security and, where possible, to transfer at least some of the financial risks by insurance. Should the risks materialize, damage can be contained by good contingency planning and crisis management, and these are the subjects of later chapters. But the best investment of all is prevention by good security, reducing the risk to a minimum.

The approach to management of terrorist risks is similar to that of fire risks. First, the manager assesses the risks, where they might occur and in what form; he estimates the cost of the damage they might do; he examines the alternative ways of reducing the risks and of transferring them by insurance; he costs the insurance policies and considers the price to be paid for the various preventive measures, not only in money but also in inconvenience, loss of efficiency, loss of profit and staff morale; he decides how much he is prepared to pay; he implements the selected preventive measures both physically and by improved procedures, briefing, training and simulation exercises; finally, in case the risk does materialize despite these precautions, he makes contingency plans for crisis management. In all of these things the manager will act through his security officer, aided by expert advice from a fire surveyor for fire risks, or a security consultant for terrorist risks. If he takes out insurance, the insurance company or underwriters will probably provide these surveyors or consultants as part of the package.

Security against kidnap and extortion involves security of premises and assets (including products) and of personnel and families. The individual is vulnerable at work, at home, at social functions and on the road between them; also while visiting outlying sites or foreign subsidiaries, especially in the vicinity of points of arrival and departure by air.

Security can be expensive and inconvenient, especially for senior executives. There is, therefore, a strong temptation to sweep it under the carpet: 'These things don't happen to me'; or 'If they want me they'll get me'; or 'How can I do my job if I'm hemmed in by security?'; or – most insidious of all – 'It's my life anyway; I'll decide what risks I'll take'. These must all be resisted, the last in particular. A chief executive who has reached the top will be tough and used to taking risks, but if by refusal to observe proper security he gets himself kidnapped, he will cause both his corporation and his family not only great dislocation and expense but also as much anguish as he will suffer himself.

THREAT ASSESSMENT

A businessman preparing to face the risk of malicious violence is like a farmer facing the risk of natural disasters – floods, fires, droughts or hurricanes. The farmer cannot forecast the weather for the year ahead but he knows that some of these hazards are likely to hit him at some time, knowing some to be more likely than others, taking account of his environment and of the record of experience in the area. He takes precautions to ensure that none (especially the likeliest ones) can bring his operations to a halt or ruin him completely.

Malicious violence and disruption can hit the businessman and his assets in many different ways: arson, sabotage and bombing, including hoax calls; armed robbery and mob violence; fraud and industrial espionage; product contamination out of malice or for extortion; abduction, assault, blackmail or intimidation of himself, his staff or their families; and extortion or political blackmail to change or curtail commercial operations by the threat of any of these forms of attack. The motives may be political, vengeful or simply in pursuit of criminal gain.

In assessing the threat he should consult and balance all available sources: his corporate headquarters; police and government agencies; his embassy (if he manages an overseas subsidiary); other corporations in the area; and professional consultancies which maintain records and analyses of past history in the area and projections of future threats. Using the same sources, he should weigh up the efficiency and reliability of the local police, intelligence and other agencies as a background for his own security precautions and contingency planning.

COOPERATION WITH GOVERNMENT AND POLICE

In countries like the USA, Britain, Germany, the Netherlands or Australia, there need be little hesitation in bringing the police into security planning provided that this is started at a high enough level to ensure its confidentiality. In some other countries, however, especially in southern Europe and the Third World, corruption may present serious problems. Yet some cooperation from law-enforcement agencies is essential. The art lies in starting with a senior officer who can be trusted (and if no such officer exists, it is doubtful whether commercial operations in the country are a sound proposition at all). For a business starting a new operation in the country, this trusted senior officer can probably be identified and vouched for by the embassy or by some other corporation, local or experienced in the country. The senior officer will then delegate authority for further planning down a chain of officers for whom he can personally vouch. In corrupt societies they are entirely accustomed to this procedure once confidence is established at the top.

SECURITY AT WORK

'The strongest castle walls are not proof against the traitor within'. Security at the workplace depends above all on trustworthy staff, control of access and control of temporary visitors and contract workers. This begins with vetting of staff who have access to potential target areas (e.g. head offices, computer centres, software stores and other key installations). Where appropriate, identity cards or card keys should be issued, with (in large installations) safeguards against unauthorized use or impersonation. A predominantly loyal staff (well-paid, well-managed, with pride and job satisfaction), trained to be alert to the unusual or to disaffection, can enormously improve security. They may also be the people best placed to give warning of any suspicious interest shown by former and possibly disgruntled staff whose inside knowledge is a natural source of information to would-be criminals or terrorists, including those intent on corruption or industrial espionage.

Protection of potential targets, e.g. senior executives or key installations, is best achieved by concentric rings of security, none of which will be totally impregnable but each of which should impose delay and give warning before the next ring is reached. The outer rings are psychological or procedural, concerned with attitudes towards security, intelligence providing for assessment and recognition of the threats, and active liaison with law-enforcement agencies. All of these lead to anticipation of attack and quick effective response to it.

The outer physical ring, the perimeter fence or the walls, doors and windows of urban installations, often give a sense of false security. An unguarded chain-link fence can be cut within a few minutes, so other things may be needed, e.g. patrols, dogs, lights, vibratory detectors, acoustic detectors, photoelectric equipment, closed circuit television (CCTV), radio-link TV, infra-red or microwave beams, buried line sensors and alarms alerting security staff and police and deterring intruders with sudden light and noise.

Within the perimeter or office block certain vulnerable areas – including executive offices – will need special protection. Some of the equipment mentioned above may be suitable for this but there is also shorter-range equipment available, some of which has the advantage of detecting movement in an area rather than in direct line of a beam. This includes ultrasonic space detectors, thermal scanners, short-range microwave devices, automatic surveillance cameras (which can also provide evidence leading to conviction – the best of all deterrents), pressure mats, proximity, impact and anti-tampering devices, metal detectors and alarm systems.

In selecting this equipment for a factory, office block, hotel, etc., or for a home, it will usually pay to engage a project manager who is neither tied to nor receiving commission from firms providing it, for obvious reasons.

As within a mediaeval castle, it will be wise to have one or more 'keeps' for final protection of certain crucial installations and the offices of potential kidnap targets. In the case of executive suites, these should have very strong access control, which may be put into full operation on an alarm, with entry controlled only from inside. The 'keep' should have independent radio and/or telephone communications. Personnel at high risk may need to carry personal alarm systems with panic buttons whose signals are received by sensors distributed within the area for onward connection to the alarm system. The receiving sensors may share the housing of fire or other intrusion detectors.

The effective protection of a VIP ends where it began – with personal attitudes to security. He should confine knowledge of his programme to those who need to know and avoid predictable habits and movements; and his staff should be vetted, selected and handled so as to minimize the risk of their being bribed or intimidated.

Finally, it is worth remembering that a kidnap will seldom be attempted unless the would-be kidnappers can predict with reasonable certainty that the victim will be at a suitable point for abduction within a limited time bracket. The point of entry or exit of his place of work, or perhaps a few hundred yards down the road from it, are attractive options, especially if he sticks to a routine. One Italian executive regularly worked late and let himself out from a side door to walk across a dark road to his car – and was kidnapped there with ease.

The problem of vulnerability when arriving at or leaving the workplace is discussed further later in this chapter under 'security on the road'.

AIRPORT SECURITY

Airport security is a special application of security of a workplace. It is a particularly complex one, of concern to hundreds of millions of air travellers, and one in which the smallest loophole can have devastating results. To do the subject justice needs a book on its own and some comprehensive professional treatises are available.* This section can do no more than indicate some of the problems to the lay air traveller to help him judge for himself between standards at one airport and another; so that, if he notices a particularly heinous lapse which puts him and his fellow-passengers at risk, he can point it out to the airport authorities; and so that he can help the airport security staff with his cooperation and support in their task.

The security aspects of most concern to the traveller are: protection against gunmen or bombers in the check-in area where there is public access (as at Rome and Vienna airports in 1985); protection against planting of guns or explosives in the hold or hand-baggage of careless or gullible passengers (as in the attempt to get a bomb on board an El Al aircraft in the cabin baggage of a pregnant woman at London airport in April 1986); prevention of a passenger getting a bomb in hold-baggage aboard an aircraft, either suicidally or, more probably, without travelling himself (as was believed to the case on the Air India 747 blown up over the Atlantic in June 1985), or leaving a bomb in

---

* Among the best is Kenneth C. Moore, *Airport, Aircraft and Airline Security* (Los Angeles, Security World Publishing Co., 1976).

the hand-baggage in the aircraft at an intermediate stop and not reboarding (as in a TWA Rome–Athens flight on 2 April 1986); prevention of hijackers boarding with guns or explosives in their hand-baggage due to lax boarding procedures; and protection against unauthorized intruders or treacherous staff with access to the ramp, baggage-handling areas, etc., smuggling weapons or explosives into an aircraft for use by hijackers or for blowing it up on its next leg.

Airfields have many miles of perimeter fence – more than almost any other installation – and control of access to the ramps, runways and facilities from the airport buildings is of limited value if intruders can reach them across the airfield. On one notorious Mediterranean airfield, airport staff regularly took a short cut to their work through a gap in the fence and their families used the same gap to collect wild flowers from the grass verges. Not surprisingly, this airfield has been the starting point of numerous hijacks (though its security has now been improved as a result). As with other workplace security, the best approach is to provide warning, by surveillance devices and patrols, of tampering with the perimeter fence, and then concentric rings of surveillance across the open and around areas which need to be secure – such as the ramps, fuel, baggage and freight-handling facilities and servicing areas. None of this can be effective, however, without a positive attitude amongst the staff and good supervision.

The prevention of unauthorized entry to secure areas is dependent on limited access points with electronic surveillance and locks, often best operated by card keys which are also identification cards. The problem of impersonation, however, has still to be solved (see Chapter 1) in the light of the large number of people – including baggage-handlers and cleaners with access to aircraft refuelling at intermediate stops. The seizure of the Pan Am aircraft at Karachi in September 1986 was a prime example of this (see Chapter 18).

The greatest threat, however, is amongst passengers (or masqueraders) and their baggage passing through the airport terminal. The route from the entry to the departure lounge to the aircraft door should be a sterile area – a 'pipeline' from which a passenger once inside cannot leave without this being detected. There should be no possibility of mingling between arriving and departing passengers who should be in separate pipelines (a precaution overlooked in some airports). In particular, no one from either of these pipelines should be able to gain access to the ramps or other secure areas. The search of the person and hand-baggage must be meticulous, though this is easier said than done because it is a desperately tedious job with nearly 3 million people boarding 30 000 aircraft from 6700 airports every day. The other problem still to be solved is the reliable detection of non-metallic (or almost non-metallic) guns, ammunition and bombs, and of explosives in hermetically sealed bags (see Chapter 1).

Control of passengers and baggage needs to be tightened at many airports, including transit passengers. So does reconciliation of hold-baggage with boarding passengers (which appears to have failed in Canada before the Air India 747 disaster). Passengers, as well as airport staff, can detect and report laxity and they should 'vote with their feet' by avoiding airports with unsatisfactory security. Airlines, too, should wherever possible avoid using such airports, including use as intermediate stops, because economic punishment is probably the best spur to better security. This is not easily achieved, however, as business passengers and airlines have little option but to use the available airports. All airline security is a balance between conflicting factors of risk and the need to attract passengers and freight by keeping costs down.

As is proved by the statistics in Chapter 2, efficient and determined action can be effective, like the American example in introducing 100 per cent checks at the boarding gates in 1973. So could a comprehensive boycott of offending airports. These, or the threat of them, have already helped to make air travel one of the safest of all means of transport. There were about 10 million take-offs in 1985 so, with less than 20 hijacks a year, the odds against being hijacked are more than 500 000 to one. The odds against a hijack of an aircraft taking off from an international airport in, say, the USA, the UK, the Netherlands or Germany are even greater. Most hijacks are from airports with a low reputation for security (even if not always a fair one) such as Athens or Cairo, because this reputation attracts the hijackers. Nevertheless each hijack has an effect out of all proportion to the casualties involved particularly in the publicity they attract, so each one encourages political terrorists to do more.

INTERNATIONAL TRAVEL

For a senior executive of a multinational corporation, the chances of being kidnapped while visiting an overseas subsidiary are generally small but may still cause considerable anxiety to those responsible for his security. Before deciding to visit at all, he should check the degree of risk in the area and seek local advice to avoid sensitive times like elections, anniversaries or predictable demonstrations. Without being neurotic, he should plan on the basis that there *are* criminals or terrorists who would like to know his travel plans.

Air tickets should be booked with a discreet travel agent and should be treated as confidential documents throughout. Travel details should be known only to those who need to know and should not be discussed openly on the telephone – especially in the country of destination. If the traveller is a corporate executive, his name should not be linked to the name of the company on any travel documents or baggage. His dress, demeanour, baggage and labels should be unostentatious. He should not display large amounts of cash and should be in possession of notes of low denomination in foreign currency before he leaves.

Airports and airlines with a good record of security should be chosen where possible, avoiding intermediate stops in airports or countries where security is known to be poor. It is best to check-in early, getting through to the secure departure lounge as soon as possible, as most airport attacks occur in the area with public access. If the risk at the departure airport justifies it, the traveller should be escorted to the departure barrier but not be treated deferentially as a VIP. He should be wary of inquisitive strangers and eavesdroppers, especially while checking in or showing his ticket. He should avoid casual conversations about his trip.

Hijacks are extremely rare, as was brought out in Chapter 2, and in the section on airport security above. Nevertheless, hijacks are very traumatic for those involved, and victims will cope better if they are psychologically prepared. To help themselves to recover from the initial shock they can remind themselves that the likelihood of surviving is extremely high; like kidnap victims, hijacked passengers are of more value as bargaining counters alive than dead. The most dangerous moment, as in a kidnap, is in the first few minutes, when the hijackers are at their most unstable and attempting to establish their dominance. To this end they will be extremely aggressive and may shoot or beat up a few passengers to subdue the others. At this time it makes sense to be as inconspicuous as possible and a window seat is better than an aisle seat – albeit not too far from an emergency exit.

Individual passengers generally react in one of three ways: with stunned disbelief; with hysteria; or with rage and aggression. Aggression is the most dangerous of all because the hijackers will react strongly to reassert their dominance and they have the means to do so. Hysteria may be almost as bad, as it will attract the attention of the hijackers and they may bully a screaming or cowering victim to frighten the rest and build up their own egos. A wise passenger will try to calm any of his neighbours who are showing either aggression or hysteria, and look as neutral as he can. He should not resist or provoke in any way, but should try to maintain his composure and dignity.

Once those first dangerous 15 minutes or so are over, he should resign himself to surviving a long ordeal (as discussed later for kidnap hostages), doing what he can to lower the tension without becoming conspicuous and/or subservient, either of which may increase his personal risk. If the hijack is prolonged, he may need to take positive action to maintain his physical and mental health. He should be especially wary of becoming dehydrated. He should relax as much as possible, do isometric exercises and play mental games to divert his thoughts from morbid contemplation. He should, however, be alert to signs of a rescue attempt and be ready to lie low and cooperate.

The other 499 999 out of 500 000 air travellers will, however, reach their destinations, and they will then statistically be at more risk than they were in the aircraft.

On arrival at his destination he should be met by someone whom he can recognize with certainty. When leaving the airport, the choice lies between full protection or a low profile. Unless the VIP needs and is given an escort strong enough to deter any anticipated scale of attack, he should leave the airport in an inconspicuous car or in a taxi which comes from the queue.

Unless he is accommodated privately (which also has its risks – see 'Security at Home' below) he will be safest in the anonymity of a large hotel. He should not accept a ground-floor bedroom and should keep doors locked and curtains drawn at night. If his stay is a long one and the risk judged to be high, he should consider changing his room or even his hotel. He should acquaint himself with all alternative means of exit (lifts, stairs, fire escapes, etc.). He should not open his door to visitors unless he recognizes their voices and is confident that they are not under duress. He should not give any information to unsolicited telephone callers or unnecessarily to hotel staff, but he should ask the manager in confidence to let him know if there are any personal or telephone enquiries for or about him. He should be wary of using public telephones where eavesdropping is possible.

If he has to leave the hotel alone he should do so in a taxi called at the last minute by hotel staff. He should never go out alone on foot and, even when accompanied, avoid dark, narrow or deserted streets. He should avoid booking long in advance at restaurants, theatres, etc. or, if such booking is necessary, get one of his hosts to do it without including his name or corporation.

To be ready for emergencies he should carry a street map and should note possible safe havens such as police stations (e.g. in case he suspects that he is being followed). He should tell someone at his destination when to expect him and telephone back to those he has left to notify safe arrival so that if anything happens action will be taken quickly. He should also have telephone numbers to ring in an emergency.

When he leaves the country he should again be discreet about his plans and avoid predictable routines. If, for example, there is only one flight, he might drive to the airport by an unusual route or arrive there with his hosts well ahead of time. He should again be accompanied right up to the departure barrier.

SECURITY ON THE ROAD

Whether at home or overseas, the largest number of kidnaps are from cars, mainly travelling between home, work and social engagements. Most of these take place on the roads within a few hundred yards of where the victim lives or works because he cannot easily avoid these points even if he varies the route in between; also because, if he can be observed leaving one of them, his probable time of arrival at the other can be predicted.

As was implied earlier, a low profile is safer than an escort which is inadequate to deal with the anticipated scale of attack. For a target known to be escorted, the kidnap gang is likely to be at least four or five strong, trained and ready to shoot, enjoying the advantages of selected fire positions and surprise. For most potential victims, therefore, the safest transport is an inconspicuous car, preferably changed regularly (e.g. one of a company fleet). If there is only one passenger he should sit in front with the driver and, if the threat warrants, a further precaution is for them to put informal topcoats over their formal clothing or travel in shirt-sleeves. It is wise for them to agree an emergency procedure in advance.

The car should be robust, reliable and fast, with heavy bumpers in case evasive driving is necessary, and a locked filler cap. It should have strong door locks, preferably with central locking, and internal window locks. It should carry a fire extinguisher, a first aid kit, a powerful torch and maps. Depending on the circumstances and degree of threat, it could also have two-way radio, anti-tamper alarm, runflat tyres, siren with internal foot switch (for use in an ambush), air conditioning in hot climates so that windows can be kept closed, and armour plate – though this is expensive and may not be consistent with an inconspicuous car.

Cars should be garaged securely and, if possible, parked in a secure place or attended by the driver. If this has not been possible, the car should be checked for explosive devices by someone trained to do so (as VIP drivers should be).

Vetting of VIP drivers is especially important. The daughter of a former Saudi Arabian General, for example, was kidnapped in London by two men whom Scotland Yard arrested as they collected the ransom. One was the family chauffeur.

If possible, the potential target should enter and leave the car within a secure compound (e.g. in a garage with an electronically operated lock and internal access to his home, hotel or company office). If a walk to or from the car is unavoidable, it should kept kept as short as possible, preferably under observation in a well-frequented street. If the police regard him as a high-risk target, they may be willing to coincide a visit by a patrol car with his approach to an isolated destination such as a residence, factory or mine.

For all journeys he should vary his route and time as much as possible, keep his movements confidential and use a simple code to notify people at the other end of his departure and safe arrival.

He or his driver should be trained in defensive and evasive driving and should wherever possible use wide roads, driving fast in the centre lane, if there is one, to avoid being boxed in. If it is possible for two cars to travel in company, the risk is further reduced. Occupants should be alert and, if they suspect that they are being followed, should check this by driving a full circuit round a block; if in doubt they should drive at best speed to the nearest police station, army post or other pre-identified safe haven.

They should be particularly wary of unexpected 'road works', 'police checks' or 'accidents', and, if possible, turn away before getting involved as these are commonly staged by kidnappers. No scruples must be expected from political terrorists – see, for example, their use of a 'young mother' with a pram in the Schleyer kidnap (Chapter 15).

In the event of an ambush, every attempt should be made to keep the car moving. The kidnappers are unlikely to have blocked the entire width of the road and sidewalks, because they will not wish to risk causing a traffic hold-up before the target car arrives. It may thus be possible to drive past it by swerving across the road or sidewalk. If not, the driver should try to drive away by reversing or doing a skid turn. Failing that, he may attempt to knock the block (almost invariably a car) out of the way with a glancing blow, but not if the angle is such that it will not move and thus immobilize his own car. Radio, sirens and horns should be used to the full.

If all these fail and the halted car is faced by armed men or women, it will seldom be wise to draw a firearm since this will immediately provoke retaliation from the armed kidnappers who will be in their most excitable and aggressive state.

HOME AS A FORTRESS

Next to being on the road, the potential victim, and especially his family, are most vulnerable at home. There is a spectrum of security ranging from living in a fortress (or even within a defended compound) to living normally but taking sensible precautions in avoiding predictable movements, admitting visitors and locking up. If there is intelligence that a person is a particular target of a determined group, or that all the staff of a particular corporation are targets, a drastic and expensive change in their life-style may be necessary. If, however, an executive is just one of a number of possible targets, sensible precautions alone may be enough to divert the terrorists or criminals to look for a softer target.

Defended compounds are commoner than people think. In lawless countries, the staffs of isolated mines or oil installations have always lived in them. In certain Third World countries, even in the capital cities, it has sometimes been politic for diplomats and corporate expatriate staffs and their families to be concentrated in defended compounds and to move in escorted convoys to work or to school. This may be easier and more relaxed for all concerned (including families) than attempting to make an isolated fortress of each individual home.

An individual fortress can be made very strong, though probably not strong enough to withstand a military assault by a large guerrilla unit with heavy weapons. But to deter anything short of this, the same defence in depth will be needed as for a factory or office as described above, i.e. concentric rings (to delay and give warning of attack) around a stoutly built house containing a 'keep' for protracted defence until help comes.

The outer ring is, once again, largely procedural. The target and his family must avoid predictable routines and keep knowledge of their movements to those who need to know them; they must not have to expose themselves getting into or out of their cars or in opening garage doors or gates, which should be electronically controlled.

The perimeter or garden wall is the outer physical ring. If possible it should not give cover for people to hide close to it, and it should be well lit, hard to cross and have a robust and reliable alarm system built into it.

There should then ideally be a well-lit ring of open ground between the perimeter wall and the house, made by clearing shrubs and out-houses. This is made more effective by an alarm system which floods this open area with noise and light, which itself may cause intruders with nowhere to hide to cut their losses. This alarm can be triggered by similar systems to those described under 'Security at Work', of which the buried line sensor is probably the most cost-effective, normally covering a 200-yard perimeter and being totally invisible. The alarm system (including the lights) should also, of course, have alternative manual operation.

The next ring comprises the walls, doors and windows of the house. Doors should be stout with strong locks, with means of identifying visitors – e.g. CCTV, intercom, wide-angle peephole, parabolic mirrors etc. – and remote-controlled opening from within the house. This should also apply to the outer gate of the perimeter. Entry points should be reduced to a minimum but there must also be alternative exits for use in case of fire or to enable the family to escape while entry is being held back at the main door.

Windows should be shuttered or curtained. If the threat includes bombing, laminated glass or adhesive polyester will reduce the risk of flying glass and wire netting can deflect grenades. Inside the 'fortress' house there should be an intercom system, alternative telephones and a radio-link direct to the police.

Once again, a corrupt or treacherous member of the household can nullify all other defensive measures. A terrorist group targeting a particular victim will without doubt try to infiltrate his household or personal staff or to bribe or coerce them at least to give inside information. Particular care should be taken in vetting to exclude those who may be vulnerable to blackmail and intimidation. The history of kidnapping and assassination is full of examples of local staff who were by nature loyal but succumbed to threats against their own kith and kin.

SECURITY OF AN ORDINARY HOME AND FAMILY

Most people, however, cannot live in a fortress, which requires the resources of a millionaire or of a large corporation – and they could in any case provide it only for a few.

For the rest, the aim must be to avoid being chosen as an easy target. The demands need not be impossible. Predictable habits and an ostentatious profile (indicating either corporate power or riches) must be avoided. A house should be chosen in a suitable area, without concealed access for intruders and amongst neighbours who can be relied upon for mutual support. They can sometimes get valuable warning that they themselves or other neighbours are under surveillance if they are alert for the unusual such as bogus delivery men, cars parked with people in them for no apparent reason, or people making suspicious enquiries. A garage with an electronically controlled door and internal access to the house will reduce the danger at the two worst moments. There must be strict attention to locking up and drawing curtains. There should be a chain on the door and a means of recognizing visitors, preferably before unlocking the door and certainly before releasing the chain. The opening of even this crack in the doorway is a vulnerable moment and the person opening it should not show himself until he has positively identified the visitors. If they claim to be, say, policemen or electricians, a telephone call should be made to their headquarters before the door is released. If there are children or servants, they too must be trained to be strict about visitors. The vetting of servants has already been mentioned, and the problem of children's friends is discussed below. A really faithful dog – of a suitably frightening breed – may be the best guardian and the best deterrent of all, because an intruder knows that he can tell a tale to a man but not to a dog.

Many difficult problems arise over families, not least that the kidnapping of beloved wife or child may well lead to a man who would readily hazard his own life to give way to a threat to theirs. Terrorists and criminals know this very well and have few scruples about exploiting this compassion.

Wives may have jobs in which they cannot hope for concentric rings of protection; or non-career wives may want to lead an active social life both for fulfilment and to contribute to their husband's work. They (or their older children) may like to drive around in conspicuous sports cars. They may not appreciate the hazard either to themselves or to their husbands, who will have to handle the crisis if they are kidnapped. Hard decisions may be necessary. If their life becomes too restricted in a high-risk area it may be better for everyone's peace of mind if they leave the country, but a top executive may himself refuse to work in the place if it means splitting his family.

Children of school age should never be needlessly exposed. They should be escorted to and from school and the school should have strict instructions never to hand them over to any unauthorized person who claims to have come to collect them. As with their parents, their most dangerous moments are on the road or at the gates of their school or their home.

Older teenagers and children at university may present special problems. They may themselves be politically subverted without realizing that the real purpose is the kidnapping or assassination of their parents. Or they may unwittingly make friends with fellow students who intend to use their friendship for that purpose. This may be more likely overseas, but two of the more chilling examples occurred at home: in Argentina, a senior policeman's daughter made a close friend, who was invited to stay overnight with the family and who put a timb-bomb under the father's mattress; and in Germany the god-daughter of Jurgen Ponto gained entry as a family friend and then with her companions shot him dead.

CONTINGENCY PLANNING AND THE ESSENCE OF SECURITY

Corporate contingency planning and crisis management will be examined in detail in later chapters. They do, however, make an ongoing contribution to security and reduce the risk of the crisis ever occurring. Contingency planning should be accompanied by training, staff briefing and simulation exercises. These will draw attention to weaknesses so that security can be improved. They will also increase everyone's awareness of the various threats and make them more alert for signs that an attack may be being planned – e.g. by spotting signs of surveillance such as cars parked outside or driving past slowly or often, visitors or contract workers asking suspicious questions or strangers whom they meet off-duty scratching up an acquaintance and seeming unduly inquisitive.

The essence of deterrence is a manifest awareness of the threat and security against it. A serious criminal or terrorist operation against corporate premises or a well-secured home will be preceded by thorough reconnaissance and surveillance. If this surveillance reveals an alert and positive attitude to security, they will probably turn away and seek an easier target. The same applies to an important individual or his family while on the move. If they are unpredictable, inconspicuous and hard to spot, there is always some other mug.

8 The Ordeal of the Hostage

BEING MENTALLY PREPARED

The ordeal of the passenger in a hijacked aircraft was discussed in the previous chapter. Unlike the individual kidnap hostage, he can do little to influence his fate apart from blending with the crowd as much as he can.

The kidnapped hostage can do a lot, and is more likely to do so if he has thought it through in advance. It is also important for those involved in contingency planning and crisis management to understand his ordeal and, when working for his release, to be able to visualize what is happening to him and how he may be reacting.

The hostage will have more chance of survival if he is mentally prepared. The shock of being kidnapped will probably be the worst he ever has to endure. A busy, comfortable gregarious and secure existence, in which he is always exercising his own options and getting a response, will suddenly be transformed into a forced inactivity and isolation, with no options at all and great discomfort and degradation. The transformation will have been violent and he may have seen his driver or bodyguards killed in trying to defend him. Worst of all will be fear, and particularly fear of the unknown. He does not know whether he will be tortured or killed or, if so, when. The ordeal is open ended, and it will be made worse by self-pity or reproach: 'Why me?', 'If only . . .'.

He will endure the ordeal better if he has thought about it in advance, rationally but not morbidly. If he has regarded the kidnap threat seriously, there is much to be said for discussing it with his wife or his colleagues, (depending on their own attitudes and personalities). The more he knows about kidnapping, the less will be his fear of the unknown. He will be able to remind himself that only a small percentage of victims have been killed and an even tinier percentage of these deliberately and in cold blood – that indeed his value to his kidnappers depends on him being alive (e.g. see Chapter 13). Finally, it will help if he remembers that the human body and spirit have remarkable powers of adaptation and that the great majority of hostages have survived without permanent damage.

Soldiers with deep penetration duties involving a high risk of capture, e.g. in the SAS, are trained to withstand the ordeal by simulation of brutal treatment (often painfully realistic), isolation, acute discomfort, degradation, mental disorientation and intensive interrogation. All who have been through this testify to its value. But even if the ordeal has only been faced in the mind, the victim at least knows what to expect, and it will be easier to bear.

THE MOMENT OF ABDUCTION

The moment of abduction offers the best – perhaps the only – chance of escape. Evasive driving has already been mentioned. The high-risk potential victim and his driver are more likely to grasp this fleeting opportunity if they have run through some scenarios in their minds, perhaps while driving to and from work. The basis of these scenarios should be to do what the kidnappers least expect in order to throw them off their stride. Curtis Cutter, for example, the US Consul-General in Porto Allegre, Brazil, in 1970, thwarted a late-night kidnap attempt outside his home when a car blocked his path and four armed men jumpd out; he drove straight at the men, carrying one of them on his bumper for several yards. The others fired and Cutter was wounded but he escaped.

Sometimes, particularly in societies in which witnesses may not dare to come forward, the kidnappers will deliberately pick a crowded street for the abduction, to give themselves more time and cover. They know that few policemen or bodyguards would fire unhesitatingly amongst a crowd of innocent bystanders. In one Latin American capital city, the victim's car was rammed by another in a long, narrow, crowded shopping street. The two drivers got out, joined by the potential victim, and a long altercation ensued. A large crowd gathered round, amongst which were the rest of the kidnap gang, who had meanwhile signalled to accomplices to block both ends of the street. Only when they were quite sure that all was set up and that they had got the right man did they produce their guns and bundle him into a car for the getaway.

Once the car has been stopped (unlike Cutter's) and the victim is facing armed men, he should do what he is told. Heroics achieve nothing unless there is a real chance of success.

THE FIRST FEW DAYS

The victim should, from the moment of capture, make a determined effort to recover his calm and alertness so that he can start making mental notes of any details likely to help the police. Even though forced to lie face down on the floor of the car, he should try to fix in his mind any clues he can get about his route: time, speed, distance, gradients, railway crossings, etc. He should try next to detect the kind of place into which he is taken, e.g. into a garage with internal access to a house, the car park under a block of flats, or through the back entrance to a workshop or warehouse. While rural guerrillas or bandits may take him to an isolated farmhouse or cave, a professional gang in a city is more likely to have selected the eventual hideout in (or in a cellar beneath) a house, flat or garage in a quiet, prosperous suburb offering more choices for a getaway route. Again the victim should consciously retain sights, sounds and smells in his memory. At least one hostage contributed to the capture of his kidnappers because he could hear aircraft taking off from a small and recognizable airfield; and another by remembering details of the wallpaper. One remarkably prescient and determined hostage scraped her fingernails over the carpet to provide incontrovertible forensic evidence for the subsequent conviction of her captors.

The treatment of the victim in the first few days after capture is likely to be at its most brutal, calculated to humiliate and demoralize. He may be beaten into submission and injected with drugs. He may be stripped to his underwear and forced to ask for a bucket in which to perform his bodily functions in front of people taking a delight in his humiliation. If it is a political kidnap he may be interrogated and, if so, his interrogators are likely to use the Pavlovian techniques of alternating light and darkness, noise and silence, brutality and kindness. They may attempt mental disorientation by sensory deprivation, keeping him permanently blindfolded, with ears plugged (or with permanent music through headphones) with no means of telling the time of day, irregular and unpleasant food and sometimes none at all, and repeated interruption of sleep. He can only steel himself to endure it, knowing that this is probably going to be the worst time of all.

He should be careful not to reveal, unwittingly, anything about likely reactions to his capture. If he is asked for a telephone number to ring, he should think hard about who is likely to react best to the first message, because this first reaction can influence all subsequent negotiations. He should avoid giving the kidnappers any clues to help them gauge the level at which to pitch a ransom demand. He may consider feeding in genuine reasons why the sum they are demanding could not conceivably be found, but any such discussion is hazardous and must be conducted with great care. Those who initiate such discussions are likely to be leading members of the gang, responsible for interrogating him and probably also directing or participating in negotiation for ransom or political concessions. His actual day-to-day guards are likely to be humbler men, probably professional criminals earning a wage, and may be more human and less hostile than the leaders, especially of politically motivated gangs. It is most important, however, that the hostage should not see – and indeed avoid seeing – any of their faces (assuming that he or they are hooded) because, if he does so, this may induce them to kill him rather than risk identification after his release.

He must do his utmost to restore his own morale. The kidnappers will try to exploit his state of shock to establish immediate and total dominance over him. He must resist this but the way he does so must be tempered by his judgement of their attitudes and his own personality; also by his fluency in their language or theirs in his. Sir Geoffrey Jackson, being fluent in Spanish, detected that his kidnappers were mainly young educated Uruguayans and was quickly able to make them laugh. By reasonableness, humour and dignity, he struck a chord with some of their deep-rooted middle-class perceptions. By contrast, Don Richardson, having detected that his kidnappers wanted to keep him alive until they got a ransom, felt confident enough to be aggressive (e.g. in his demands for drugs for his heart condition and in giving them ultimatums that he would go on hunger strike) – reinforced by the fact that he felt intense hatred for the woman who was one of the gang leaders and was their English-speaking negotiator. William Niehous, on the other hand, judged it wise to try to establish human relationships – and survived 40 months in captivity before he was rescued (see Chapters 13 and 14).

Some hostages, like many prisoners of war, have been convinced that their morale depended upon making immediate and repeated plans for escape from the start, however unlikely this might be to succeed (Richardson was one of these) while others have judged it best to try to build up a rapport with their kidnappers (and especially their guards who probably harbour no hatred and to some extent share their ordeal) without compromising their own dignity. Each may have been right in his own prevailing human and physical circumstances.

Certainly, the more that the hostage can bring the kidnappers to regard him as a human being, the less likely they are to kill him.

SURVIVING THE LONG NIGHT

Surviving the Long Night (Vanguard, 1974) is the apt title of the US edition of Sir Geoffrey Jackson's inspiring account of his 8-month kidnap by the Tupamaros. Anyone facing a high risk of kidnap, especially in Latin America, will gain enormously from reading this book, both in avoiding kidnap and surviving it if it occurs. He will survive it best if, while remembering that statistically the ordeal is likely to be short, he steels himself to endure it for a long time.

The rapport which often develops between kidnappers and their victims (the 'Stockholm syndrome') is now well known and its psychological roots well established. It is, however, more likely to develop with criminal kidnappers (or the guards employed by political kidnappers) than with terrorists with a fanatical religious or political motivation. The case of Dr Herrema described in Chapter 15 and some of those involving Arab hijackers are awe-inspiring examples of what religious and political indoctrination can do to the human spirit.

A major concern for the hostage is demoralization by inactivity and morbid contemplation. He should do his utmost to find positive things to do within his limitations. Exercise programmes like the Canadian Air Force 5BX system can be done in any space in which a person can stand up and lie down. Mental exercise, such as memorizing details of his cell, or composing a diary or letter or (Jackson again) short stories to be written later, or designing an ideal home, can all help to keep the mind from unhealthier thoughts.

Provocative non-cooperation is likely to be counter-productive, but the victim may be able to restore his own morale by little victories, such as persuading his captors to allow him a pencil and paper or to alter a phrase in a letter or tape cassette which they are compelling him to send out.

The problem of providing written or taped communications is a difficult one. On the whole, it is best to give them fairly freely. Some will prefer to resist making statements which could be of propaganda value to their enemies; and all should clearly avoid saying anything which will give away important secrets or put someone else's life at risk. Apart from this, however, resistance may not be worth the price in exacerbation of the captor–hostage relationship. Statements will be recognized by everyone as being made under duress and will carry no weight. On the positive side, they will help the police and the negotiators to judge the hostage's state of mind, either from his voice-print or analysis of his handwriting.

It is possible to arrange to memorize a system of codewords whose use can transmit a particular meaning, e.g. 'I am well' can be coded to mean something different from 'I am fine'. So can different forms of endearment. These can be recorded in the potential victim's personal file (see Chapter 11). There are hazards, however: the hostage may find it difficult to insist on the right phrase without exciting suspicion, and the kidnappers may, deliberately or by chance, dictate something which sends a dangerously misleading message.

The conditions of a hostage are calculated to develop total dependence upon his captors. According to their whim, he eats or starves, sleeps or wakes, washes or urinates. He reverts to the dependence of a baby on its mother. His captors can assume the mantle of gods with, literally, the power of life and death over him. This can be deeply demoralizing to a person who has enjoyed power and status, especially if his new gods are young enough to be his children and their doctrines and life-style represent all that he most detests.

One of the reasons why his psychological pendulum may swing so sharply from hostility to rapport arises from this power of life and death. Because the kidnapper has power to kill him but spares him, his reaction may be a subconscious submission to him – a phenomenon known to psychiatrists as 'pathological transference'. A parallel is the way in which a defeated wolf will lay bare his throat to his conqueror – a submission which (as Konrad Lorenz has pointed out) wolves accept more humanely than humans. This submission is, of course, just what the kidnapper, by his aggression and brutality, is trying to achieve so that he will not be bothered by further resistance. Nevertheless, the criminal and even sometimes the terrorist 'god' may in due course respond with at least a vestige of human feeling.

Hostage release, rescue and rehabilitation are discussed later in Chapter 12.

9 Response to Kidnap: Morality and the Law

CONFLICTING INTERESTS

Many institutions and individuals are involved in the response to a kidnap and their interests will often conflict.

The victim has interests which conflict in themselves: as a potential victim assessing the risk of kidnap, he has to balance cost and inconvenience against how seriously he takes the threat. He may prefer to take the risk rather than prejudice the efficiency of his work or sacrifice the freedom of his life-style; or he may be reluctant to appear scared or to place a burden on his firm or family. Once kidnapped, of course, he will place a far greater burden on them. He will be fighting for survival and may be under extreme coercion, persecution or torture.

His family may be less willing to abandon his life than he is himself. If the victim is a child they will not sacrifice it in any circumstances. The family will, however, be best advised not to negotiate for themselves because emotion would play too big a part, but they will be able to give indispensable information and support to those negotiating for them.

His company will be involved if the victim is kidnapped to extort money from it, and it has to balance its responsibility to the victim against its responsibility to its other employees and stockholders. It has to maintain commercial operations during the crisis or face bankruptcy. It may have a legal responsibility for adequate protection of its personnel (at least one victim and another victim's wife are known to have sued their firms). It has also to preserve its reputation and the morale and confidence of its staff. It may face a conflict between some of these obligations and observance of the law.

Corporate headquarters – if the company is a subsidiary – may see the problem differently from the people on the ground. The corporation has ultimate financial responsibility, and has to consider not only morale, but the threat to its other subsidiaries if it gives way too easily. A communication problem may arise at vital moments of decision during negotiation.

The negotiator is appointed by the person to whom the extortion or coercion is being applied (e.g. the company or family of the victim).

His duty is to act in the best interests of his client within the law of the land. For that reason a local lawyer is often the best person for this role, as he is also accustomed to negotiating. The selection, briefing and operations of the negotiator are discussed in later chapters. It is preferable that he should be not too closely related to the victim or he may become emotionally involved.

Consultants specializing in kidnap and extortion are often valuable because, with experience of other cases, they can advise a family or firm which has never faced this kind of crisis before. Their role is discussed in more detail in Chapter 12. Once confidence is established they may, with the negotiator, be able to free corporate executives to continue commercial operations with only periodic reference to the incident management team.

The **lawyers** of the firm or the family (one of whom may, as stated, act as negotiator) must be involved in all important decisions in view of the complex legal liabilities which are discussed later in this chapter and in Chapter 11.

Stockholders' interests must be protected if decisions on large ransom payments or on suspension of certain commercial activities are involved. **Other corporations** and **joint venture partners** may also be concerned and their legal rights must be borne in mind.

The police have a dual responsibility: to the victim and to society. In countries where there is reason to suspect corruption, ways must be found to guard against this as discussed in Chapters 7 and 11, but the police must be involved, both for legal reasons and because the pressure on the kidnappers will be severely reduced if they are not. In some countries several police forces may be involved (e.g. in Italy, the *caribinieri*, the city police and the finance police). Their primary aim will be detection and conviction, but they can only achieve this if they gain the cooperation of the victim's family or firm, and this may be hampered by local laws inhibiting negotiation as will be discussed later in this chapter. The police will wish to emerge with their reputation for firmness and efficiency intact, and they should welcome and repay any cooperation which helps them to achieve a successful result.

The army may also be involved and may in some countries take over responsibility for anti-terrorist operations from the police.

Intelligence services will also be involved. Contact with them, however, is unlikely to be direct but is made through the police or other government agencies or, occasionally, in the case of expatriates, through the embassy. If channels for such contacts can be established this can be of great mutual benefit.

In the case of expatriate kidnaps, the local **government** and its agencies, sometimes **the legislature** and almost always **the judiciary** will be involved. If the kidnap is by a criminal gang the government may try to keep out of it, but if there are political objectives they may take a tough line, even demanding full control of the negotiation process. Problems of the law affecting this will be discussed later but if the government strongly disapproves of any action (such as payment of a ransom or publication of a political manifesto) the penalties could include imprisonment of local executives, expulsion of expatriates or confiscation of assets.

The media will almost always play a crucial role which can be of positive assistance, or harmful. In the case of a company, much will depend on the relationship it has built up with the press, radio and TV companies. Public relations planning is discussed in Chapter 11. The **parent government** of an expatriate victim or company may also be involved, directly or through its **embassy**. It may be anxious not to damage its relationship with the host government or to prejudice the prospects of future commercial activities. It will also be concerned with discouraging further attacks on its nationals. It will, of course, be even more involved if the victim is one of its employees (e.g. a diplomat). For companies and individuals, however, their embassy is likely to be one of their primary sources of help and advice.

GOVERNMENTS, CORPORATIONS AND FAMILIES

Most governments now adopt a policy of not releasing convicted terrorists even if this means the death of a hostage. Bitter experience has shown that they are unquestionably right. In 1975, for example, five German terrorists were released to secure the release of Peter Lorenz, a candidate in the West German mayoral election due a few days later. Within a few months one of these five, from the 2 June Movement, had shot two more people dead (during the abduction of 11 OPEC oil ministers in Vienna). Since then the West German government has always stood firm, with public opinion behind it. When Dr Hanns-Martin Schleyer (president of Mercedes Benz and of the German employers' organization) was kidnapped by the Red Army Faction in 1977 with demands for release of the RAF's convicted leaders, he courageously left letters asking that there be no concessions for his release and, even in letters from captivity under duress, he maintained this attitude and asked only that his ordeal should be brought to a head quickly. He died rather than see killers released to kill again and Helmut Schmidt's government took the same line.

Chancellor Schmidt did, however, show considerable subtlety. Ministers and senior officials were despatched to certain Arab countries which could be seen as possible destinations for released prisoners, where they were spotted and reported by news-hunting international journalists. The kidnappers – despite Schmidt's public reiteration of a 'no concessions' policy, nurtured hopes that he might give way and kept Schleyer alive for six weeks, during which time the police twice narrowly missed chances to rescue him. Arab hijackers then seized a Lufthansa airliner to reinforce the demand and Schmidt despatched the GSG9 commando for a successful rescue mission at Mogadishu airport, whereupon the prisoners committed suicide in jail and Schleyer was murdered. Other aspects of the Schleyer kidnap and the Mogadishu hijack are discussed in Chapters 14 and 18.

Governments may also be justified in showing flexibility over meeting demands for publicity for the terrorists' propaganda, not necessarily directly but – as in the London Iranian Embassy siege in 1980 – by assisting the broadcasting authorities to obtain the material (see Chapter 18). Governments should not, however, pay ransoms, and most now follow this policy, though some have not stood in the way of families and their friends finding ransoms (see the Starr and Schleyer cases in Chapters 14 and 15).

In a perfect world no one would ever give way to extortion because to do so provides funds for criminal and political terrorists to mount further operations and encourages them to do so. Brian Jenkins has estimated that $1 million can support 20 full-time terrorists for a year.* The Peronist–Marxist Montoneros obtained $240 million from ransoms during 1973–76 and the guerrillas in El Salvador (see Chapter 14) financed the launching of their prolonged rebellion by a concentrated series of ransoms (totalling over $40 million) extorted by kidnapping expatriate executives of multinational corporations during 1978–80.

Soldiers and diplomats accept that their governments cannot be expected to make concessions to save their lives, but sometimes the government is the target for extortion while the hostage is not a government employee and the government faces a very difficult dilemma.

* Brian Jenkins, *Terrorism and Personal Protection* (Boston and London, Butterworths, 1985) p. 227.

It is, however, unrealistic for governments to imagine that corporations and families will take this view. A corporation which is seen to abandon its staff to their fate in high-risk areas will, in the end, lose far more in terms of staff morale and recruitment than the cost of paying even a seven-figure ransom. Though in theory they might expect that this would invite their being chosen as targets again, this is in fact rare because, once bitten, they improve their security so much that they become less attractive targets than other companies.

If corporations are ready to give way to extortion in the belief that life is more important than money (on both humanitarian and commercial grounds), families are even more so. Few parents would consider a bank balance as comparable in value to the life of their child – and, like corporations, once bitten, they will take care not to be picked again. Kidnappers seeking ransoms know these things very well.

LAWS INHIBITING KIDNAP NEGOTIATIONS

Laws designed to inhibit the payment of ransoms have been tried in many countries where kidnapping has been high especially in Italy where most of the kidnaps have been by criminals for money, and in Latin America where more of them have been politically inspired. Some governments have tried to make communication with criminals or illegal political organizations a criminal offence and have arrested the people negotiating for release of a hostage. Others (especially the Italians) have attempted to ban the payment of ransoms to such organizations, and to ban insurance against kidnap and ransom (discussed later in this chapter). Judges in Italy have also had the power to freeze the assets of companies or families when one of their members has been kidnapped and to block the release of currency to them.

The result has been uniformly counter-productive. In Italy, firms and families which perceive themselves to be under threat have, by one means or another, built up funds outside the country. When someone has been kidnapped they have avoided telling the police since any action to secure the release of the hostage would render them liable to arrest. They have therefore settled as quickly as they can, often for the full amount demanded. Since no one knows who or where the kidnappers are, the only source of information about them will be through the negotiators with whom they choose to make contact (they will certainly not contact the police). Thus the police get no information and therefore have no hope of detection, arrest and conviction, which are the only effective deterrents against kidnapping. As a result of this, at the peak of kidnapping in Italy in the late 1970s, the conviction rate of kidnappers averaged less than 10 per cent.

By contrast, in the USA, the FBI have always followed the principle that convictions will only come from full cooperation with the hostage's colleagues or family who, they know, give overriding priority to his safe release. So the FBI make it clear that, for them too, the hostage's life has priority over detection and arrest. They cooperate to the full, actually helping rather than inhibiting both in negotiation and, if need be, in payment of a ransom, which is therefore often recovered. The British police have taken the same line – as in the Kaloghirou and Xuereb examples in Chapter 15. The results speak for themselves. The head of the FBI reported in 1974 that, of 647 cases of kidnapping in the previous 40 years, 1934–74 (following the kidnap and murder of the Lindbergh baby in 1933), all but three had been solved and over 90 per cent of the kidnappers had been arrested.* There can be few crimes anywhere in the world with a 90 per cent arrest rate. A major reason for the FBI's success was that, by cooperating with the firm or family during negotiation for the release of the hostage, they were able to use the information gained in the process to arrest the kidnappers *after* the hostage's release.

The question of banning payment of ransoms by corporations was discussed in the California State Senate after the kidnapping of Pattie Hearst in 1974. Three bills were brought before the Senate to outlaw the payment of ransoms either from the assets of a charitable trust or from corporate assets. Trustees or corporate officials who made or approved such payments would become personally liable for the amount paid.

Brian Jenkins, of the Rand Corporation, was asked for written comments before the bills were discussed, and these were published (see footnote below). He argued most convincingly against the bills. He considered first that they would not deter the kidnappers, who cared not at all whether the person paying the ransom was breaking the law; secondly that the victim's family or firm would not be deterred

---

* Cited by Brian Jenkins in *Should Corporations be Prevented from Paying Ransoms?* (Santa Monica, Rand Corporation, 1974). The difference between the 90 per cent arrested and 'all but three solved' was that some of the kidnappers had died, fled the country, etc., though the police knew who they were.

from paying if they believed that his life was at stake; thirdly that, since they would be forced to keep the payment secret from the police, the prospects of detection and arrest of the criminals would be greatly reduced and the greatest deterrent of all – conviction – would thereby be made less likely.

The Senate followed the same line and the bills were defeated.

INSURANCE

Insurance against kidnap and ransom began in 1933 after the Lindbergh baby case and grew rapidly in the 1970s with the growth of kidnapping (see Chapter 2). Currently the premium income averages $60 million per year of which over 70 per cent is placed with Lloyd's of London.

Various governments have at times tried to make this form of insurance illegal and at first sight this may sound sensible. The arguments are that kidnappers may pick insured persons as victims in the belief that they may pay higher ransoms more quickly and that they may be less ready to cooperate with the police.

None of the arguments, however, are borne out by experience. There are no documented cases known to Lloyd's in which insurance has been the basis of selection of the victim, and no criminal or terrorist appears ever to have mentioned insurance either during a kidnap or after they have been caught, except in one case where they read conjecture in the press that the hostage they were holding was insured – and in this case the hostage was in due course rescued by the police without a ransom being paid.

Lloyd's conditions for kidnap and ransom insurance are, in fact, tightly worded to ensure that none of the arguments do apply. They only issue policies of indemnity within the proven resources of the person insured, i.e. Lloyd's underwriters do not pay ransoms but merely reimburse (up to the limit of the sum assured) what the person has paid out of his own resources, and he is barred from using the policy as a collateral for borrowing money. The policy is conditional on its existence being kept secret and if this condition is broken it is invalidated. It requires that the law enforcement authorities be involved as soon as is practicable consistent with the personal safety of the victim; and payment is only made when those subjected to the extortion are able to show that they have in fact paid ransom. If any payment is forbidden by local law it is an illegal act and no reimbursement will be possible in this case even if payment of ransoms is legal elsewhere.

The business of an underwriter covering kidnap risks depends upon his having the reputation of increasing the chances of the hostage being safely released – as the great majority are – otherwise he would get few clients. The underwriter and his agents will also do their utmost to minimize the chance of the client being kidnapped at all, to limit the damage and to help the police to catch the kidnappers – and again the cooperation they themselves can expect to get from the police will depend upon their reputation for this. As discussed earlier in Chapter 7 under 'Risk management', the parallel with fire insurance is a valid one. No one would suggest that fire insurance makes fire more likely; on the contrary, it reduces the risk and, should a fire occur, helps to limit the damage. This is because fire insurers send experts to survey the premises covered and often piovide incentives in the form of reduced premiums if the insured carries out the recommended fire precautions and installs fire-fighting equipment (sprinklers etc.) to limit the damage.

The Lloyd's syndicate which handles 70 per cent of the world's kidnap and ransom insurance (Cassidy, Davis) follows the same principle. The syndicate retains a firm of consultants (Control Risks) who survey the risk, often at no cost to the client, and recommend ways to guard against it; they advise the client on preparing contingency plans and setting up a crisis management organization and assist him in practising this organization in simulation exercises. In the event of a kidnap a consultant is immediately provided to advise the client throughout the crisis management and negotiation at the underwriters' expense.

As a result it is very rare for an insured client to be kidnapped: of some 2400 kidnaps recorded worldwide since kidnap and ransom insurance burgeoned in 1976, less than 3½ per cent of the victims have been insured. Of those who are, the great majority are released safely, in cooperation with the police. Where ransoms have been paid, the average for cases advised by Control Risks, for both insured and uninsured clients, has been about one-third of the sum originally demanded and a great deal less than the average for all cases, since a large number of kidnaps in the world go unreported and many of these are settled for the full ransom demanded without any reference to the police.

The banning of kidnap and ransom insurance by the government of a particular country does not, in fact, prevent insurance – it merely drives potential victims to place their insurance and pay the ransoms outside the country, and there will always be insurance companies somewhere who are ready to insure and reinsure these risks. Many of these companies will not, however, impose the conditions which Lloyd's do, especially the insistence on cooperation with the police, and will not provide the expert advice from the consultants provided by Lloyd's. The likely result is that there will be more successful kidnaps, higher ransoms paid and fewer arrests and convictions.

LAWS WHICH HELP TO DEFEAT TERRORISM

Laws inhibiting the freedom of action of negotiators and police are clearly counter-productive, but laws which inhibit the operation and support of terrorists are to be encouraged.

The first essential is effective control of firearms and explosives. In some countries the laws are so bad that they lead to a vicious circle, in which ever-widening possession of firearms by criminals is taken to justify wider possession by others, making it still easier for criminals to get them. This is the situation in the USA, where the homicide rate with firearms is one of the highest in the world.

The second essential is for the law to facilitate the detection, arrest *and conviction* of terrorists. The expectation of arrest and conviction is a far greater deterrent than the scale of punishment. Useful laws can inhibit the movement of criminals and terrorists, internally and across frontiers; they can facilitate the custody of suspects to give time for investigation without prejudicing the civil liberties of innocent people; they can empower judges to authorize tapping of telephones to obtain evidence for arrest and conviction of kidnappers; and they can preserve liberal processes of the law by preventing the intimidation of witnesses and juries, the deliberate delaying or disruption of court proceedings and the abuse of privileges enjoyed by lawyers in a free society.

Intimidation of witnesses and juries forced the Republic of Ireland to try terrorist offences before judges without juries in 1962 and the same was done in Northern Ireland 11 years later in 1973. In Great Britain, the Prevention of Terrorism Act has since 1974 permitted the detention of suspects for two days, with provision for extension to seven days with the personal approval of the Home Secretary, for questioning about terrorist offences. After the murder of Dr Schleyer, the West German government introduced an effective package of laws, including restraints on lawyers abusing their privileges in court to disrupt the process of law and using prison visits to act as couriers for convicted terrorists; they also established a highly effective computerized intelligence system. All together, these measures kept Germany virtually free of terrorism for the next seven years. After the murder of Aldo Moro in 1978 the Italian government also introduced laws to improve intelligence, deter intimidation and control deliberate disruption of the judicial process; and, most effective of all, they provided for leniency for 'repentant terrorists' prepared to give information, resulting in the arrest of over 400 left-wing and 150 right-wing terrorists in 1982 and the abandonment of the armed struggle by the Red Brigades in 1983. This last, based on comparison with the years before and after, (e.g. 135 terrorist murders in 1980, 27 in 1982 and 3 in 1983) must have saved hundreds of lives.

Other laws and measures to help the fight against kidnap and extortion might include the means to facilitate immediate tracing of threatening telephone calls. This could be initiated by the person receiving them pressing a panic button which would trigger immediate and, where possible, automatic action in the telephone exchange and in the police station to locate the caller. For crimes involving extortion or intimidation there should be measures to protect the identity of witnesses to protect them from retaliation, especially where the kidnappers are members of a larger criminal or terrorist group; procedures for the recovery of assets of the kidnappers to repay the victim; international cooperation for the loan of specialist resources to assist in investigations; limitation of liability in suits brought by third parties arising from resistance to kidnap; a sentencing policy to reflect the treatment of hostages, duration of captivity and level of ransom demanded; and making it an offence to misuse the media recklessly in such a manner as to put lives at risk.

The dilemma facing a liberal society is where to strike a balance between the essential measures to protect the lives, the freedom from abduction and poisoning, and the tranquillity of the public, and the preservation of their civil liberties, including the civil liberties of minorities. On no account, however, must the 'right' of a militant minority to kidnap, coerce and kill be given priority over the right of the majority to live in peace.

INTERNATIONAL COOPERATION

Various attempts have been made to establish international treaties with binding commitments to cooperate against terrorism, to extradite or prosecute terrorists and to exclude certain offences (e.g. hijacking, kidnapping) from being regarded as political offences providing grounds for evading extradition. Conventions against hijacking and attacks on diplomats were signed by many countries at Tokyo (1963). The Hague (1970) and Montreal (1971). The Convention for the Suppression of Terrorism (1977) was signed by most member countries of the Council of Europe but was largely nullified by exclusions.

The Economic Summit Meeting (of the USA, Canada, Britain, France, Germany, Italy and Japan) at Bonn (1978) agreed to extradite or prosecute hijackers and to boycott both the airports and airlines of any other country which failed to do so. Since these seven countries operate 80 per cent of the non-communist world's air traffic this was potentially a powerful weapon. Later summit meetings in London (1984) and Tokyo (1986) made further agreements, especially to improve cooperation between each other's police and intelligence services.

None of these agreements have had much practical effect because most governments will act primarily in what they believe to be their national self-interest. If, for example, the extradition or imprisonment of a proven Arab hijacker, kidnapper or bomber would prejudice a delicate and lucrative deal with some other Arab country, a government may try to find a way to release him and send him home. They are happy enough to sign an 'extradite or prosecute' agreement if they believe that they can influence the handling of the prosecution or the proceedings of the court in such a way that the accused will be acquitted. Alternatively they will ensure that any agreement not to regard certain offences as political (e.g. kidnapping and bombing) is nullified by a loophole that 'notwithstanding' any such agreement they retain the power to treat *any* offender or offence as political at their own discretion. An article to this effect, inserted during the debate of the Council of Europe Convention for the Suppression of Terrorism, rendered the agreement virtually useless.

There is no prospect of the United Nations achieving anything in this field because the countries which sponsor and support terrorism and regard it as a legitimate international political and economic weapon (including some Arab, African and Latin American countries) will block, or at least never be bound by, any agreement which would curtail their ability to use or support the use of that weapon.

Similarly, most countries in the world would gladly amend the Vienna Convention of 1961 to provide effective safeguards against abuse of the diplomatic bag to smuggle weapons and explosives, but those few (mainly Arab) countries which do abuse it would either not agree to the amendment or would ensure that there were loopholes to enable them to evade it.

The best hope lies in informal bilateral cooperation on a professional level (e.g. police and intelligence services) of countries which have a common interest in countering terrorism, such as the seven countries of the Economic Summit and the other members of NATO. The Economic Summit agreements of 1978, 1984 and 1986 have provided top-level political endorsement for such cooperation and, given this, the professionals will welcome the opportunity to cooperate. Generally, bilateral cooperation between these countries is excellent and is only frustrated when their governments, in pursuit of national interest, override them and find ways of evading their obligation. This will only be cured if the terrorist threat becomes serious enough to alarm them.

10 Response to Product Contamination

EXTORTION AND MALICIOUS CONTAMINATION

There is a fundamental difference in the threat, and therefore also in the response, between extortion by product contamination and politically motivated malicious contamination.

Where the aim is extortion, the threat is to publicise the contamination unless the ransom is paid. Once the story has been blown by the media (which it certainly will be if any poisoned products actually reach the consumer) or by the company warning the public, the criminals have no further lever for extortion. They will therefore usually take some pains, first, to ensure that no contaminated items do in fact reach the consumer, and, secondly, to keep the story out of the media, at least until the ransom has been paid. Successful handling lies in cool-headed and responsible crisis management in the light of these factors.

Where the aim (e.g. of animal rights activists) is to inflict maximum economic damage, the first anyone usually hears of the incident is when the contaminators *do* inform the media that there are polluted products on the shelves (whether this is true or a hoax) and urge them to give this maximum publicity. The key to successful response lies in a good relationship of trust, confidence and discretion between the target companies, the police and the media.

ASSESSING THE CREDIBILITY OF THE THREAT

The first essential on receipt of a threat (in either case) is to establish its credibility. If it is a hoax, huge losses may be incurred unnecessarily. On the other hand, if there really are contaminated products at large, the cost of delay in warning the public and withdrawing suspect stocks, in moral, commercial and legal terms, could be very heavy.

Judging the credibility of the threat is an art, rather than a science, which can be greatly facilitated by good background knowledge of the type of crime and the aims, motivations, problems and perceptions of the criminals, whether their aim is extortion or damage (e.g. animal activism).

It is rare for either animal activists or extortioners actually to want to poison members of the public, not because they are compassionate but because this would be counter-productive. The animal activists do not want to forfeit public sympathy for their cause and extortioners do not want to lose their main bargaining counter. Exceptions to both of these may occur: where, for example, animal activists or malicious poisoners are contemptuous of public opinion and wish simply to inflict maximum damage on the company by arousing enduring public concern about the safety of the product; or where the extortioners are embarked on a phased campaign in which the first phase is not intended to gain money but to establish the credibility of the threat with a view to encouraging capitulation to a heavy ransom demand in a second phase. Both, however, are rare, because they carry greater risks of the operation failing and of the criminals being caught.

CONFLICTING FACTORS

Four conflicting factors must be balanced against each other in the response to product contamination: public policy, and commercial, moral and legal factors.

As with kidnap and ransom, everyone in a perfect world would resist coercion by product contamination and refuse to pay ransoms, since these both finance and encourage further crime. If governments were the victims of product extortion (which they virtually never are) this would be their public policy and they will certainly encourage corporations to adopt it too. Nevertheless, there will be occasions when corporations consider that the risk to life or public health is such that moral considerations make it imperative to buy off the threat, and other occasions when they judge that the negotiation of a small ransom will avert far greater losses to their stockholders while playing for time in order to keep open the best chance of detection and arrest of the extortioners.

Commercial losses can be potentially enormous. Some examples were given in Chapter 6 and there are others in Chapter 19. If real or suspected contamination of food or pharmaceutical products comes to public knowledge, whether because the target corporation warns the public or by any other means, the direct losses in sales may run into millions of pounds. Continuing public anxiety may result in a prolonged or permanent loss of market share – or even the total abandonment of manufacture and sale of an established and successful product. At the same time, if a crisis is prolonged or the threat recurs, there may be large hidden losses arising from diversion of management effort away from marketing the product into the defensive activities of prevention and crisis management. The heaviest and most tragic (in every sense) case of lasting damage was the repeated contamination of Tylenol, involving the murder of eight innocent members of the public in the USA (see Chapter 19). On the other hand, there is encouragement in the resilient adaptiveness of Woolworths (Australia) to repeated attempts at extortion, leading them to establish a permanent contingency planning and crisis management structure which relieves the main stream of management from diversion from their day-to-day task of continuing commercial operations (see Chapter 19).

Moral considerations, however, may outweigh the direct commercial factors. Whatever action the company takes must in the end be publicly defensive, whether it succeeds or fails and whether it comes to light immediately or later. If someone dies as a result of failure by the company to issue a warning or to withdraw suspect stocks, even though the extortioner or animal activist who injected the poison is the real murderer, the public may not regard the company's action as morally defensible and the ultimate commercial losses could be higher than the cost of recalling and withdrawing the product. The legal costs, if the company is held to have been negligent, could be even greater.

THE LAW

Although it is the victim of a crime, a corporation whose products are contaminated may incur legal liabilities to consumers, to its staff, to stockholders and to other corporations or trading partners. It is therefore extremely important that legal advisers are involved throughout in contingency planning and crisis management.

There are, in fact, two aspects of English law which are in need of amendment or, at least, of clarification.

Under current English law, if a criminal (whether for extortion or political purposes) injects a lethal dose of poison into a consumer product available for sale to the public and then warns the manufacturer or the retailer or the police or the media that he has done so, his defence counsel can argue that his warning shows that he did not have the *intent* to kill anyone. If someone did eat the product and die, a jury might find him guilty of murder but, if counsel persuaded them that, say, a retail corporation, having been warned that there were contaminated products at large, had failed to recall or destroy them or warn the public, they might acquit him of murder and find him guilty only of manslaughter (i.e. negligent or reckless action resulting in death). If the corporation, having been warned, were judged to have been criminally negligent or reckless in permitting contaminated goods to fall into the hands of an unsuspecting customer, the persons responsible in the corporation could themselves be charged with manslaughter.

The Criminal Damage Act of 1971 specified up to life imprisonment for criminal damage with *intent* to endanger life or *recklessness* about doing so, but a court might regard a warning as evidence of no intent. The Public Order Act of 1986 comes into force in 1987 and section 38 tightens the law on contamination, including hoaxes. The section reads:

(1) It is an offence for a person with the intention—
   (a) of causing public alarm or anxiety or
   (b) of causing injury to members of the public consuming or using the goods or
   (c) of causing economic loss to any person by reason of the goods being shunned by members of the public or
   (d) of causing economic loss to any person by reason of steps taken to avoid any such alarm or anxiety, injury or loss

to contaminate or interfere with goods or make it appear that goods have been contaminated or interfered with, or to place goods which have been contaminated or interfered with or which appear to have been contaminated or interfered with, in a place where goods of that description are consumed, used, sold or otherwise supplied.

It will also now be an offence, with those intentions, to threaten to commit, or claim to have, or suggest that someone else has committed, such offences; or to be in possession of materials with which to do so.

The maximum penalty is 10 years' imprisonment and a fine.

It remains to be seen how effectively the courts implement this act. It should also cover the consequences of repeated malicious damage to, say, the plate glass window of a butcher's shop to make his insurance premiums too high for him to bear – a frequently declared ALF aim.

There is also a strong case for the government to cover these extra premiums or a 'stop loss' on claims arising from such damage.

PRODUCT RECALL, WITHDRAWAL AND INSURANCE

On receipt either of an extortion threat based on product contamination or of a notification that products have been contaminated by animal rights activists, the first step, again, must be to assess whether it is a hoax or whether it is necessary to accept that it may be real. In the latter case the next most urgent assessment is whether there is a chance that some of the contaminated product may already have got into the hands of the public.

In the early stages, at least, the extortioners or animal activists will probably be anxious to avoid this happening, for the tactical reasons discussed earlier, i.e. that the extortioners will not want to lose their leverage and the animal activists will fear the public fury which would result. There is, however, always the rare possibility that a man with a deep grudge or mental disorder may want to kill people, as in the Tylenol case. From the terms of the threat or warning and from the other evidence (e.g. poisoned products on the shelves, traces of poison in syringes, as were found in some of the turkey contamination cases) it may be possible to make a fairly reliable judgement of whether there is any real risk of poisoned products being at large. If there is any such risk, it is clearly essential to recall all items that may have been affected.

At the same time it will be necessary to withdraw items of suspect stock from retailers' shelves for inspection and, if necessary, destruction; also to place an embargo on movement of stock in warehouses. This decision and its extent will depend again on the judgement of the credibility of the threat, on the assessment of the ease with which the particular products could be contaminated and on the reliability with which they could be inspected and passed as clear. It was because of the ease of contamination that Johnson and Johnson, after the second Tylenol contamination and murder in 1986, decided to cease production of the drug in capsule form.

The problems of withdrawal of stock by retailers vary a great deal. If a large chain of supermarkets or pharmaceutical stores has a good crisis management organization, this can be both quick and efficient; one such chain with over 100 stores in the UK is confident that, from the moment of decision to withdraw a product from sale, there will be no item of that product on the shelves after 40 minutes. At the other extreme, popular items of confectionery on display at tens of thousands of retail outlets down to small kiosks on railway stations and ice-cream vans cannot be withdrawn easily or quickly. The only solution lies in widespread warnings by radio, television and the press to both the retailers and the public.

This problem is, of course, already familiar to retailers because it is sometimes necessary to recall and withdraw items found to have been contaminated accidentally during manufacture. There are consultancies which specialize in this subject, such as Product Safety Ltd (PSL).

It is also possible to insure against product contamination and its consequential costs, including extortion, on conditions similar to those already described for kidnap and ransom insurance. The costs covered can be extended to include the cost of recall, withdrawal and destruction of the product and loss of earnings resulting from the incident. The same Lloyd's syndicate which covers the majority of kidnap and ransom insurance, (Cassidy, Davis), when covering product extortion and related risks, will again provide Control Risks consultants to advise the client on security measures, contingency planning for crisis management and, in the event of an incident, for negotiation and resolution of the crisis.

RELATIONS WITH THE POLICE AND THE MEDIA

Relations between the target corporation, the police and the media are crucial in the case of product contamination and extortion. Animal activists will probably tell the media in the first place but if the call is simply a hoax by an individual, hasty and irresponsible publicity by the media without first consulting the target corporation could cause needless loss and disruption and encourage further hoax calls. There are many such calls and in most cases they are treated responsibly. If, after consultation between the corporation and the broadcasting or newspaper office concerned, the corporation does consider that there is a real chance that the risk is a real one, they will almost certainly decide to warn the public and recall, withdraw and inspect the product, regardless of loss, for the commercial, moral and legal reasons described earlier. In warning the public and retail outlets (particularly if there are a lot of small ones involved) cooperation between the corporation and the media will be of great importance.

A similar need for responsibility and cooperation arises if a product extortion threat comes directly to the knowledge of the media. This will not usually come from the extortioners for the reasons given earlier. Again, responsible journalists will usually consult the corporation before acting on the information. If they disclose it hastily without proper consultation, this will almost certainly result in a further extortion demand, whether such a two-phase operation was originally intended or not.

The record of responsible handling by the media of these and similar crimes (e.g. blackmail) is a reassuring one. Journalists generally do not like blackmailers, extortioners, poisoners or hoaxers, and do not wish to be used by them as pawns. They do not usually, therefore, rush into print.

A relationship of trust between the target corporation and the police is, if anything, even more important but, as with the media, this will be severely prejudiced if the corporation has reason to doubt police discretion. In at least one case a junior police officer doing, no doubt, what he judged to be his duty, did by indiscretion cause a scare, inflicting heavy losses on a corporation over what they were convinced was – and which proved to be – a hoax. This has only to happen occasionally to deter other corporations from trusting the police, leading to crises being handled without police involvement at all, with resulting forfeiture of the chance to arrest and convict and the encouragement of further crimes.

The police, like the corporation, have to reconcile a number of conflicting responsibilities: first, to protect the public from danger and crime; secondly, to arrest criminals and secure evidence for their conviction; thirdly, not to encourage crime by allowing it to reap rewards; and fourthly, to deter future crime – for which by far the best deterrent is a high prospect of detection and conviction. And – as with kidnap – this detection and conviction is unlikely to be achieved without the cooperation of the target of the extortion or malicious contamination or hoax.

Generally the police, like the media, have a record of responsibility and discretion in handling these crimes, the revulsion for which they share with journalists and the public. It is clearly in the interest of corporations to bring in the police at an early stage and, as with kidnap, the initial approach is best made during contingency planning (or failing that when the crisis occurs) to a senior officer – in Britain at Chief or Assistant Chief Constable level – where they can be sure that the need for discretion will be fully understood.

11 Contingency Planning

MINIMIZING MANAGEMENT DIVERSION AND COST

When suddenly faced with a kidnap or other extortion crisis in which lives and millions of pounds may be at stake, management can become obsessed and diverted from the pursuit of its commercial objective. This diversion can be greatly reduced with sound contingency planning and the prior establishment of a crisis management organization. The aims of contingency planning and crisis management are:

   (a) to preserve lives;
   (b) to resolve the crisis with minimum loss of assets;
   (c) to minimize disruption of commercial operations.

Crisis management is a matter of policy, organization and procedures. It must go hand in hand with stress management, which is a matter of communication, to share the load on those responsible and to sustain the morale and cooperation of other executives and staff involved.

Quite apart from direct losses, such as payment of a ransom or destruction of contaminated products, indirect costs can be enormous. These include loss of management time, disruption, cost of communications, travel and accommodation, specialist advisers, legal costs and liabilities, family welfare, publicity and public relations and – arising from the crisis – an enduring loss of market share. During the prolonged kidnap of expatriate executives from five multinational corporations in El Salvador in 1978–80, it was estimated that the average cost to each corporation worked out at $100 000 per day, (though the cost to those who employed specialist advisers was about half that amount).

ESTABLISHING CORPORATE POLICIES

An extortion crisis siezes management by the throat, throwing up unfamiliar problems requiring urgent solutions. A great deal of management time and stress can be avoided if as many policy decisions as possible have been discussed and agreed in advance by a Crisis

Management Committee (CMC), whose structure will be discussed in the next chapter. This committee should meet to make contingency plans, which would include procedures for activating the committee as the executive authority should a crisis arise. Kidnap, short-term abduction, product contamination, bomb threats or warnings should all be considered, along with plans for evacuation of various kinds as appropriate, e.g. of buildings in which bombs are suspected, of isolated premises or residences where security cannot be maintained, or of families and non-essential staff in the face of a more general deterioration of the situation such as occurred in Iran and El Salvador in 1978–80.

Some of the factors which must be taken into account have been discussed in earlier chapters – such as the conflict between commercial, moral, public policy and legal factors; local laws which may lead to criminal or civil proceedings; and legal liability to hostages, families, staff, clients, the public, stockholders, and other corporations including trading and joint venture partners.

The extent and the methods of cooperation with local government and law-enforcement agencies must be decided. If the adversary is an extreme political movement, the government in some countries may demand control of negotiations. Where there is a possibility, policy decisions should be taken in advance on how to respond to such a demand, bearing in mind that the extortioners will be clandestine and will have the initiative in deciding with whom they will and will not negotiate. Insistence by a government on having a representative at the side of the company's or family's negotiator can present problems.

A bomb warning or threat, whether for extortion or malicious disruption will require an urgent assessment of its credibility (i.e. is it a hoax?) and policy decisions on response, particularly on immediate search procedures and the criteria on which to decide on partial or total evacuation of premises.

Extortion demands of all kinds require a similar assessment of credibility. If it is a case of kidnap, this will involve a 'proof of life' question (see next chapter) as early as possible to establish that the extortioners really are the people who hold the victim, not imposters, and that he is alive. It is easier to seize the brief opportunities available for these enquiries if some suitable material for them is already to hand.

In the case of product contamination, criteria should be established for reaching decisions on whether to warn retailers and consumers, whether to recall, withdraw or freeze the product; and procedures for inspection and for tightening security precautions to limit further contamination of other products and in other locations.

For all kinds of extortion, policy decisions should be taken on negotiating strategy, e.g. whether to talk or refuse to talk, whether to be prepared in certain circumstances to pay and, if so up to what limit; and the problems that might arise over raising the money in various currencies. All this will require consideration of what risks should be accepted – risks to life, to staff, to the public, to assets or of legal liabilities. These decisions are seldom black and white, and will be easier to finalize when the time comes if policies have already been thrashed out – often best done in simulation exercises as discussed later in this chapter.

ADMINISTRATIVE PREPARATIONS

The process of contingency planning will indicate the need for a number of administrative preparations. One of these is to design a proforma to be placed by every telephone with instructions on how to proceed if a bomb threat or warning or an extortionary call for kidnap or product contamination is received. An operator or secretary will probably be the first to answer the telephone and may want to transfer it to an executive but the caller will probably refuse to wait and will give a terse and aggressive message, e.g. declaring that there is a bomb or product contamination or kidnap and demanding that a ransom be ready for payment on a certain date when instructions for delivery will be given; there is usually also a warning of dire consequences if the police are informed.

The telephone proforma should list the kind of information the recipient should take note of in addition to getting any details the caller will give about the bomb, contaminated products, etc., especially anything which will help to decide whether or not it is a hoax; information about the caller, e.g. sex, description of voice, accent, whether agitated or calm, young or old; and whether there was any background noise.

The proforma should also give a list of executives and others who should at once be informed, in order of priority. A selected number of these people will have a confidential list of trusted police officers, so the recipient of the call should not normally notify the police direct. Some of these same selected people will also have instructions about who else should be informed – e.g. families in the case of a kidnap –

and on alerting key members of the Crisis Management Committee (see next chapter) who will put certain emergency measures into motion (e.g. inspection or recall of products, or extra security for possible 'second victims' of kidnappers). In the case of bomb warnings, search and possibly evacuation procedures will also need to be considered. In the case of kidnap and other extortion, the immediate taping of telephone calls, if possible including the first, should be amongst the standard contingency preparations, as should urgent arrangements for tapping by the police. In Italy, now, this normally happens within 30 minutes of a kidnap being notified.

In countries where kidnapping is common it is wise to prepare a Confidential Personal File on every individual who is regarded as a high kidnap risk (including data on his family in case they become hostages). The file should include address and telephone numbers; particulars of wife and children, including schools and regular activities (e.g. dancing class on Tuesdays); numbers of their passports, credit cards, identity cards, etc; details of cars; names, addresses and telephone numbers of family doctor and lawyers and of close neighbours and trusted friends; full medical data for emergencies including blood groups of all the family, special problems (e.g. weak heart, diabetes) and any drugs required for them; also an up-to-date photograph, samples of handwriting and voice recordings which, after a kidnap, may assist experts in assessing the victim's health and state of mind and to what extent he is acting under duress. The subject can be invited to insert, if he so wishes, a sealed envelope containing strictly personal data to be opened only if he is kidnapped and then only to be seen by named people. (At least one distinguished hostage in a Latin country had a mistress whose address was known to the police but not to his wife). These files would all, of course, be stored so as to ensure that no one had access to them except named people in an emergency or with the subject's approval.

Since contingency planning will be done by the Crisis Management Committee, or by the shadow Incident Management Team of a subsidiary (see next chapter), it will ensure that individual responsibilities are allocated and recorded, e.g. for liaison with police and the media, care and protection of a hostage's family, etc. It will also review security precautions (see Chapter 7), legal liabilities and insurance policies (e.g. against damage, malicious or otherwise, product contamination, kidnap and ransom, etc.) as described in Chapters 9 and 10.

In overseas subsidiaries in some countries it will be wise to have contingency plans for evacuation in case terrorism or civil strife get out of hand – of families and non-essential staff, or of all expatriates and any local employees who may be victimized. If the need for it does arise, there will be great urgency and little time to organize anything that has been overlooked. Yet such planning will have to be done with great discretion, both to safeguard staff and family morale and to avoid, in a delicate situation, any impression that the company is looking over its shoulder.

A great deal of useful preparation can be publicly justifed, should that be necessary, as a precaution against more general and less sensitive contingencies, not necessarily involving evacuation, such as floods, fires, earthquakes or *coups d'état*. A checklist of preparatory actions should be drawn up by a confidential evacuation committee, headed by a senior executive, with members covering transport, communications, legal and medical matters. One member should, if possible be a trusted locally-born executive.

JOINT PLANNING WITH THE POLICE

Joint planning with the police and other government agencies is an important part of contingency planning, and will depend a great deal on their discretion and reliability in the country concerned, both of the agencies as a whole and of selected and trusted individuals. In the case of a large company or a high-risk individual target, the police are likely to welcome direct alarm links and/or radio and to be willing to advise and help in preparing for telephone calls to be taped or tapped (though this will depend on the local law). The police should themselves be helped to make their own contingency plans, based on detailed reconnaissance, for quick and effective response, e.g. to a bomb threat or a break-in.

LEGAL LIABILITIES

In all contingency planning it is essential to take professional legal advice, probably best achieved by including the corporate legal adviser in the CMC. Local laws affecting dealings with illegal organizations (see Chapter 9) could result in criminal proceedings and there have been civil law suits as a result of both product contamination and kidnap. One hostage sued his corporation for failing to protect him and then failing to secure his release earlier. He lost his case, but the widow of another kidnap hostage, in Guatemala, who had been killed when the police attempted to rescue him, was awarded £1.25 million against his corporation in a 'wrongful death' settlement. Both of these were US-based corporations operating in Latin America.

Care must also be taken over legal liability to local trading or joint venture partners for any decisions which may have to be taken. To guard against being successfully sued by stockholders, it is important that the board of directors give and record their authority to their crisis management committee and incident management teams to negotiate and, if necessary, to pay a ransom up to a resolved maximum. Such suits, whether successful or not, can throw a heavy load on senior executives and, even if the plaintiff loses the case, he may well go bankrupt without paying the costs awarded against him. All of these legal liabilities – criminal and civil – should be foreseen and considered in contingency planning to ensure that they do not add unexpected problems to the crisis.

PUBLIC RELATIONS PLANNING

In either a kidnap and ransom or a product or bomb extortion, some of the media and some individual journalists, if well handled, may act as positive and valuable allies, while others may be damaging and put lives at risk. On the positive side, their reports can be phrased so as to make a psychological impact on the kidnappers, and to influence the climate of public opinion; they can, on occasions, provide the quickest or even the only channel for attracting the attention of kidnappers during a long period of silence. On the harmful side, they may arouse the kidnappers' expectations by exaggerating the wealth of a company or family; or they may endanger the life of the hostage by revealing that his negotiator is cooperating with the police, or by publishing details of police surveillance or of projected rescue operations. They may also damage the image of the company and the morale of its staff. The media themselves are also under many pressures, in some countries from rival media and in others from government control.

It can pay great dividends if a company can nourish friendly contacts with trusted editors and journalists, because both sides can benefit. If the company shows its willingness to trust the journalist by giving him privileged information in times of tranquillity and crisis, he knows that betrayal of that trust will lose him a highly valued source in the future.

Once such a relationship has been established and proved (except where the journalist has devious motives from the start, and these usually become apparent) experience has shown that it is very rare for it to be deliberately betrayed.

One member of the CMC will be made responsible for public relations. It will be important for him to go through all the likely scenarios in the contingency planning stage, and to establish agreements on PR policy. This is probably best done by means of simulation exercises.

TRAINING AND SIMULATION EXERCISES

To reduce the risk and to effectively handle a crisis if it occurs, executives and staff must be trained and practised. Discretion will be needed, both to avoid causing alarm and anxiety and to avoid arousing trade union opposition or demands for danger money. The best approach is to convince the staff that the better and more evident the standard of security and alertness, the smaller is the likelihood of being picked as a target.

Crisis management committees, incident management teams and evacuation committees can best be trained by simulation exercises. One of the best techniques is termed a 'hypothetical', which was developed by the Harvard Law School and promoted by the Ford Foundation. The members of the CMC and others who may have responsible roles in a crisis are seated round a horseshoe of tables facing inwards, each ready to play his own role. The exercise depends on a highly skilled moderator who has done comprehensive preparation. He presents a hypothetical situation and throws problems at individuals as they arise. For example, the moderator plays the part of the kidnapper at the other end of the telephone. He then carries the situation forward in the light of the responses of the role-playing members. Such a hypothetical is normally done continuously for about three hours.

A highly successful example was a hypothetical run by the BBC in November 1979, at which the key role-players were journalists and police officers, government officials and politicians. The hypothetical situation was the seizure of an embassy by Middle Eastern terrorists in London and was an uncanny prediction of the actual situation which was to arise six months later at the London Iranian Embassy siege. The hypothetical was off the record and amongst those taking part were the editor of BBC Television News (Alan Protheroe), a BBC TV reporter (Kate Adie) and the police officer who was later in charge of the actual siege (John Dellow). All of these three, and many others (e.g. the editor of the *Daily Mirror* and one of his reporters) were destined to be intensely and personally involved in the real thing six months later. There is no doubt that the hypothetical exercise, in which these 20 people reacted to each other in the precise problems they were to face, contributed enormously to their successful cooperation and handling of the Iranian Embassy siege when it came.

A variant of this type of simulation is the 'paper chase', much used by the British police and military staff colleges, in which a series of pre-planned situations on paper are handed out to the participants who are, once again, playing the roles they are likely to play in practice. Given the necessary exercise staff, these paper situations can be adjusted and revised to take account of the responses of the participants. Normally carried out as a one-day-exercise, a crisis management committee is presented with, say, six or eight situations in turn, with an imaginary gap of several days or weeks between them. Each situation presents a crisis which the CMC discusses, moving on through each in turn to a dénouement.

Since all the key executives in the CMC should be playing their own roles – security, PR, finance, personnel, legal, etc. – a simulation can be best planned and conducted by someone from outside. This could be a consultancy specializing in security against kidnap and extortion who could devise scenarios based on their experience in actual crises in which they have been involved. Periodic simulation exercises could be part of a package in which the consultancy advises and assists the corporation in reviewing and improving its security, making contingency plans and setting up a crisis management organization, including a commitment to assist training and to attend as advisers on crisis management and negotiation if a crisis does occur.

12 Crisis Management

CRISIS MANAGEMENT STRUCTURE

To achieve the aims set out in the previous chapter – to preserve life and to resolve the crisis with minimum loss of assets and minimum disruption of commercial operations – a two-tier structure is desirable: a Crisis Management Committee (CMC) at corporate level and Incident Management Teams (IMT) at local or subsidiary level. Both should have been established previously to conduct contingency planning and will be activated immediately if a crisis occurs. The following should normally be represented:

CMC (Corporate policy)
Chairman ⎤ in case one
Deputy Chairman ⎦ is absent
Coordinator (full-time in crisis)
Security
Financial
Legal
Personnel
Regional/International
Public Relations

IMT (Local day-to-day management)
Manager
Security
Legal
Negotiator
Specialist Consultant
Representative from
    corporate HQ when necessary

In the CMC the role of the full-time coordinator is crucial. He must be nominated during contingency planning which must also include plans for his immediate relief from other duties in a crisis. In many corporations he will be the director responsible for security. He must be sufficiently senior to take most of the decisions himself (in the light of policy decisions already taken) because his primary function is to leave the other CMC members free to concentrate on maintaining commercial operations, referring to them only when necessary for confirmation of major decisions or for periodic updating. If the IMT is in a distant subsidiary he will no doubt visit it from time to time.

The subsidiary also has to continue trading and here the key figure is the negotiator, who will most often be a local lawyer (probably the subsidiary's legal adviser). Once negotiating contacts are established, it is often possible for the negotiator, assisted by the specialist consultant, to handle the crisis without diverting the management from commercial operations except, as with the full-time coordinator in the CMC, for referral of major decisions (such as a ransom offer) and periodic updating.

IMMEDIATE REACTION TO A CRISIS

The means by which threats or extortion demands are communicated were discussed in Chapter 4. The first demand is usually an extremely brusque and aggressive telephone call, and the use of a proforma to guide the reaction of whoever first receives such a call was recommended in Chapter 11.

Depending on geographical considerations, such a call may come direct to the corporate head office. In the case of a kidnap of an overseas executive of a multinational corporation it will usually come to the subsidiary company, or to the hostage's family or to a local newspaper, any of whom will quickly inform the company office. The IMT will then at once be activated and information sent to the head office, who will activate its CMC. The rest of this chapter, except where otherwise stated, is based on the kidnap of a member of a subsidiary located in a different country from its parent corporate head office. Variations applicable to negotiation by governments or families, and in product contamination and other forms of extortion are discussed later in the chapter.

Both the CMC and the IMT will need at once to assess the threat. They have to decide quickly whether to treat it seriously or as a hoax and whether the callers really do hold the hostage they claim to have taken. Once any extortion incident has reached the media, it is commonplace for other gangs and individuals to try to extort money by a false claim to hold a hostage (or to have the power to release contaminated products, if that was the basis of the extortion).

If the CMC/IMT decide to treat it seriously they will, at their first meeting, review any prior policy decisions concerning negotiation; also regarding notification of staff, families, government agencies, police and the media. The CMC will establish its full-time coordinator and the IMT will select (or confirm the appointment of) its negotiator. Both may decide to call on the services of a specialist consultant, whom they may already have consulted during contingency planning and who will be provided at underwriters' expense if they are insured.

It will be urgent to establish secure communications between the CMC and IMT, between the IMT and the police and, of course, with the extortioners. The last will hold the initiative in this matter but it should be possible to agree upon a telephone number for them to ring and, if possible, upon a time at which they should use it.

It will be necessary to establish an organization to collect and collate information and to keep a log from the start of the crisis, so that patterns and trends can be discerned and so that, if the crisis is prolonged and requires reliefs and shifts, those coming on duty will be in the picture. As part of this organization it will be wise to install tape recorders on any telephones which may be used for negotiation and, depending upon the relationship with the police and confidence in their discretion, to arrange for these telephones to be tapped.

This information organization will be closely linked, or may coincide, with the organization for handling public relations. As soon as any inkling of the crisis reaches the media, the officer of both the headquarters and the subsidiary will be inundated with calls and requests for interviews. As discussed in Chapter 11, some of these will be positive and useful but others could be harmful and dangerous. To avoid rumours and the creation of hostility in the media, and to nurture and develop useful and positive journalistic liaison, it is essential that one or more people are earmarked to handle these calls (and to protect others from being troubled with them) and are fully briefed on the policy lines to be taken.

The load imposed by a major crisis will necessitate other special staffing arrangements, including preparation of rosters and appointment of deputies.

Because of the open-ended possibilities of immediate or subsequent legal problems, as discussed in Chapters 9, 10 and 11, it will be essential to involve legal advisers both at corporate and subsidiary levels from the start.

In the case of product contamination or the threat of it, amongst the most urgent decisions at the first meetings of the CMC and IMT will be those concerning warning, recall, withdrawal, inspection and notification of the police and the media as discussed in Chapter 10.

Immediate consideration must also be given to tightening security to meet the extra threats imposed by the crisis (e.g. in a kidnap case the possibility of a second victim being taken, such as another executive or a family member) as this would greatly strengthen the hand of the kidnappers in negotiation. At the same time, security of communications and of documents will need to be tightened and all staff warned to be discreet, in view of the intensification of the quest for such information both by accomplices of the extortioners and by the media.

THE ROLE OF THE NEGOTIATOR

The selection of a negotiator is probably the most important single decision of the IMT. Ideally, where the kidnap risk is high, this selection will have been made in advance during contingency planning, but in practice this does not often occur, either because the threat does not seem to be sufficiently urgent, or because the choice may be affected by the circumstances, by what is known of the kidnappers, what they are demanding and the identity of the hostage (who may in the event be an expatriate, a locally-employed member of staff, or a wife or child). It is not uncommon for the kidnappers to ask the hostage to suggest the first person to be notified and the person to conduct negotiations. In the case of Leon Richardson's kidnap (see Chapter 13), which was totally unexpected, this request was made and his choice – though by no means conventional – proved to be an inspired one.

In normal circumstances, the best choice for negotiator is a local man because he knows not only the language, but also the social structure and the detailed geography; he should be accustomed to negotiation so a local lawyer is often chosen. Sometimes an intermediary who is likely to be trusted by the kidnappers may be a wise choice, provided that he is trusted by the company or family concerned and preferably also by the police.

Above all, the negotiator must be willing to do the job, which is exhausting and may place him at risk, and he must have the necessary personal qualities. He must be reliable and discreet and have the determination and the nerve to handle what are often aggressive and very brief telephone calls during which his instant reactions may be decisive. He must be capable of detached judgement and should therefore not be a member of the hostage's family nor emotionally too close to him (though there have been successful exceptions to this, notably in the Richardson case). He must have intelligence at least matching that of the kidnappers (which in the case of some political terrorists is high), patience so as not to provoke them and the initiative to spot, seize and exploit any opportunity, however small. He should not, however, have too cold a personality. A sense of humour and the ability to show warmth and feeling may help him to develop a working relationship with the kidnappers' negotiator, which can greatly facilitate negotiations and may save the victim's life. He must, on the other hand, have the necessary iron in his personality to seize the initiative and dominate the kidnappers when he senses that they are beginning to become anxious to reach a settlement before the police close in on them.

The negotiator should not normally be the person responsible for making policy decisions, (though again Richardson's negotiator was an exception) because it is useful for him to be able to play for time by saying, for example, 'I have no power to agree to that. I will put it to the company and, if you telephone again at the same time tomorrow, I will give you their reaction. I am doing my best to put your arguments to them but you must understand my position.' He needs precise instructions before every communication as to how far he may and may not go. The timing and location of the next contact should, if possible, be agreed with the kidnappers so that the negotiator can take it in a secure environment and at a time that will not unacceptably disrupt any other commitments he has. Here again, any rapport with his adversary will be valuable because they may well feel that their chances would be set back if he were replaced by another negotiator.

THE ROLE OF THE CONSULTANT

Though there have been a number of exceptions, it is rare for a family or corporation to be picked twice as a target for extortion by kidnap, because after one experience they so improve their security that future would-be kidnappers will turn away and choose an easier target. The corollary, however, is that when the firm or family do face a crisis they are usually facing it for the first time. As a result, they may have little idea what to do and may react in a state of shock. This can have a disastrous effect, increasing the risk to a hostage's life, the duration of his ordeal and the prospect of paying a very large ransom.

During the dramatic growth in kidnapping in the 1970s and 1980s, many families and firms paid out enormous sums in ransoms accompanied by a damaging diversion of management time and effort and, sometimes, a catastrophic effect on trading. The demand for specialist advice, both for preventive security and crisis management, has grown. A number of security companies were formed to meet this demand and some of these have now built up a large fund of experience. They are able to put this experience at the disposal of a client who has never previously handled such a situation. A relevant comparison is with an accountant, doctor or lawyer who applies his experience both to pre-empt his client's troubles and to help him to handle them if they occur.

In describing what should and should not be expected of such a consultancy the author has drawn on the experience of Control Risks Ltd with which he has been associated since its foundation in 1975. About 85 per cent of their work comprises threat assessment and preventive surveys and 15 per cent response services, i.e. assistance in handling an actual crisis. At the time of writing they have carried out preventive surveys for over 1100 corporate and family clients and participated in crisis management and negotiation in over 200 extortion-related incidents (about 110 kidnaps and 90 product contaminations and other forms of extortion). These have included a proportion in which their services were provided to the clients free by the Cassidy, Davis Syndicate at Lloyd's. Approximately half of Control Risks' work has been done for insured clients and half for uninsured. Their consultants are recruited almost entirely from people with experience in public services, notably the police, the armed forces and the security and intelligence services.

There are, of course, other consultancies which provide some of the same services and some different ones. Inevitably, in a field which has expanded rapidly in response to a surge in demand, quality varies. The best way of choosing between them is to ask other corporations or individuals who have had occasion to use professional consultants in a similar situation. Other considerations are: to be wary of consultants who have links with equipment manufacturers since their advice may not be wholly objective; to find out the number of cases handled by the consultancy, particularly in the country concerned or in neighbouring countries; and to find out as much as possible about the professional background of the individual consultants they employ.

Control Risks have a number of divisions, the ones most relevant to this chapter dealing with information, prevention and response. The information service provides regular assessments of political and security risks all over the world, available on-line or in hard copy. The prevention division carries out surveys of corporate security, advises on improving it, undertakes project management of physical improvements on an agency basis if required, assists in contingency planning and setting up a crisis management organization, and provides education and training. These are provided in the form of seminars and simulation exercises (see previous chapter) for top and middle management, covering contingency planning, crisis management, hostage survival, evacuation planning and travel security. Training courses are also run for management and staff taking up appointments overseas; for security, office and domestic staff; and for bodyguards and drivers.

The response division provides consultants to advise on crisis management and negotiation if a crisis occurs (e.g. a kidnap or product contamination). Fees are on a daily consultancy basis (except where they are provided at underwriters' expense) or can be covered by a security agreement under which an annual subscription guarantees the fees (but does not insure against ransom) for a priority service by the consultants up to an agreed maximum which will normally cover the duration of the crisis.

The consultant's role is to advise and assist the corporate security director (not to duplicate him) in his tasks of training, prevention or response. When help is provided in response to a crisis, a consultant will go at once to the place where the negotiation is being handled – i.e. the IMT – and, if the crisis is prolonged, he will be relieved from time to time by another. As described earlier, once the IMT is in its stride, this consultant and the negotiator will probably be able to handle things without the need to bother the higher management in the IMT except for major policy decisions.

At the same time, another consultant will probably go, as soon as the call comes, to the corporate head office (if that is separate from the out-station where the IMT is operating) to advise the CMC on setting up its organization and communications, providing relevant up-to-date information and discussing strategy; he would thereafter visit periodically as required.

In the case of insured clients the consultant has one further role – that of insurance assessor. As with fire insurance there is always a possibility of fraud – the equivalent of arson – by staging a bogus kidnap, paying a 'ransom' and claiming it back. Since the consultant provided by the underwriters (at any rate by the Cassidy, Davis Syndicate at Lloyd's) is closely involved and sees that the police are involved too, there is in practice no chance of such a fraudulent claim being undetected.

NEGOTIATING TACTICS

In the setting of a kidnap crisis in an overseas subsidiary it is assumed that the negotiation will be conducted by its IMT, though the principles will be the same if the kidnap is nearer home (e.g. of a senior executive at the head office) and the CMC also acts as IMT. As soon as it is activated, the CMC or IMT will need to establish or confirm a negotiating strategy with a realistic objective and a tactical plan to achieve that objective.

The first demand from the kidnappers will be aggressive, and their technique will aim to demoralize the negotiator and the executives holding the responsibility for the hostage's safety. They will alternate between brutal threats (including threats to kill or dismember) and sometimes long periods of silence, which can be very frustrating (see Chapter 4). They will attempt to coerce by fear, exploiting the appetite of the media for human drama to maximize the stress on the hostage's company and family. Threats to kill and mutilate the hostage or of indefinite detention are standard practice.

If the kidnappers have done their homework, they will have made a judgement of what the corporation or family can afford or are likely to pay. They will have studied any weak points and their aim will be to establish a psychological domination. They will use every strategem, direct or indirect to keep up the pressure to settle. If the hostage is an executive, for example, they may send recorded messages direct to his wife in the hope that she will harass the company. The Montoneros in Argentina, who have extorted more in ransoms than any other movement on record, advised their members to select executives for kidnap who had determined and articulate wives who would put pressure on the corporations or government to give way. All this, coupled with the threat of the hostage's wife or children being taken as second hostages, strengthens the case for moving the family out of the country where the hostage is held.

The kidnappers may also try to influence the media with similar objectives – to further the impression amongst both families and company staff that the company cares less about the lives of its staff than about hanging on to its money. As was discussed in the previous chapter, the IMT should try to establish positive contacts with editors and journalists to foster helpful and responsible comment on the case. If they can persuade an editor that a certain line is likely to be seen by the public as adding to the risk to the life of the hostage he will probably refrain from that line to avoid the odium that this would incur.

The CMC and IMT and their negotiator should seize every chance to build up the psychological pressure on the kidnappers in cooperation with the media, the police and other security forces. The kidnappers are unlikely, despite their threats, to kill their hostage so long as they still have hopes of getting a ransom for him, so they will, as time goes on, feel a growing fear that unless they get their money soon they may lose everything. They will, however, be reluctant to settle for anything less than enough to cover their costs and commitments (e.g. the payment of hired abductors and guards) plus at least some profit. To keep these hopes alive (lest they do decide to cut their losses, kill the hostage and abduct another), it may be wise to make some kind of offer quite early on in the negotiations. They will no doubt indignantly reject this but it can then be made clear to them that this offer will only be raised in response to a lowering of their own demand.

Though the negotiator, the IMT and the CMC will hope that, given time, the police will be able to rescue the hostage without any payment at all (as in the Guinness case in 1986 and many others), they should set themselves a target towards which to push the negotiation while this time is gained. Experience has shown that tensions amongst the kidnappers build up and, after an apparently implacable attitude to start with, they start to lower their demands more quickly. As this begins to happens the negotiator should be able to increase his domination over them. As the kidnappers become more worried about the risk of detection, the urgency of their desire to settle increases and becomes more apparent.

Throughout the negotiations, and especially as the case approaches its climax, the consultant should provide the negotiator and the IMT with a regular reappraisal of the risk and, in the light of this, a position paper deducing what line the kidnappers are likely to take next, how to respond to it and how to increase the pressure on them and gain the initiative. The kidnappers will still try to keep their telephone calls brief, to avoid them being traced, so a good consultant will brief and rehearse the negotiator in readiness to handle the next call before it comes.

Proof-of-life calls are an essential feature of negotiation, i.e. questions which only the hostage could answer (e.g. 'What is the name of your aunt who lives in Eastbourne?'). These are more reliable than, for example, photographs of the hostage holding the morning paper with its headline visible. These can be fudged, and there is at least one case of a dead hostage being propped up to be photographed in this way. The kidnappers will expect to be asked proof questions and, regardless of angry objections, will not refuse to get the answers if the victim is alive because it is in their interest to do so; they know that people will not pay a ransom for a dead hostage. Proof calls are necessary throughout, as a prelude to any offer during negotiations and especially at the start (to establish that those demanding the ransom do actually have the hostage), and before any final deal to resolve the case.

NEGOTIATION BY FAMILIES AND GOVERNMENTS

Where a ransom is demanded from a victim's family rather than from a corporation the principles for negotiation remain the same but there are some important differences in procedure. The family will be more limited in resources and money and will probably have no obvious office in which to establish the negotiator. They may well use the office of a lawyer to whom the task of negotiation is delegated or, if the hostage or one of his close friends or relations is a businessman, his business office may be used. On some occasions (e.g. see the Richardson case, Chapter 13) there is no clear distinction between the firm and the family. On other occasions, the kidnappers may be trying to extort ransoms and concessions simultaneously from the family, a corporation and a government.

Although it is usually unwise for an emotionally involved member of the family to be the negotiator, the head of the family or the next-of-kin of the hostage will inevitably remain responsible for negotiating policy because, ultimately, they are the only people with power to offer money in negotiation. Some families have established a full CMC structure and operated it successfully. In other cases communications between the family and whoever they may delegate as negotiator have been more informal. As with a corporation, a family and its negotiator can gain both comfort and tactical expertise if they are advised by an experienced consultant.

When a government official is kidnapped in his own country, most governments activate the crisis management organization which they will already have in being to control all such incidents, be they hijacks, kidnaps, hostage seizures, bomb threats or natural disasters. In Britain this is known by the acronym COBRA and is headed by the Secretary of State for Home Affairs. Its permanent executive secretary is a senior civil servant in the Home Office and it includes representatives of government services as appropriate (e.g. police, military and intelligence) and of other ministries if they are likely to be involved (e.g. foreign and transport ministries). Most governments have well-publicised policies that no ransoms will be paid and no concessions made and this is both practical and wise (see Chapter 9).

They should and generally do, however, show some flexibility in negotiation, exactly as corporations and families do, to gain both time and information to increase the chances of rescue of the hostage and arrest and conviction of the kidnappers. A good example of this was the German government's handling of the Schleyer case, which was described in Chapter 9.

Due to the high incidence in recent years of hostage siege situations (especially in embassies) and of aircraft hijacks (a form of hostage siege) the British government and many others maintain a pool of highly trained police negotiators. Since not only the hostages but also their captors are surrounded and cannot escape, there is less pressure of time and this is a very different kind of negotiation from that with kidnappers in a secret hideout. Though there have been some bloody exceptions, governments have a high record of success in hostage siege situations because they do hold most of the high cards and know how to play them.

Governments have had a more mixed record of success in handling negotiations with kidnappers in secret hideouts. In the case of kidnapped ambassadors, there are at least two governments involved (host and parent), and the kidnappers may be subjecting both to different pressures. After some initial faltering during 1968–73 (see Chapter 2) governments have generally stood firm, and diplomats and other public servants accept that this must be so. Many governments require their ministers to sign a letter to this effect before taking office.

Greater problems arise when the victim is not a government official but the concessions are demanded from a government. Examples of this are the Starr and Schleyer cases discussed in Chapters 14 and 15. In the Schleyer case, the family tried to secure his release with a ransom, but the kidnappers were only interested in coercing the government to release convicted terrorists and Schleyer was murdered. In the Starr case, a private consortium raised the money on behalf of the family and he was released. In both cases the governments gave their approval to these offers but made it clear that they would make no concessions themselves.

Negotiation for the release of victims of anti-development abductions (see Chapter 5) often have to be done by governments, especially where the demand is for recognition of a dissident movement or for publicity. Sometimes, however, the demand is for money from corporations. The special problems involved were discussed in Chapter 5 and are illustrated in the case studies in Chapter 16.

NEGOTIATION IN BOMB AND PRODUCT EXTORTIONS

Negotiations in cases of extortion by bomb threat and product contamination follow the same principles of coercive argument but the underlying nature of the threat is very different. In particular the duration is usually much shorter and, although there may be an implied threat to the public, the immediate drama of a pistol to the head of an individual is missing.

In the case of a bomb threat, the extortioners will usually try to avoid killing people, either by setting off bombs when premises are closed except for skeleton guards, or by giving warning so that buildings can be evacuated. The threat is to repeat the bombing when the premises are crowded unless a ransom is paid. The extortioners will realize, however, that this would arouse such public fury that maximum police effort would be devoted to catching them, so they are in practice unlikely to carry it through without warning. Negotiatiors are therefore facing a threat of possible disruption of trading and damage rather than threat to life and, assuming that they are covered by insurance, they will have a strong hand to play, though both nerve and determination will be needed.

Negotiating with product extortioners was discussed from the viewpoint of the extortioner in Chapter 6. The crucial factor is the relationship between the company, the police and the media, as was discussed in Chapter 10. If a relationship of trust and confidence has been built up, experience suggests that there is a good chance of successful negotiation and arrest of the extortioners. That is why, when the target corporation indicates its determination to resist, the extortion is so often abandoned. To pay immediately in secret, though it may seem the easiest option to reduce the chance of heavier commercial losses is, in fact, bad tactics.

PAYING A RANSOM AND RELEASE OF THE HOSTAGE

The time may come when the payment of a ransom offers the best opportunity for the arrest (or, at least, to get leads towards a future arrest) of the extortioners. Kidnappers and other extortioners are themselves well aware of the risk and will go to great lengths to minimize it. In many product extortions they have taken fright in the course of negotiations and abandoned the whole operation. Police forces, too, are well are of the opportunities offered by ransom payments. Some have made such clumsy use of the opportunity that it has been thrown away; others, such as the FBI, have consistently handled it with sophistication and skill, coupled with sympathy and cooperation with those paying it, resulting in their remarkably high rate of hostage survival and arrest of kidnappers.

The most difficult problem to be solved in paying a ransom may be raising the necessary currency. In many countries the banking and finance regulations may make it hard to do this without it leaking out (especially if, as often happens, the demand is for payment in a hard foreign currency). If it does leak out, the kidnappers may abort the operation and demand a completely fresh negotiation, possibly adding to the hazards and hardships of the victims and reducing the prospects of successful rescue and detection.

Modern international methods of electronic transfer of money now make this an increasingly attractive method of demanding payment, but only by sophisticated criminal gangs or political movements with access to the banking systems in both the country in which payment is to be initiated and that in which it will be secretly banked.

The majority of ransom payments are still made in currency, either foreign or local. The extortioners will demand that the ransom should be in used notes of low denominations, not with consecutive numbers. Two dilemmas arise: first, whether the notes should be real or counterfeit or a mixture; secondly whether they should be recorded and marked. The danger with counterfeit money is that, if a police operation to intercept the ransom collectors fails, there may be retaliation against the hostage, so, though it has on occasions been used in product and bomb extortion cases, it is seldom if ever used in kidnap cases. The problem with recording and marking is the time this takes. For this reason and to gain more all-round flexibility in negotiation, it may be wise to put the process of collecting currency in motion earlier in the negotiations, even though in the event the need to deliver it may be averted. Special care, however, will be needed to ensure that this is known only to carefully selected people in the banks, etc. who can be trusted not to reveal it.

When the detailed negotiations for the actual payment of a ransom begin, the kidnappers may try to reduce their risks by insisting that the negotiator switches instantly to a different telephone number, or they may change the method of communication altogether without warning. They will make more than usually aggressive threats and may well try to insist that a specific person whose face they know must deliver the ransom alone. The negotiators, however, can make it clear that no one can be forced to volunteer for this job and, bearing in mind that kidnappers are likely to be anxious to get this dangerous phase over as quickly as possible, the demand can be resisted.

The instructions for delivery will be like those in a treasure hunt. The deliverer will be directed to find a clue at a spot chosen to make police surveillance difficult and detectable. This clue will direct him to the next one and he may well be ordered to switch to a different car which he will find near his own in the car park. If the kidnappers are at all suspicious they are likely to abort the ransom collection. If not, the deliverer may be told to drop the ransom at a named point and move on. Some have been ordered to drop it from the window of a train or even by landing a helicopter briefly in a jungle clearing. If he meets the kidnappers at all, it may well be in a sudden ambush by masked men at a point on the route where he least expects it – and nearly always in darkness.

The negotiators should insist that there be a proof-of-life call immediately before delivery of the ransom; also some proof that the ransom is going to the people who hold the hostage – e.g. by those who collect it handing over something unique to the hostage such as his passport or credit card or, at the least, that this identification be included in one of the final written directions in the 'treasure hunt' series.

The police will almost always press for facilities to keep the ransom vehicle under surveillance. In some of the cases described in Part III a police officer successfully masqueraded as one of the deliverers. The kidnappers, however, will be extremely wary and, while doing their best to cooperate with the police, the CMC and IMT must ensure that whatever arrangements they may make do not impose unacceptable risks. In countries with an efficient and responsible police force this will be well understood. Bearing in mind that collecting the ransom is an operation which the kidnappers are going to carry out in any case, a good police force, with discreet cooperation, has a good chance of obtaining the information it needs to make arrests and recover the money.

Once the ransom is in their possession, the kidnappers will search it for electronic devices and try to detect if part or all of it is counterfeited or marked. They may put in motion a laundering process to disperse the money through criminal or commercial outlets before they release the hostage. On some occasions they may double-cross and try to extort a second ransom. This has been attempted, mainly by criminal gangs in Italy but it is rare (about one case in twenty) because it adds considerably to the kidnappers' risks at their most dangerous juncture.

The hostage is seldom released immediately. The delay may vary from a few hours to several weeks but is, on average, one or two days after payment of a ransom. He is almost always released from a car in a place where the car is unlikely to attract any attention or its details be observed or reported. The commonest place is on a deserted road in an urban area, within walking distance of a telephone, in the dark, with the hostage ordered not to remove his blindfold for a stated number of minutes.

SIEGE AND RESCUE

If the location of the hideout is detected and it is surrounded, the nature of the situation is radically changed. The matter will thereafter be handled by the police or the army. They now have the initiative and no longer have to wait for the next message at the whim of the kidnappers. The kidnappers themselves become the prisoners, even though they hold a hostage within the prison; and they become utterly dependent on their besiegers. If they have more than one hostage they can kill one (and have sometimes done so) to force the pace, but if they do they realize that they are sealing their own doom. If they have only one hostage they are unlikely to kill him, because they will then not have a card in their hand to deter the police from coming in shooting.

Most sieges have therefore ended successfully, with the release of the hostages alive and with the arrest of the kidnappers – and this includes the majority of hijacks once the aircraft has landed in a country unsympathetic to the hijackers. A number of cases are examined in Part III.

Unless the kidnappers can be surprised and overwhelmed in the first few minutes (in which case it is a raid rather than a siege), the essence of a successful siege is patience. There are three stages: containment, negotiation and release. The containment is the most dangerous stage, because the kidnappers, shocked at finding themselves surrounded, may go berserk if rushed, turning upon their victims and then, possibly, upon themselves.

Care should be taken not to use force too soon or escalate it too quickly. Once any particular level of force has been reached, it is hard to reduce it. Once the kidnappers have decided that they want to get out alive the most dangerous period has passed. The police will normally be advised by a psychiatrist, and he may be able to identify this moment. Thereafter the aim should be to soothe the kidnappers, taking all the time in the world. They should, however, be given no hope for any reward but to emerge alive – and then only to a prison cell. The only incentives are negative ones. The longer or more violently they resist, the longer their sentence is likely to be and the more likely they are to die.

The negotiator should be a police officer who, though trained in kidnap negotiations, is of fairly junior rank, because he must (like any other negotiator) be able to play for time by saying, 'I have no power to agree to that; I'll have to ask'. On occasions, close friends or relations have been used to try to persuade kidnappers to surrender, but this can be counter-productive because it may arouse their emotions and increase the risk of their behaving irrationally.

The kidnappers may try to push the hostage into acting as negotiator on their behalf. This should be resisted; first, because he is not a free agent; and secondly, because this would deny the police and their psychiatric adviser some of their opportunity to analyse the kidnappers' state of mind.

The negotiator, while constantly encouraging surrender, should give nothing away too easily. The kidnappers should not be given food or water unless their need is becoming desperate; they should be driven into the same relationship which they imposed on their victim: that of a baby dependent for everything upon its mother.

It may, on occasions, be wise to give them a transistor radio (unless they already have one). Political terrorists, in particular, may become frustrated to the point of violence if they are isolated; but the knowledge that their siege (and with it their cause) is known to the outside world may be enough to lead them to surrender. Also, with lives at stake, radio stations will usually broadcast responsibly in response to police requests, and this can be a positive asset.

During the siege the rapport between the kidnappers and their hostage may increase, because they now share much of the same predicament. This should be given every encouragement, no matter how galling it may be to the police to be abused by the hostage, because it may save his life.

At the same time, a skilled negotiator may be able to build up a kind of rapport of his own with the kidnappers, especially if the impression is given that his higher authority is being hard-nosed; he can exploit the 'mother and baby' relationship to the full.

The police should try to wear down the resistance of the kidnappers. Negotiators should work in shifts. Lights should be beamed through the windows and noise – such as vehicle engines or loud-hailer tapes constantly urging surrender – can be used to keep them awake.

The police psychiatric adviser should, if possible, be with the negotiators throughout. The room should be bugged as soon as possible and all conservations between the kidnappers and with their hostage should be taped. This helps the psychiatrist to judge how they are likely to react to new negotiating ploys or to an assault. At the original Stockholm siege, for example, the psychiatrist, Dr Bejerot, had to pick the right moment to advise the release of tear-gas into the locked bank vault – a risky operation as those inside would have suffered severe lung damage in such a confined space if not out within 90 seconds. But the kidnappers did surrender at once without harming the hostages.

RAIDS

If the police locate a secret kidnap hideout they have to decide whether to put it under discreet surveillance, or besiege it openly, or mount a surprise raid. In the Kaloghirou case (see Chapter 15) they chose discreet surveillance and waited for the ransom to be paid and the hostage to be released before going in to arrest the kidnappers and recover the ransom. With an efficient and confident police force, this is the safest way.

Protracted sieges usually end in surrender. Raids are particularly likely to be necessary when the hostages are in an aircraft on the ground with fanatical hijackers who may go on killing hostages until allowed to take off for another country more sympathetic to them. The Dutch Marines did several successful raids (on a prison, a hijacked train and a besieged office) in 1974–78, timed again on the advice of a very able psychiatrist (Dr Richard Mulder). Others (e.g. on an Egyptian aircraft hijacked to Malta in November 1985) have been less successful. Some of these are examined in Part III.

The essence of a successful raid, whether after a long siege or out of the blue, is the momentary confusion of the kidnappers or hijackers by surprise and shock. This can be aided by stun grenades, which momentarily dazzle and stun both the kidnappers and the hostages without doing them any lasting harm. These were used in the successful rescue of the hostages in the hijacked German aircraft at Mogadishu in 1977 and in the Iranian Embassy siege in London in 1980 (see Chapter 18).

REHABILITATION OF THE HOSTAGE

The handling and rehabilitation of a hostage after his rescue or release must take account of the ordeal he has suffered, which was discussed in Chapter 8.

In the immediate aftermath of his rescue or release the hostage should be insulated from the media for two reasons: first, in his highly disturbed and yet euphoric state, he may make remarks (such as expressing sympathy with his kidnappers or criticism of the police) which he will later regret. Secondly, the best therapy is for him to relax in the secure companionship of those nearest and dearest to him and with access to simple and familiar things, such as his own clothes and shaving kit.

Whether or not they have succumbed to the Stockholm syndrome, most hostages harbour some feelings of guilt. They may feel guilty about failing to taker proper precautions to avoid being abducted, about failing to resist or escape, about their feelings of warmth towards their persecutors or about the trouble and expense they have brought to their family or firm.

Most do, in time, recover from their ordeal and may even gain from it in a heightened zest for living, deeper family relationships and greater tolerance and generosity. Some acquire or reinforce profound and enduring religious beliefs. Others will carry psychological scars for ever, such as a loss of ambition and drive. This is sometimes wrongly assumed to be the case and has prejudiced some corporate victims' careers, but it is often quite unfounded and unfair. William Niehous, held hostage for the longest period on record (40 months) was back at work in an executive position within three months and was grateful that his firm thereafter treated him as if nothing had happened.

Many, however, retain a lasting fear of terrorist organizations and attribute exaggerated powers to them, even when they have moved thousands of miles away from the country where they operate. Most will also show the effects in smaller ways, such as nervousness of people coming up behind them or over-reaction to minor irritations. Some have a compulsive desire to talk about their experiences but are discouraged from doing so by well-meaning but misguided friends and relations.

Dr Martyn Symonds, Director of Psychological Services to the New York City Police Department, writing in *Terrorism* published in 1983 by the American Psychiatric Association, wrote:

> Some individuals . . . experience their victimization as a personal affront to their pride. Their feelings are compounded by their perception that society is indifferent to their plight. They embrace their feelings of rage and injustice, and constantly seek reparations, even revenge, for their victimization. In this sense they will remain psychologically disabled.

> These, however, are a minority. Brian Jenkins, who interviewed a large number of former hostages for his Rand Corporation study, found that most of them, having had some problems initially, found that 're-entry difficulties were mild and disappeared within a few months, swept away by the joy of being alive'.

Part III
Case Studies

13 Leon Don Richardson

The kidnap and release of Leon Don Richardson taught so many valuable lessons that it will be recounted here in more depth than the other case studies. The American-born head of a company based in Hong Kong and Australia, was kidnapped in Guatemala. His partner and son-in-law Tom Dundon (also American-born, based in Australia) negotiated for his release. Don Richardson displayed remarkable courage and perception in his ordeal, matched by that of Tom Dundon and his office manager in Sydney, Gloria Donaldson. Negotiations were conducted by telephone, first to Sydney, then to Mexico city. The case also illustrates the role of the consultant who assisted Dundon throughout the crisis.

KIDNAP AND DETENTION

Leon Don Richardson was abducted in Guatemala city on 10 February 1981 by the left-wing Guerrilla Army of the Poor (EGP) or its associates. He was founder and chairman of the Magna Group, a multinational metal group based in Australia and Hong Kong with operations worldwide. He had only been in Guatemala two days, but his visit was scheduled and the kidnap was set up by a recently employed Guatemalan junior manager, possibly acting under coercion. As they came out of one of the factories they were visiting he was seized by eight armed terrorists dressed in military combat jackets and was taken away in a truck. He noticed that before they turned off the main roads on to a bumpy track they changed the tyres, presumably to confuse the police, which confirmed his impression of their professionalism. He was imprisoned for 100 days in a barred cellar beneath a farmhouse.

He met in all five people, all of whom were hooded. Three were guards, who seemed keen to be on reasonable terms to make their job easier, one telling him that it was quite a good job, better paid than the average in Guatemala with plenty of free time for football, etc. The other two were clearly educated, one (a Guatemalan) being the boss and the other a most unpleasant woman speaking fluent English with a Canadian accent, who later did most of the negotiating on the telephone.

In his initial questioning it became clear, to his immense relief, that they did not intend to kill him and that they regarded him as 'merchandise' (the word by which they always referred to him) to be sold for money to fund their movement. He had a heart condition and he told them that, if they wanted him to survive, they had better get him the medicines which he needed – which they did with alacrity.

Thereafter, he set about a calculated pattern of behaviour to unsettle them and gain psychological dominance over them, alternating between cooperation and rage – a mirror image of what they were trying to do to him (he was convinced that the two leaders had been trained in psychology). Because he sensed that their greatest fear was the loss of their 'merchandise', he provoked them (knowing that they would only shoot if his escape attempts got him above ground), and gave them ultimatums threatening to kill himself. He also alarmed them with accounts of the degree to which his company was mortgaged so that it could not conceivably raise any substantial ransom. All of these things greatly assisted negotiation for his release as the kidnappers felt increasingly under pressure. (It must be said, however, that, in general, aggressive behaviour by a hostage can easily rebound and is of use only after making a dispassionate assessment of the psychological state of the kidnappers – which Don Richardson did.)

Soon after his kidnap he was asked to name a negotiator. He named Tom Dundon, giving his address and telephone number in Sydney. It was, however, six weeks before the kidnappers made any contact.

SEEKING ADVICE AND ESTABLISHING CONTACT

During these six weeks Tom Dundon had naturally not been inactive. After initial reports that his partner had been arrested, it soon became clear that he had been kidnapped. On the third day this news broke and he was besieged by the media, whom he used to publicise Richardson's heart complaint. Having asked advice from the Australian Department of Foreign Affairs, he made contact with a firm of specialist consultants, met the managing director in Mexico city and was much impressed. The managing director advised him on strategy and on how best to cope with the situation while still keeping the business operating commercially; he asked Dundon whom he thought Richardson might suggest as negotiator and Dundon rightly guessed himself. Dundon decided to retain the services of the consultancy and one of the consultants then accompanied him to Guatemala to try to set up arrangements for making contact with the kidnappers, including hiring a post office box number, an office with telephone and a tape recorder; they also arranged for people they could trust to run it and to put advertisements in local newspapers, etc. as necessary.

They discussed the likely form of the first call the kidnappers might make and how it should best be handled. Dundon was advised to make himself 'hard to get' in order to give himself more time to think and to gain the initiative while, at the same time, working out what might be a sensible first offer if this proved tactically desirable. Thereafter a member of the consultancy briefed Dundon throughout the negotiations which, in the event, were conducted from Sydney and Mexico city.

The consultant, before each call, rehearsed Dundon and his colleagues in every possible scenario, including aggressive threats to cut off Richardson's fingers or kill him, and the possibility of their putting Richardson himself on the line (though they never did).

The first call came through to Sydney on 20 March while Dundon was in Hong Kong (where Richardson based himself) trying to help Mrs Richardson and to ensure that he had her support in his role as negotiator. The call was answered by his extremely capable Sydney office manager, Mrs Gloria Donaldson who was, of course, fully prepared for it. The message was for Dundon to go on 22 March to a room the kidnap gang had booked for him in the El Presidente Hotel, Mexico city.

Lest this be a trap for a second kidnap, the consultant advised Dundon not to go to Mexico city and his place in the hotel room was taken by another Magna executive accompanied by the consultant. When the woman with the Canadian accent rang she said she would only speak to Dundon and slammed down the telephone. Two days later she telephoned Sydney and again demanded angrily that Dundon should go to Mexico city. Gloria Donaldson said she would tell him and asked a proof-of-life question. The woman, after a pause, gave an indeterminate answer, which clearly meant that she was not in immediate contact with the farmhouse. She was in fact ringing from Mexico.

GAINING THE INITIATIVE

It was three weeks before the next call (14 April). The woman gave the correct answer to the proof call, again demanding to speak to Dundon. Gloria Donaldson said she would get a message to him and asked the woman to ring back next day. The gang in fact rang back later the same day. Unknown to them, Dundon (and the consultant) were sitting beside Gloria Donaldson during both calls.

The gang was clearly now getting edgy, and called two days later. Dundon again sat silently beside Mrs Donaldson when she took the call. She said that Dundon *would* go to Mexico city, but to a hotel of his own choice; that the hotel room nominated by the kidnappers would be occupied by a colleague who would give them another number where they could reach Dundon. Mrs Donaldson gave them a further proof question to be answered when they spoke to Dundon in Mexico city in three days' time.

Dundon arrived in Mexico city on 17 April, travelling under a false name. It was clear to him, however, that he was under observation at the airport and a car followed him to the hotel he had chosen and remained parked outside. On the consultant's advice, he told the Mexican police of the position and they were sympathetic and helpful throughout.

It had been decided to try to establish a secret telephone number in a place whose location the kidnappers would not know and they picked a lawyer's office about an hour's drive out of town.

They then rehearsed every possible scenario for the next call. They decided that, when the kidnappers rang the room they had nominated and booked (at the Holiday Inn) this should be answered by Dundon himself, not the intermediary they were expecting, to achieve surprise. Dundon went to the Holiday Inn and when the call came the woman (whose voice, of course, he knew well from the tapes of previous calls) was thrown into confusion by his presence and said she would ring back. She did so within an hour, and Dundon immediately demanded the answer to the proof question given three days earlier. Before answering she, in turn, asked two questions which could only have come from Richardson. He then told her the secret number, told her to write it down, and dictated the times at which he would be there, tacitly establishing that he was now giving the orders. She agreed to ring back there in an hour.

Though clearly followed out of the Holiday Inn he shook off the pursuit by darting down a side street and jumping into a passing cab, which he directed round a circuit to check that he was no longer being followed.

The consultant had already reached the secret telephone so they again rehearsed the call, the consultant simulating the kind of aggressive questions he expected the woman to ask. When the call came, she tried to regain control by demanding that Dundon return to the Holiday Inn. Dundon refused, saying that she could get him only at the secret telephone number between 8.30 p.m. and 10 p.m. the next two nights but that if she did not she would have to start again by telephoning the office in Sydney. She then ordered him to go to a stated restaurant to receive a package at 11.30 p.m. that night. He refused, that night or any other night. He then heard the woman arguing angrily in Spanish with her colleagues in the background and she then shouted, 'You will go to the restaurant and you will go now', and hung up. But he did not and went back to his hotel.

Next day he went back to the secret number at 8.30 p.m. and she called at 9 p.m. It was agreed that the package (a tape) would be delivered to the Holiday Inn but that someone other than Dundon would collect it. She agreed to ring the secret number again two days later to discuss it. The package contained letters written by Richardson and by the kidnappers, setting out their demands, a photograph of Richardson holding the current issue of *Time* magazine and a tape of his voice, which Dundon could sense was made under duress using a script, though it did include some recognizable phrases of his own.

The demand was for $10 million and at the next call Dundon said that there was no question of this amount being raised. Richardson himself (as described earlier) was stressing the firm's debts but said that, by selling their inventory they might raise $750 000 or $1 million. He formed the strong impression that they were in a hurry to settle.

Negotiations thereupon gathered pace. On the consultant's advice, Dundon opened with an offer of a small fraction of the original demand, only raising it slightly each time the kidnappers lowered their demand. After three weeks (mid-May) they had more or less agreed on a figure.

RELEASE

At this stage the case took a dramatic turn. Members of the gang who were in Mexico city for convenience of negotiating with Dundon, passing him the tapes, etc., were spotted and arrested by the Mexican police who in turn urged them to warn their comrades in Guatemala by telephone of what was in store for them. At the same time Richardson played a risky but, in the event, effective card. Putting on one of his 'rage' acts, he warned the kidnappers that, unless he was released within two days he would commit suicide. Thereafter, things moved fast. His clothes were taken away and cleaned and he was allowed to have a bath and shave – which he did at gunpoint. He was taken, blindfolded, to a vehicle after being searched to ensure that there was nothing on him which could give the police any clues. After a long drive which he thinks was designed to confuse, he was dropped outside the Red Cross offices in Guatemala city.

This peremptory release was due to a combination of Richardson's ultimatum and the terrorists' awareness that both the Guatemalans and Mexican police were closing in on them. They were no doubt alarmed at the prospect of being caught in possession – and especially in possession of a dead body. Richardson was released, having lost 38 lbs, tired but in good health. No ransom was paid.

DON RICHARDSON'S ADVICE FOR BUSINESSMEN AT RISK

Don Richardson has written and collaborated in writing quite a lot about his ordeal. In a chapter of Brian Jenkins' *Terrorism and Personal Protection*, he has set out some advice to businessmen, which includes, in summary, the following:

(a) He advises businessmen to check that they are spending enough on security. If in the slightest doubt, he says, hire a professional security firm to survey the premises, office and home and having paid for his advice, follow it.
(b) He commends taking out kidnap insurance.
(c) Assess the risks, he says; define danger zones; study kidnapping and how to reduce the risk; decide how you would react if you or a family member were kidnapped. Prepare for dealing with a crisis. Keep on file such information as fingerprints, blood groups, passport numbers, credit card numbers and medical history.
(d) He stresses that the police should be brought in when a kidnap takes place and adds: 'Anti-kidnap consultants are worth their weight in gold. Contact them or have their telephone numbers handy should they have to be called in.'

(e) He gives encouraging advice on hostage survival, urging victims to beware of self-pity and to fight back mentally; to play mental games, plan escapes and exercise vigorously; above all, never to give up hope and to remember that the chances of eventually being freed are high.

(f) He advises paying a ransom if there is no other way, since human life is more important than money, though governments should not release prisoners or make political concessions. He advises the businessman to discuss with his firm and his family how they should handle a demand for a ransom and, should they decide to pay, how they should raise the money.

14 Kidnapping: Latin America

In the 1970s and early 1980s there were a very large number of politically motivated kidnaps in Latin America, specifically targeting foreign businessmen. Though there still are a number of these, criminally motivated kidnaps now greatly exceed them. There is some brutality but generally nothing like the bestiality of some of the Italian kidnappers described in the next chapter.

As shown in the statistics in Chapter 2, the number of kidnaps in Latin America has been enormous, and only a handful can be picked as short case studies to illustrate various different aspects.

GUATEMALA

Mrs Marta Elena **Rios de Rivas** was abducted on 26 June 1983 in Guatemala city by armed men as she was leaving the primary school where she was a teacher. She was five months pregnant at the time, which her kidnappers clearly did not know.

She was the sister of President Rios Montt and her kidnappers were the Castroite Rebel Armed Forces (FAR), who demanded that an FAR communiqué should be published. Members of the family tried to contact the kidnappers secretly to negotiate but their attempts were met with silence. The government then publicly confirmed the kidnap.

Six weeks later (on 8 August), while Mrs Rios de Rivas was still held, President Rios Montt was overthrown in a military *coup* by General Mejia Victores. A few weeks later (10 September) the new President's sister, Celeste Aida Mejia de Valasco, was also kidnapped. President Mejia said that he had no intention of negotiating with terrorists, either for the release of his own sister or the sister of his predecessor; that if the family of Mrs de Rivas managed to secure the publication of the FAR manifesto abroad, that was their own affair but that he would certainly not consent to its publication in Guatemala.

FAR then sent a note to the family demanding that they publish a communiqué from the group in newspapers in Canada, the USA, France, Italy, Venezuela, Argentina and all the Central American countries. They announced in the press on 12 September, as their only means of getting it to the attention of the kidnappers, that they had done so, calling upon the kidnappers to keep their bargain. In due course they showed Mrs de Rivas a newspaper containing the communiqué (her first knowledge of anything happening outside during her 119 day imprisonment) and released her on 25 September.

The kidnap of an expatriate businessman (Richardson) in Guatemala was described in the previous chapter.

EL SALVADOR

Ian **Massie** and Michael **Chatterton**, manager and assistant manager of Lloyds Bank International in El Salvador, were kidnapped in San Salvador as they approached Massie's car in the car park on leaving their office at 6.35 p.m. on 30 November 1978. The kidnap was carried out by the Armed Forces of National Resistance (FARN) as part of the series of kidnaps of expatriates to raise funds for the current guerrilla war by FLMN, of which FARN are a constituent part (see Chapter 3). They demanded the release of prisoners, publicity and a ransom of $40 million. During the same period, they held expatriate hostages from multinational corporations based in four other countries (Japan, Netherlands, Sweden and USA), skilfully playing off one against the other. Each operation was meticulously planned, with a build-up of intelligence about the target and a strong logistic organization (safe houses, etc.) based on a secure secret cell structure.

Negotiations for the release of Massie and Chatterton lasted seven months, the Salvadorean government and the British Embassy being kept informed throughout. Amongst their pressure tactics, the kidnappers after 5 months sent a video film of the hostages to the BBC. Some modifications were accepted to the publicity (e.g. no publication in El Salvador) and the demand for release of prisoners was dropped. The ransom was eventually reduced to a fraction of the sum originally demanded, to be paid in parts on the day of release. The first payment was made at 10 a.m. on 2 July 1979 upon which Chatterton was released. Then the second payment was made and four hours after that Massie was released.

Following these kidnaps and the outbreak and continuance of the civil war, the guerrillas have largely confined their kidnapping to Salvadoreans.

COLOMBIA

There have been a very large number of kidnaps in Colombia, and the case of Richard **Starr** is selected because it illustrates the particular problems arising when there is a conflict of interests between the government and the family of a hostage.

Richard Starr was a 31-year-old American biological scientist provided by the US government's Peace Corps to carry out research at the request of the Colombian government. He was kidnapped on 14 February 1977 at La Maracena in the Andean Mountains by a large group of FARC guerrillas who were storming a small police post (killing one policeman and wounding another). Starr did not appear to be the target but was taken away as a hostage. Only when the guerrillas discovered that he was an American did they start to think about what publicity, concessions or ransom they might obtain from the incident.

Because of the remoteness of the area and the poor communications, everything moved very slowly. Initially the guerrillas confined themselves to propaganda, getting reports into the press that they had captured a 'CIA representative' (a standard accusation against Peace Corps volunteers). After about a year they demanded that Starr be exchanged for Jaime Guaracas, an FARC member in prison for murder. Both the Colombian and US governments refused to consider this as it was in breach of their policy of no concessions. Later, however, Guaracas was released on a legal technicality, but an indirect attempt to arrange the exchange on this basis failed as FARC knew that the US government had nothing to do with the release of Guaracas.

Later – in May 1978 – FARC sent a letter to the US Embassy demanding a ransom of $250 000, instructing them to place a specified advertisement in a Bogota newspaper. The US government, fearing that Starr would otherwise be killed, placed the advertisement, though they had no intention of paying the ransom. One effect of this was to torpedo a parallel negotiation by Starr's mother, Mrs Charlotte Jensen, who had raised $50 000 in conjunction with her Congressman which Starr believed FARC would have accepted. After the newspaper advertisement, however, they refused to consider anything less than $250 000. There seems to have been considerable lack of understanding between the State Department, who were willing to assist and encourage the family's efforts to raise and pay a ransom privately, but not to compromise their policy of never paying a ransom themselves, and Mrs Jensen, who regarded this attitude as inconsistent.

Eventually a well-known newspaper columnist, Jack Anderson, in cooperation with Mrs Jensen and her Congressman, raised $250 000 privately and paid the ransom. Starr was released on 12 February 1980 after three years in captivity. His ordeal, however, left its mark and he died at his home in the USA in 1983.

VENEZUELA

The only hostage known to have been held for longer than Starr was William **Niehous**, kidnapped from his home in Caracas on 27 February 1976 and rescued by Venezuelan police in June 1979 after 1219 days in captivity. He was vice-president of the Venezuela subsidary of Owens–Illinois. His kidnappers were a splinter group of the far-left Red Flag movement and Owens–Illinois agreed to publish a manifesto and a condemnation of the Venezuelan government in newspapers in Venezuela, London, Paris and New York. The Venezuelan government thereupon announced that it would nationalize the assets of Owens–Illinois in Venezuela for breach of their national law. But Niehous was not released and contacts ceased.

He was held in remote jungle, living on basic guerrilla food, and chained to a tree every night. Living in a large group of guerrillas, moving frequently and with no idea where he was, he realized that he had little hope of survival if he escaped so, being a Spanish speaker, he did his best to develop a relationship with his captors in the hope that, if they came to regard him as a human being, they were less likely to kill him.

Despite his conditions and his seemingly interminable ordeal, he managed to keep himself physically and mentally fit. Within the confines of his chains he devised exercises and he kept his mind alive by talking to his guards about the weather, politics and international sport; he wrote letters to his family (though only one was ever delivered). Above all, he was determined to live and return to his family, and was sustained by his religious faith. He was rescued when a Venezuelan patrol came across his hiding place, apparently by accident.

He made a remarkable recovery. Within three months he was back at work with Owens–Illinois in a management post and the company treats him no differently because of his experience as a hostage – which is as he wants it to be. He believes that his family life has been strengthened by the ordeal that they all suffered. To some extent he blames himself for failing to spot the signs that he was a kidnap target and take the advice he was given on reducing the risks. He is a remarkable man and his fortitude not only enabled him to survive and recover but also provides hope and encouragement for others facing the trauma of kidnap.*

PERU

Jose Antonio **Ourubia**, president of the El Pacifico Insurance Company, was kidnapped by armed men on 7 November 1983 at about 7 p.m. as he left a club and approached his car in a narrow one-way street in Lima. They battered him over the head with a pistol and shot his chauffeur dead. There were about five people in the abduction squad who were probably hired for that task alone by the sophisticated criminal gang which comprised another seven or eight in the 'command and holding group'. The hostage was taken, after a change of car, to what appeared to be the buildings of a disused mine and he was imprisoned in one of a number of prefabricated wooden rooms in a cellar. The kidnappers demanded a ransom of $10 million, by letter, on the sixth day, with instructions for placing an advertisement in a newspaper to signify assent.

Jose Ourubia and his family were known to be very rich. He was a director of at least ten other companies and public speculation on the combined wealth of the family has valued it at more than $500 million. Bearing this in mind, the family negotiated with great skill. After long periods of silence the kidnappers appeared to become anxious and Ourubia was released after 154 days on payment of a small fraction of the sum originally demanded. The money was delivered by a doctor nominated by the kidnappers, who took it to a point as directed where two motor-cyclists came and picked it up. The hostage was released next day.

---

* William Niehous has described his ordeal in Brian Jenkins (ed.) *Terrorism and Personal Protection* (Boston and London, Butterworths, 1985) and in Martin Herz (ed.) *Diplomats and Terrorists: What Works, What Doesn't* (Washington DC, Georgetown University, 1982).

URUGUAY

As described in Chapter 2, the wave of diplomatic kidnappings in 1968–73 was broken because governments hardened their attitudes towards it, generally with the staunch support of their ambassadors; an outstanding example was the British Ambassador in Uruguay, Sir Geoffrey **Jackson**, kidnapped by the Tupamaros on 8 January 1971 and held for eight months. This kidnap teaches many enduring lessons, notably about detecting surveillance and about hostage survival, which are light-heartedly but movingly described in his book (see bibliography).

In the prevailing climate, Jackson had realized for some time before his kidnapping that he was under surveillance as a target. In a piece of parkland opposite his residence he noticed that there was always a young family – father, mother and baby – having a picnic. The 'family' varied but the pattern never did. Almost daily as he drove to work, he and his security staff noticed a scooter following and cutting in, carrying different couples (boy driving, girl watching) but always with the same registration number. Later, heavier vehicles would cut in, evidently testing the reactions of his driver. In a doorway opposite the entrance to the embassy he noticed a canoodling couple who did not quite ring true, with a parked scooter bearing a registration number traced to a student with known links with the Tupamaros.

He and his wife found occasion to visit the Foreign Office in London and explained the situation, warning them that he thought it unlikely that the Uruguayan police would be able to prevent him being kidnapped. It was agreed that, if he were, he, she and they would immediately announce that there would be no concessions, nor pressure on the Uruguayan government for concessions, for his release; he would tell his kidnappers, she would tell the Uruguayan government and the British government would announce it to the media. This, in the event, they did.

He decided (wisely in view of the number of armed terrorists the Tupamaros were likely to deploy for his abduction) that neither he nor his bodyguard should carry arms. Otherwise he took sensible security precautions, such as varying his routes and times of travel – so effectively that the Tupamaros did not attempt a kidnap on the open road but chose a narrow street in the city close to the embassy. This involved a major operation to ensure a getaway, multiple teams being coordinated by radio to stage hold-ups (e.g. by fake accidents or a van stalling across the road) to block traffic feeding on to the getaway route at the critical time. The actual abduction was carried out by a van pulling out in the single-lane path of his limousine and crashing into its wing, armed terrorists appearing from the van and amongst shoppers on the pavement.

He was held (in two places) in extreme squalor and discomfort, in cellars sometimes ankle deep in water or sewage. He kept physically and mentally fit, with exercises and by composing children's stories (later published). His strong Catholic faith was a lynchpin in his survival. Being a fluent Spanish speaker, he was able to make his young student jailers laugh, particularly by drawing cartoons, but kept his distance.

Twice, they brought left-wing journalists to interview him in captivity but the propaganda rebounded due to the picture of his dignity and courage which emerged. Eventually, the Tupamaros realized that they were going to get no concessions and that, if they killed him, this would have a strong adverse reaction both in Uruguay and outside, so they found an excuse (a prison break by some of those whose release they were demanding) to let him go. Some people have suggested that the prison escape was arranged by the government in cooperation with the Tupamaros to get both sides off the hook. If so, this could have been an example of government flexibility but, be this as it may, there is no doubt that the Tupamaros realized that their operation had failed and were desperate to bring it to an end.

Following this, there was a general election in which the left-wing party lost heavily. The resulting right-wing government cracked down and destroyed the Tupamaros with few public regrets, but was taken over by its own army, and Uruguay was for the next decade denied democratic government for the only time in its history.

ARGENTINA

In Argentina in 1971–76 two terrorist movements, the ERP and the Montoneros, conducted a series of kidnaps and extortions of business executives to raise money for future operations, a pattern copied successfully in El Salvador in 1978–80 as described earlier in this chapter. In short-term financial gains the Argentine movements did very well, the ERP netting $30 million and the Montoneros $240 million. One other result, however, was to provoke the military *coup* in 1976 and both movements were destroyed in 1976–78 in a ruthless campaign, which included the notorious 'disappearances', by the military regime.

Of the many kidnaps only a few can be mentioned, selected because of their significance or their scale or because of lessons they taught. In March 1972, the ERP kidnapped the president of Fiat, Dr Oberdan **Sallustro**, and demanded both government concessions and a ransom from the company. The government rejected their demands and banned the payment of a ransom. Three weeks later Sallustro was killed by his kidnappers when police discovered the hideout. One of the results of this was that companies become more reluctant to report kidnappings to the police.

The following year (1973) Juan Peron was re-elected president and declared an amnesty, releasing 500 terrorists including the murderers of Sallustro. This further reduced the confidence of business firms in the government.

In May 1973 the ERP claimed to have extorted $1 million in goods from the **Ford** Motor Company, after murdering one executive and wounding another; but five months after the payment they killed another Ford executive and his three bodyguards. Only after Ford had threatened to close down their operation in Argentina altogether did Peron agree to direct his army to take part in protecting their plant.

Thereafter kidnaps for huge ransoms followed thick and fast, with ERP receiving $14.2 million for the release of the **Exxon** general manager kidnapped in December 1973. The biggest ransom on record, however, was paid by an Argentine firm, Bunge **Born**, whose founder-president paid $60 million for the release of his two sons in 1975.

Jorge and Juan Born were in the process of taking over the business from their ageing father. Every morning they used to drive to work from their home 24 kilometres from Buenos Aires with their general manager sitting in front with the chauffeur, followed by an escort car carrying two bodyguards. They were often initially accompanied by a third car, which dropped off the Born family children at school. This, though it gave great security to the children, meant that their route regularly passed the school at the same time in the morning.

The kidnap took place on the morning of 16 September 1984 and lasted seven months. A few days before the hostages were released a leading member of the Montoneros, Mario Eduardo Firmenich, gave a one-hour press conference in a suburb of Buenos Aires, describing how the kidnap was done and announcing the terms of the settlement.

The Montoneros used 19 terrorists for the kidnap itself plus another 20 or 30 guarding the hostages and on auxiliary duties (another example of lavish manpower where there is no wage bill). The kidnap group worked in five teams. They picked a wide boulevard, an unlikely site for a kidnap, but there were narrow service roads each side. On a radio message that the car was on its way, they closed the boulevard under pretence of tree lopping and established portable traffic lights to divert traffic through the service road. Two trucks were used to collide with the Borns' car and the bodyguards' car. Terrorists dressed as police 'arrested' the bodyguards and handcuffed them under their own car. They shot the general manager and the chauffeur dead and took away the Born brothers. In a country where such scenes were commonplace, bystanders preferred not to notice.

About a week later, the Montoneros established a system of secret telephone and written communications and on 2 October they demanded $100 million plus distribution of goods to the poor and changes in the corporation's labour policies. By 26 December Bunge Born had offered $17.5 million and raised it to $30 million on 30 December. The Montoneros said that the minimum offer even to start negotiations was $50 million. The company replied that they could not raise that amount of cash so the Montoneros said that one of the brothers could be released if they paid half the ransom. They then hardened their line, demanding $80 million and warning the company that if they continued to resist, this would be bad for the brothers' health.

Meanwhile Jorge himself was negotiating with the kidnappers and wrote a memorandum offering $60 million which was sent on to the company, to which his father said he had no option but to agree. Some of the money was paid in Argentina and the rest in Switzerland and the younger brother, Juan, was released on 22 March 1975. The Montoneros then announced that they would not release Jorge until their other demands had been met. Food, clothing and blankets were delivered to 150 places and striking workers were paid for the time they were on strike. On 20 June 1975 Jorge was released.

No one gained very much. Following the military coup and crack-down in 1976–78, most of the surviving ERP and Montoneros leaders, including Firmenich, fled to Mexico or Europe, where they had banked much of the money from their ransoms, and many stayed there.

15 Kidnapping: Western Europe

GREAT BRITAIN

Great Britain (as distinct from Ireland, North and South, see next section) has suffered relatively little kidnapping, but its experience contains a number of useful lessons, particularly in the fields of hostage negotiation and rescue, police surveillance and handling the media.

Lesley **Whittle** was the 17–year-old daughter of a prosperous family (though not a rich one). Her father was dead and she lived with her mother and brother. While alone in bed in the house, she was kidnapped in January 1975 by a dangerous lone criminal, Donald Neilson, who left a demand for a ransom of £50 000 ($75 000). In full cooperation with the police her brother, Ronald Whittle, followed detailed instructions to deliver the ransom money to a rendezvous at 2 a.m., about 60 miles from their home. The rendezvous, however, was in a different police district (Staffordshire) from their home (West Mercia). The West Mercia police had arranged for 12 unmarked CID cars from Scotland Yard to establish surveillance around the rendezvous. Due to a communications failure a Staffordshire traffic police car, unaware of the operation, drove round the area, with blue lights flashing, taking the numbers of each of the 12 'illegally' parked surveillance vehicles. This was before Ronald Whittle arrived with the ransom. Neilson was watching, having hidden the girl nearby in an underground drainage system, secured by a steel wire round her neck. Seeing the patrolling police car (ironically nothing to do with the operation) he took fright, killed the girl and ran away. Her body was found hanging in the shaft some weeks later and Neilson was eventually arrested and convicted of her murder – and of a number of other murders committed during robberies.

This ghastly case illustrates two things above all: first, that a lone criminal, having fewer options and resources to fall back on, may be more dangerous to the victim than an organized gang; and secondly that, if the police do try to monitor the delivery of the ransom it must be treated as an intensely delicate operation, requiring great skill, discretion and coordination. Any bungling, as on this occasion, is likely to prove fatal.

Later in the same year, on 6 November 1975, Alio **Kaloghirou**, an 18-year-old Cypriot girl, was kidnapped from her family home in London, where the kidnappers left a demand for £60 000 ($90 000) with a warning not to tell the police. The family did tell the police (but no one else). The Commissioner of the Metropolitan Police, realizing that the story was likely to leak out, invited the editors of all the London national papers and broadcasting stations to Scotland Yard and asked them to observe a media blackout. The police, with full cooperation from the family, tapped the telephone over which ransom negotiations were conducted, located the hideout and placed it under discreet surveillance. Under police instructions the family paid the ransom and the girl was released. The police (who had deployed more than 100 detectives on the case) arrested the kidnappers three hours later and recovered the money.

Throughout the case (11 days) the media respected the blackout. All were invited to daily briefings at Scotland Yard, so that each could see that all their rivals were also respecting it. All were told together the news of the release and the arrests. Everyone – the family, the police and the press – emerged with credit. The reason for the success was that all were cooperating on the basis that the life of the hostage took priority over everything else – so the police gained the time and information to detect and arrest the kidnappers without interference by the media.

Since then, there have been three other cases in which Scotland Yard have used the same procedure for media blackout with the same success (though more often doing their raid before the victim is released). Provided that they know that the blackout will only be requested if lives are at risk, and that their rivals are observing it, the media will respect it. Sometimes, however, to persuade the media to accept their request, the police have felt it necessary to promise to release more details than may be wise after the operation is concluded and this may give ideas to other criminals. It is not always an easy balance for the police to strike but they do rightly give priority to the safety of the hostage.

One of the most successful cases of police–media cooperation was that of Emmanual and Maria **Xuereb**, son and daughter-in-law of a diamond merchant, Anthony Xuereb. Three kidnappers were awaiting them when they came home on 4 January 1984 and took them to a house in Croydon (south London). They demanded £2 million ($3 million) from the father with a threat to send him one of Emmanual's fingers each day until he paid, and that if he refused his son's head would arrive in a box. The father told the police, who asked the media for a blackout. After further telephone calls and delivery of alarming photographs and a cassette, the kidnappers, presumably fearing that the police might close in before they got their ransom, released Maria on 8 January with orders to her father-in-law to pay £200 000 in cash, £200 000 in pure gold and 500 Krugerrands. Maria (who was 25 years old and very determined) was able to tell the police that she heard the noise of two railway lines and of church bells, and that she glimpsed some grey curtains under her blindfold. She had also had the presence of mind to scratch her fingernails along the carpet to gather forensic evidence. Aided by her information the police located the house and raided it at 5.30 the next morning, rescuing Emmanual and arresting the three kidnappers.

An unusual case illustrating the role of international banking in kidnap and extortion began on 6 January 1986 when Mohammed **Sadiq al-Tajir** was kidnapped in London. Sadiq was the brother of Mohammed Mahdi al-Tajir, the United Arab Emirates (UAE) ambassador to London. Next day the ambassador (one of the world's richest men, reputed to be worth £2000 million) received a telephone demand for £50 million. He consulted the Metropolitan Police, who advised him against paying the ransom and requested the media to observe a blackout, which they did. Negotiations therafter continued by telephone for several days between the ambassador and an Arab businessman domiciled in New York. Eventually the ambassador agreed to provide a bankers' draft for £2 million ($3 million) for payment to a bank account maintained by an intermediary in Lebanon. When the money had been duly transferred, Sadiq was released in London, still chained to a bedstead, after 11 days as a hostage. The telephone calls had been tapped and taped and a man was later arrested and held in custody in New York pending proceedings on a demand for extradition to UK. The ambassador said that he had paid the ransom both to save his brother's life and to facilitate the arrest of the kidnappers.

IRELAND, NORTH AND SOUTH

On 3 October 1975, Dr Tiede **Herrema**, manager of a Dutch steel plant in the Republic of Ireland, was kidnapped from his car on the way to work by IRA men posing as police. He was held for six weeks in three houses in turn, the third being in a suburb of Dublin. The police spotted the house by detecting accomplices supplying food and the kidnappers surrendered after an 18-day siege, in which police officers from Scotland Yard advised on the basis of their experience of sieges earlier in the year in London (see Chapter 18).

The kidnappers were Eddie Gallagher, wanted for several bank robberies on behalf of the IRA, and Marion Coyle, a 20-year-old woman politically indoctrinated by the IRA from childhood. Their demand – to release their respective IRA girlfriend and boyfriend from prison – was refused by the government. Initially their treatment of their hostage was brutal and they made some vicious threats (e.g. to cut off his foot if the government required proof of life). Later, however, Dr Herrema succeeded in developing some rapport with Gallagher (who was essentially a criminal employed by the IRA). Marion Coyle, however, though the three were cooped up under great stress for six weeks, never spoke a word to Dr Herrema or acknowledged a word he said to her. This confirms a more general experience that the Stockholm syndrome is more likely to work with criminals, who maintain some spark of humanity, than with politically indoctrinated terrorists who, as in this case, become totally dehumanized.

In November 1982, the IRA were becoming alarmed by the effects of evidence being given by former members who had defected, including Raymond Gilmour, so they kidnapped his father Patrick **Gilmour** to deter the son from giving evidence. He persevered with his testimony, however, and after ten months, his father was released, unhurt but in poor health having lost 14 lbs in weight. The attempt at coercion failed because Patrick Gilmour had already condemned his son's defection and was seen by IRA sympathizers to be a loyal republican, so to have killed or harmed him would have done them no good. His son was no doubt well aware of this.

The INLA tried the same strategy in May 1983, (before Patrick Gilmour had been released), when they kidnapped Elizabeth **Kirkpatrick** to deter her defecting husband Harry, but he too, continued his testimony and she was released after 116 days – probably for similar reasons. In this case (while she was still held) the INLA also kidnapped Kirkpatrick's stepfather and sister in the Republic, but they were rescued by the police after 14 days and three men were arrested. This may have been a further reason for the release of his wife a week later.

Shergar, a Derby-winning stallion valued at £10 million ($15 million), was kidnapped from the Ballymanny Stud Farm on 9 February 1983, and a demand for £2 million ($3 million) was received next day. The significance of the case, no doubt well appreciated by the kidnappers, was that the bloodstock industry brings £1000 million ($1.5 billion) into Ireland every year, employing 250 000 people – a very big element in the economy of a country with a total population of about 3 million. There were fears that owners of valuable horses might withdraw them if the case were not resolved.

The day after the kidnap *The Sporting Life* offered a £10 000 reward for the safe return of Shergar and the conviction of the criminals. There were numerous calls from people claiming to be or to speak for the kidnappers, most of them probably hoaxers. The syndicate who owned Shergar and the police, however, made it clear that there could be no negotiations with anyone without proof of life. None was ever produced and the likeliest presumption is that Shergar was injured while being transported – or possibly the kidnappers became alarmed that he had been spotted and could not be concealed – so they put him down and disposed of his body. Lloyd's met an insurance claim for theft, but no ransom was paid.

On 8 April 1986 three armed raiders broke into the home of John and Jennifer **Guinness** in the Howth Peninsula not far from Dublin, tied up Jennifer and her daughter Gillian, and waited until her husband came home an hour later, when he was overpowered after the raiders had opened fire. They intended to take the daughter but Mrs Guinness persuaded them to take her instead, saying, 'My husband will pay more for me'. They told Mr Guinness that they required a ransom of IR£2 million ($2.6 million).

She was held for eight days during which the gardai (police), convinced that this was not an IRA case, placed various known criminals and their associates under surveillance and found that one had hired an Opel Kadett which was seen being driven by two brothers also under suspicion, and that a flat in Waterloo Road, Dublin, had been rented by the girlfriend of another. The gardai surrounded this flat and one of the gang tried to shoot his way out but surrendered when the gardai returned his fire. Then after about five hours of negotiation the remainder of the gang surrendered.

Mrs Guinness, aged 48 with a strong, agreeable and persuasive personality, played a positive part in these negotiations. She was not helped by the media, e.g. after seeing TV coverage, the kidnappers commented 'Jesus, lady, you're worth millions'. Nevertheless she managed to build up a rapport with some of them and was able to exert a calming influence. The gang appeared to be surprised that her husband had not paid up at once and had informed the gardai. The gardai have handled many kidnaps and short-term abductions since the IRA campaign began, and every hostage has been safely released or rescued, though at the cost of the lives of one policeman and one soldier. In handling the Guinness case they fully lived up to this record.

THE NETHERLANDS

There have been two notorious cases of Italian kidnappers operating in the Netherlands.

On 28 October 1978, Mauritz **Caransa**, a 61-year-old millionaire property-owner in Amsterdam, was kidnapped as he left a hotel at 1 a.m. after playing bridge. He negotiated his own ransom with the kidnappers, lowering it from 40 million to 10 million guilders ($4 million) and then wrote a letter dictated by them requesting the company to pay it. They did so and he was released. One abductor, an Italian, was arrested in Rome on 29 November and two more four months later.

On 27 November 1982, Antonia **Van der Valk**, 51-year-old wife of a motel owner, was kidnapped by four armed men in her home after her husband had gone to bed. The first he knew was when he received a telephone call early next morning, demanding a ransom of 10 million guilders ($4 million). After five days of negotiation he agreed to pay it but the kidnappers detected police presence and aborted the operation. They then furiously telephoned the family and said that they had killed the hostage but, after three days of silence, they rang again, raising the ransom to 12 million guilders. The 'treasure hunt' instructions led from Amsterdam through Luxembourg to the German border where the money was left. Mrs Van der Valk was released, after 21 days in captivity. Nine Italians were arrested and charged just over a year later.

At 7 p.m. on 9 November 1983, Freddy **Heineken**, head of the brewing firm, was kidnapped as he left work, with his chauffeur, Ab Doderer. The firm had been built up by Heineken personally and the board negotiated more in the manner of a family than of a corporation. The police, throughout, maintained excellent cooperation, making it clear that their first priority was the release of the hostages, leaving all policy and tactical decisions to the company. As a result, the company kept them fully informed and discussed every decision with them. They sat jointly on their committees.

Three hours after the kidnap a package was dropped on the

pavement outside The Hague police station containing Heineken's watch and Doderer's passport, with a demand for 35 million guilders ($13 million) and instructions for the wording of a newspaper advertisement to indicate compliance. The company inserted this advertisement on 11 and 12 November but requesting contact. At 3 a.m. on the 16 November they received orders to start the payment run but they ignored them and inserted an advertisement refusing payment without further contact, repeating it on 22 November. On 22 and 23 November the kidnappers telephoned and conditions were agreed for the payment, which included proof of life of both hostages and a guarantee that both were to be released.

All of this gave time for police investigations, helped by an anonymous lead which enabled them to place surveillance on a number of known criminals. The ransom was paid in accordance with instructions in the early hours of 28 November and on 30 November the police raided the hideout (a warehouse) rescued the hostages and arrested two of the kidnappers. They later arrested three more, and recovered most of the money. The kidnappers proved to be members of a rich and highly professional criminal gang who had previously got away with a number of other spectacular and lucrative crimes.

WEST GERMANY

Dr Hanns-Martin **Schleyer**, president of Mercedes Benz and of the Employers' and Industrial Associations, was kidnapped at 7.30 p.m. on 5 November 1977 in Cologne by the RAF, at the peak of its professionalism. It was known that he had been a target for some time and he was provided with three police guards and an escort vehicle. In a one-way street near his home, the road was partially blocked by a white minibus and a girl terrorist masquerading as a young mother pushed a pram off the pavement into the path of his car, while a yellow Mercedes came fast in the opposite direction, finally blocking the way by the side of the parked minibus. About five terrorists emerged from the minibus and the Mercedes and from behind. They fired about 100 rounds in 90 seconds, killing the driver and all the bodyguards. They did not hit Schleyer, who was taken away in the minibus. They demanded the release of 11 convicted RAF terrorists from prison.

The first hideout was a masterpiece of anonymity – a flat on the 26th floor of a block of 960 flats housing 2500 people including 650 university students; and there was a lift direct from the basement car park where the terrorists had hired a parking slot a month earlier, rent paid in advance, along with the flat and key to the basement elevator, which took them direct to the 26th floor without having to pass the concierge. The hostage was no doubt drugged, and carried up in a rolled up rug or cupboard – not an unusual sight in the lift with five or ten flats changing hands every week.

The police searched the block when routine checks revealed a car in the basement registered in an alias known to be used by an RAF member still at large. The car was not linked to the kidnap nor to the 26th floor flat, so the search of the 43 stories and 960 flats took eight days – by which time the terrorists had moved to a flat in Liblar, a quiet suburb ten miles out. Here again a piece of routine information led to a search but they had moved out – probably to Belgium or Holland – a day earlier.

This near miss was due to delay in processing the mass of information which poured in from the public during the kidnap – 3826 messages which were logged and filed. These included a report from a Liblar neighbour that this flat had been taken, rent paid in advance, some weeks earlier but not occupied until now. That in itself seemed of no great significance to the police but, had they had the computerized intelligence system which was introduced the following year, the message would have been automatically linked with others affecting this block and would have resulted in immediate action probably saving Schleyer's life.

The government had no intention of giving way, but they clearly kept the kidnappers hoping that they might do so, as described in Chapter 9. They also made no objections to Schleyer's family offering to pay a ransom, but the RAF insisted that the prisoners must be released. Eventually, Schleyer was murdered six weeks later, after the failure at Mogadishu of a hijack designed to force the pace (see Chapter 18), and his body was found in a car near the German border in France.

As a result of this case the German government introduced the highly effective package of laws, with the computerized intelligence system, which kept Germany almost free of RAF terrorism until 1985.

On 18 December 1981, Christina **von Gallwitz**, the 8-year-old daughter of a merchant bank manager, was kidnapped as she was walking to the school bus in Cologne. A ransom of DM1.2 million ($450 000) was demanded. Three attempts to deliver it failed, one due to police intervention, whereupon the kidnappers called off negotiations and were silent for a month. Then a final demand was made in a letter to a newspaper. The family asked the police to withdraw and obeyed the kidnappers' instructions to throw the ransom (now DM1.5 million) out of a train. Christina was released four days later at a motorway service station, where she was given an alarm clock and told not to remove her blindfold until it rang. She had been held for 139 days in small cupboards in which she could not stand up, so that when released she could hardly walk.

On 6 September 1982, Sven **Lehne**, 13-year-old son of an employee of the Munich Transit System, was kidnapped by two men while cycling along a deserted woodland path. He was held in an apartment block, chained to the bed for six days. A ransom of DM1.7 million ($0.6 million) and a Porsche car were demanded. A payment was arranged under police surveillance and the men were arrested. Sven was found on a nearby park bench. This kidnap followed an attempted bomb extortion of the Munich Transit System when three bombs were placed on a train and in buildings, doing relatively minor damage. The two men demanded DM1.8 million as the price for stopping the bombing. When this was refused they kidnapped Herr Lehne's son Sven.

FRANCE

Baron **Empain**, a 41-year-old Belgian multimillionaire, was kidnapped from his car in Paris on 24 January 1978 by three armed men. A ransom of $1.5 million, was demanded. The baron had left instructions with his wife that if he were kidnapped no ransom should be paid, but on the third day they cut off the little finger of his left hand and sent it to her. After two months of negotiation his wife agreed to pay $8 million and this was delivered under surveillance by the police, who shot one kidnapper dead and arrested another. The French have the death penalty for kidnap and murder, and the arrested man telephoned the rest of the gang from the police inspector's office, warning them that their only hope (and his) of escaping the guillotine was to release the baron at once. He was dumped without payment on the outskirts of Paris. Eight more of the kidnappers were later arrested and sentenced to long terms of imprisonment.

Baron Empain suffered severely from his ordeal. Ill-health forced him to give up the presidency of his company and he spent five years in the USA before he had recovered enough to resume it.

This case illustrates the value of time gained by negotiation, and of efficient police cooperation. The family could well afford to pay the ransom and the kidnappers knew it but, due to the staunchness of the baron and his wife, they chose to give the police the time and information to secure his release without ransom and to convict the kidnappers. The police attitude (and perhaps the availability of the death penalty) have had much to do with the low rate of kidnapping in France.

SPAIN

As recorded in Chapter 3, ETA have kidnapped about 40 Spanish officials and businessmen (no foreigners) since the 1960s, mainly for ransom to raise funds; this includes short-term abductions. There have also been some kidnaps by non-political criminals. Two examples will be given briefly in this chapter (one ETA, one not) and one of a short-term abduction (by GRAPO) in Chapter 17.

On 10 January 1983, in San Sabastian, Miguel Ignacio **Echevarria**, 20-year-old son of an industrialist, was kidnapped by two armed men who broke into his home and left a demand note for pesetas and French francs equivalent to $1.3 million. Police tried to stop the family negotiating and one man was arrested, but a friend of the family negotiated a payment of 162 million pesetas ($1 million) which was dropped from a train. Miguel was released on a deserted country road eight days after his kidnap. ETA denied responsibility and even launched their own investigation but neither the police nor, so far as is known, ETA, ever did detect the criminals.

On 25 March 1983, Diego **Prado**, a 53-year-old banker, was kidnapped from his flat in Madrid by four armed men, two posing as policemen. ETA claimed responsibility in telephone calls to the Bilbao press, and demanded 65 million pesetas ($400 000). The family negotiated and a ransom (size unknown) was paid. Diego Prado was released in a dishevelled state, probably drugged, on the outskirts of Madrid after 74 days as a hostage. In June 1984, two men were convicted of the kidnapping and received long prison sentences.

ITALY

On 22 March 1977, Paolo **Lazzaroni**, aged 40 and a director of a family biscuit manufacturing business in Milan, was kidnapped from his car near the factory, at about 7 p.m. His wife and children were away skiing and he had told his brother that he was going to the gymnasium and then to a cinema, so his absence was not noticed. Just after midnight the kidnappers telephoned his father-in-law, Aurelio Manzoni, demanding $5 million, giving him a password and telling him not to talk to anyone else nor to inform the police. Meanwhile, his wife had telephoned home and got no answer so rang Paolo's older brother Luigi (also a director) who informed the *carabinieri* that Paolo was missing. This was at about 11.30 p.m. and soon afterwards Manzoni and Luigi were both summoned to *carabinieri* headquarters.

Next day, after two more calls (in one of which Manzoni got proof of life), the kidnappers told him to find another negotiator and another telephone, and not to tell the police. The *carabinieri*, however, were watching Paolo's wife and, seeing her go several times into a block of flats, tapped all the telephones in the block until they identified the one being used.

The family played for time and made a low offer ($150 000) which the kidnappers angrily rejected, saying that they would not ring again for six months.

At this point the family played a masterstroke, inviting the press to attend a meeting of employees at the factory. The workers, including the Communist Party trade-union leader, condemned the kidnap, saying that the payment of a ransom would threaten their jobs, and organized a march to the city hall to protest against the failure of the police to find the kidnappers. This was headline news in six newspapers the next day.

The kidnappers, clearly alarmed, rang the negotiator and within two days had agreed on a ransom of $730 000 – about one seventh of the original demand. After final proof of life, this was delivered by the usual treasure hunt process. Two days later, on his 16th day as a hostage, Paolo was released. He had developed some sympathy for his guards who were clearly small fry hooked into a criminal gang and, when he left them, one threw his arms round Paolo and said, 'I wish I could work for someone like you'.

Meanwhile the police surveillance had identified some of the gang and four weeks later they made 34 arrests.

On 16 March 1978, Italy's most distinguished statesman, Aldo **Moro**, six times prime minister and expected to become president, was kidnapped by the Red Brigades (BR) near his home as he drove to mass, as he regularly did, with five bodyguards and an escort car. The technique was almost identical to that used to kidnap Dr Schleyer six months earlier. Whether there was RAF participation or whether BR simply copied what they had seen in the numerous press reports and diagrams of the Schleyer case is uncertain. Like the RAF, BR demanded release of prisoners.

Moro was held for 55 days before being murdered and contemptuously dumped between the Christian Democrat and Communist Party headquarters. BR regarded both parties as enemies of the Left and Moro had been the architect of their *modus vivendi* in parliament. He almost certainly spent the 55 days hidden in Rome and the police failure to find him was due largely to the Italian government's emasculation of the intelligence services – ironically when Moro was prime minister – in 1976. In that year many top directors of the intelligence services had been dismissed, some no doubt deservedly, for abusing their positions, but no effective new management was installed. The morale of the rank and file slumped as they were still expected to do a difficult and dangerous job. Worse still, a law was passed giving any examining magistrate the right to see the intelligence file of anyone involved in a case he was handling. This meant that a criminal or political terrorist had only to get one of his friends to persuade a corrupt or gullible magistrate to ask for his file and he could read it, no doubt easily guessing the sources of the information as the best police informers are those whose lives overlap with those of the people on whom they are informing. As a result, few informers after 1976 dared give information, and the lack of intelligence cost Moro his life.

The Moro case – and the horrific surge of criminal kidnapping – fortunately convinced the Italian government that they must control 'freedom of information' more effectively. From 1978 onwards the intelligence services (fully rehabilitated) could challenge the release of any file on security grounds, and could be over-ruled only by a cabinet committee on terrorism headed by the prime minister and the minister of the interior. Other effective laws were introduced at the same time as discussed in Chapter 9.

Rolf **Schild** was a British businessman who had a vacation villa in Sardinia. Returning there in the early hours of 21 August 1979, he and his wife and daughter Annabel were kidnapped by Sardinian bandits and taken into the mountains. Such kidnaps are not uncommon and the bandits had probably set their sights on a ransom of about £200 000 ($300 000) within a few weeks.

Normally the Italian media, living with so much agony over kidnaps, avoid discussing the financial resources of the family of a victim. This time, however, some of the British media behaved disgracefully, publishing wild and grossly exaggerated conjectures about Schild's wealth – reporting, for example, that he had recently sold one of his companies for £2.75 million without mentioning that, like many businessmen, he had borrowed heavily in raising and developing this company so that most of this money was owed to the banks. The Italian press and radio understandably quoted the British media and the kidnappers, overjoyed with their 'catch', demanded £11 million ($16.5 million). They released Schild to raise the money. Instead of a few weeks he had to negotiate for seven months to get his wife and daughter out and then only for a ransom believed to be a great deal higher than the bandits would originally have expected.

The kidnap in Verona on 17 December 1981 of US army Brigadier-General James **Dozier** and his subsequent rescue formed a watershed in the history of the Red Brigades (BR) and proved the value of the inducements to repentant terrorists. It also yielded evidence that the kidnap had been planned for several months in advance with a budget of 18 million lire (about $9000) – which shows how cheap political kidnaps are compared to criminal ones in which the abductors, guards, etc. have to be paid. He was kidnapped from his flat by eight BR terrorists, the first two gaining entry by claiming to be plumbers. He was held for 43 days in a tent inside a room in a flat, hooded, chained and forced to wear headphones playing loud rock music (which permanently damaged his ears).

Massive police investigations resulted in the arrest of several BR members, one of whom proved to be the driver of one of the vehicles used by the kidnappers. He 'repented' and gave information which helped the police to locate the flat. After keeping it under surveillance they mounted a highly professional raid, rescuing Dozier and arresting his four guards. This led to further arrests and capture of documents, resulting in the virtual elimination of BR as a fighting force by 1983, though some splinter groups have continued to fight and up to 300 members have taken refuge in neighbouring countries, especially in France.

Dozier showed great courage and endurance but he was remorseful after his ordeal in that he had failed to heed warnings and advice to take proper security precautions, on the grounds that he was very busy but, thanks to the Italian police and intelligence services, he survived.

Anna **Bulgari** Calissoni (heiress to the Bulgari jewellery empire) and her 16-year-old son Giorgio were kidnapped by three armed men who broke into their house near Rome on 19 November 1983. They were held in a tent in woodland, blindfolded and sometimes chained. When the family refused to pay the 3 milliard lire demanded they increased the demand to 4 milliard ($2 million), cut off Giorgio's ear and sent photographs of him and his mother with chains round their necks, also showing his ear and blood streaming down the side of his face. At this the family, fearing that both would be killed if they continued to resist, paid the 4 milliard lire and the hostages were released on 24 December after 36 days in captivity.

Pietro **Castagno**, a 76-year-old restaurateur, was kidnapped from his car on his way to work in Turin on 21 January 1984. The kidnappers were Calabrian criminals who quite often take their victims from the prosperous northern cities. Castagno was kept in a damp hole dug out of the rocks in the Aspromonte Mountains, chained by the neck and ankle. His guards never spoke to him and he spent his time killing rats and mice. After six months of negotiation, a ransom of 1 milliard lire ($0.5 million) was paid but the hostage was not released and a second demand of 1.5 milliard lire was made. The police arrested eight Calabrians in September and three more in October, in whose flat they found banknotes from the first ransom. Also in October the police blocked the payment of a second ransom and made nine further arrests bringing the total to 20; and they made public statements that those arrested would get life sentences unless Castagno were released at once. Eventually (in March 1985) a second ransom of 400 million lire ($200 000) was paid and the hostage was released in rugged country in Calabria after 415 days in captivity. This case demonstrates the depth and resources of one of the large southern Italian criminal fraternities.

Stefania **Bini**, 16-year-old daughter of a working-class family, was kidnapped on 20 October 1984 on her way to school in Rome. The family heard nothing for 45 days when they received a ransom demand for 300 million lire. The family paid 10 million lire ($5000) but Stefania was not released. Ten months later her body was found buried under the floor of her uncle's flat. He admitted that he had kidnapped her and shot her soon afterwards, quoting phrases from her diary thereafter to give the impression that she was still alive. This case is a reminder that by no means all Italian kidnaps are of rich people. In the south, particularly the kidnapping by bandits of farmers' children is not uncommon and the whole village clubs together to raise a few thousand pounds to get them released.

AN ANONYMOUS CASE

This case took place in two European countries whose identity, and those of the people involved, cannot be stated. The case taught a wide range of lessons in 'how not to do it'.

The president of a company was kidnapped by armed men lying in wait in the communal car park under the block of luxury flats in which he lived with his family. He was following a regular routine, no doubt noted by surveillance, returning from his sports club at the same time most evenings. He was driven away in his own car which was later abandoned. Ten minutes later, the kidnappers telephoned his son, who was already in the flat, demanding a ransom of $750 000. They told him to get the money ready and that they would contact him again in 72 hours.

His son, who was also a director of the firm, decided to pay at once without informing the police but next day, after a board meeting, another board member did tell the police, who immediately surrounded the block, with one policeman inside the flat. The telephone was tapped and taped.

Someone in the company also leaked the story to the press and the next day there was press speculation: 'Why are the kidnappers only asking $750 000? The family could easily afford $4 million!'

The kidnappers then directed the son to send an intermediary to a named hotel in a neighbouring country. The intermediary obeyed the instructions but was disconcerted to find himself being followed on to the aircraft by two very obvious plain-clothes policemen. The arrival airport was also crowded with police and, when he arrived at the hotel, he found six policemen in his hotel room. 'We are here to protect you', they said, 'and to stop you paying a ransom'. He followed instructions to go to a rendezvous at a café but, not surprisingly, the kidnappers did not appear, sent him a sardonic message saying that he clearly did not seriously want to see the hostage released, telling him to 'go home and wait', and raising the ransom to $2.25 million. Later, they raised it further to $4 million.

Back in the home country, the police were somewhat shamefaced. They insisted on retaining contact with the incident management team, but promised to be discreet. The kidnappers named a lawyer to act as intermediary for face-to-face negotiations. After seven weeks the family, with police agreement, settled for a ransom of $2.1 million. This was dropped from the window of a train at an agreed spot and the hostage was released four days later.

The glaring mistakes made included: a potential target following a predictable routine; poor security on arrival home; lack of discretion inside the company; confusion over dealing with the police and the media; gross irresponsibility by one newspaper; and clumsy surveillance by the police in both countries. The victim was lucky even to escape with his life and a ransom nearly three times more than the original demand.

16 Anti-development Abductions

KURDISTAN

Eight million Kurds live in a mountainous region straddling five countries, Iran, Iraq, Syria, Turkey and the USSR; they have an ethnic and cultural identity of their own and wish to be united in a single state of Kurdistan. Since 1980 Iraq and Iran have each exploited Kurdish aspirations in the territory of the other to draw troops away from the Gulf War. The Kurdish Socialist Party of Iraq (**KSPI**), who carried out the abduction described in this study, is thus encouraged by Iran.

During 1981–83 more than 30 foreign workers from Britain, France, Germany, Poland, Austria, Hungary and Yugoslavia were abducted by Kurdish guerrillas. None were harmed and, though ransoms were paid for some of them, the main aim was undoubtedly publicity for the Kurdish cause.

Two of these expatriates were Guy Boisvert (aged 22, Canadian) and Renaldo Franceschi (aged 40, US citizen), both employed by the Canadian-based **Atco** Corporation, supervising a number of dispersed construction projects in Iraq.* Their truck broke down in north-eastern Iraq and they were abducted on 2 May 1982 by three armed Kurds who took them to a remote Kurdish village whence twelve days' march through the mountains took them about 160 km to the headquarters of the KSPI in Doletu, a small group of mud huts and tents close to the Iraq–Iran border. Here they were given Kurdish clothes and were allowed to walk freely about the camp, living under the same rugged conditions and disciplines as the guerrillas but otherwise treated fairly and with increasing friendliness. The guerrillas clearly hoped that they would take away some sympathy for their cause, which they did.

In the camp they met Michael Powell, an Englishman who they were dismayed to learn had been a hostage for 15 months. Powell had some books and they were allowed to listen to the BBC and Radio Monte Carlo.

* There is a detailed account of this abduction by Barry Nelson in 'Kidnapped', *Canadan Business*, June 1983.

Boisvert and Franceschi were told to write to their families, to the company, to their governments and to papers or press agencies of their choice. Those to their families and Atco arrived on 1 June, about a month after they were kidnapped. They were told to say that they were with the Kurdish Socialist Party which had representatives in Beirut, Damascus and Europe, whom Atco should contact within five days or the hostages would be put on trial as spies of the Saddam regime in Iraq; and that in order to break the barriers to the world media the partisans were seizing foreign experts sent to help Saddam. There was no demand for a ransom.

Meanwhile, it seemed in no way unusual to Atco's construction superintendent in Iraq to hear nothing for a week from people on tour of remote sites, but after ten days he became concerned and started a search of hospitals, prisons and morgues. He then telephoned his headquarters (Atco's transportable building subsidiary in Texas) who in turn informed the US State Department and Atco's head office in Calgary, Alberta, who informed the Canadian Department of External Affairs in Ottawa. Both governments told them that the likeliest explanation was that the men had been kidnapped by Kurdish guerrillas, but no one had any idea how to contact them.

Atco immediately convened their Crisis Management Committee (CMC) which was constituted on the lines described in Chapter 12. Headed by the executive vice-president, it included Art Roberts, vice-president for special services and Kenzie MacLeod, chief of security, both of whom were former police officers; also finance and administrative vice-presidents and an experienced confidential secretary; a legally qualified director and the public relations manager were called in as necessary. Roberts also called in a firm of specialist consultants which had been recommended to him, and they advised the company throughout the crisis. Regular contact was made with the families of the hostages and with the US and Canadian governments.

Discussion with other companies which had had people taken by the Kurds quickly established that self-styled representatives in London, Paris and Damascus had proved unreliable. This was to be the experience of Roberts and MacLeod, who met large numbers of them, some of whom asked for ransoms varying between $500 000 and $750 000. They applied a test of giving each a numbered letter with proof questions which only Boisvert or Franceschi could answer, saying that they would only continue negotiations if answers came back signed by the hostages. None ever did.

Meanwhile the English hostage, Michael Powell, was released, along with five Germans and two Frenchmen. All were handed over, unusually, to the Iraqi police (KSPI normally sent its hostages to Iran). Powell came out on 24 June and gave the first information to the press that a Canadian and an American had been hostages with him.

Here, Atco took a shrewd and original line. They had decided to withhold publicity as this was their only negotiating card – it was what the kidnappers badly wanted. The publicity following the release of Powell and the others had come only *as a result of their release* so, when the press telephoned Atco and the Canadian External Affairs Department about 'the Canadian and the American' they stalled the questions and Atco asked the two hostages' families to do the same.

This may have been why, in mid-July, Franceschi was told he was to be released. Boisvert had been taken away for treatment of a serious skin disease and was released separately.

Franceschi, two Hungarians and a Yugoslav were escorted on a three-day march to a border post where they were handed over to teenage Iranian Revolutionary Guards. They were then driven to Tehran and shunted around from one Revolutionary Guard base to another. Boisvert, who did not meet Franceschi again until they were home, had a similar experience. It was not until 10 August that Atco heard, through Ottawa, that it was believed that they had been transferred to Iran but the Iranian authorities, when approached, denied this. (It was possible that this was just because the Revolutionary Guards chose not to, or found no channel to, report that they had them.) Concern grew that the Iranians might suspect them of being Iraqi agents or be holding them as a reprisal for the Canadian Embassy's help to six Americans in escaping from the US Embassy seized in Tehran in 1979.

Meanwhile, Boisvert and Franceschi were taking every chance to get messages out to foreign embassies in Tehran and, in the somewhat disorganized conditions, some unexpected messengers were used. The Danish Embassy was the first to get news to Canada that they were in Tehran. Eventually it was the astute seizure of an opportunity by the Canadian ambassador to Pakistan which got the hostages released. He was due to see the Iranian foreign affairs minister on 16 December to discuss the re-opening of the Canadian Embassy in Tehran and brought the subject up. Playing on his knowledge that the Iranians were keen to re-open diplomatic relations, he persuaded them that they would acquire merit for a humanitarian gesture and secured Boisvert's release. He and the Danish ambassador collected him from the Iranian foreign ministry on 20 September. Franceschi was released on 9 October.

This case illustrates the extraordinary difficulty of communication in this kind of kidnap. Success came because the company, the Canadian and US governments and the hostages themselves tried every possible channel, testing them for reliability and pursuing those which were promising. The governments were able to play their parts without being involved in discussing concessions. The media were used wisely and skilfully. The whole operation was well handled by Atco's crisis management team which was in being before they were hit by a crisis; and its chairman said in an interview with *Canadian Business* (see previous footnote) that the specialist consultants were 'worth every penny they charged'.

The Kurds also achieved their aim. Boisvert and Franceschi, while disapproving of their methods, both sympathized with their cause so, since the publicity was kept in check until after they were released, it was better publicity.

ANGOLA

In 1983–85, Jonas Savimbi's **UNITA** movement, occupying the south-eastern half of Angola, kidnapped 312 hostages, to embarrass the MPLA government and to gain world publicity and recognition. They came from Brazil, Bulgaria, Canada, Cape Verde Islands, Colombia, Czechoslovakia, Mexico, the Philippines, Portugal, Spain, the UK, Uruguay and the USA. The longest any were held was 458 days.

On 23 February 1984, 77 hostages were taken from the Cafunfo diamond mining centre in north-east Angola; 16 were British, 15 Filipino and 46 Portuguese. They were marched 700 miles to the UNITA camp in Jamba in the south, taking nearly eight weeks. On their arrival there, Savimbi ordered the release of all except for the 16 British men and a Portuguese woman who was married to one of them. The 60 released hostages were flown to Johannesburg under arrangements by the International Red Cross and thence home.

Savimbi's demands were the same as for all the other hostages taken by him to Jamba: for all foreign technicians to leave Angola and for their governments to recognize UNITA.

The British government did make a concession by sending a senior foreign office official, Sir John Leahy, to visit UNITA in Jamba on 12 May 1984. He was photographed shaking hands with Savimbi. The hostages were required to sign a document undertaking not to return to Angola so long as the civil war continued. They were released on 13 May, having been held for 80 days, and were flown home via Johannesburg. They said that, while the march from Cafunfo had been exhausting, they had otherwise been well treated and all looked tanned and healthy.

SUDAN

As indicated in Chapter 3, the Sudan is divided between the Christian or animist Black African south, where the **SPLA** is fighting for independence, and the richer Arab-dominated Muslim north. In 1983, the SPLA, as a matter of policy and after clear threats to do so, launched a campaign to disrupt development projects which, they claimed, would in fact further enrich the north at the expense of the south. They also hoped thereby to bring about the overthrow of President Nimieri and his imposition of strict Islamic law – which indeed came about in 1985. Despite the apparent inadequacies of the Sudanese army, the companies involved in the projects were naturally loath to abandon their investments and accepted Nimieri's encouragement to continue and his guarantee of army protection.

The first attacks came in November 1983, when the SPLA kidnapped four Frenchmen and three Pakistanis working for a French consortium on the construction of the Jonglei Canal. On the same day two Britons engaged in preliminary work for Chevron in connection with the Bentiu oil refinery were also abducted. All the hostages were released within a few days with lists of SPLA demands which included cessation of work on the projects.

Early in 1984, further attacks were made on both projects involving the deaths of several locally-employed workers and eight more kidnaps. Two of the hostages, from the Chevron project, were condemned to death when the sister of one of them tried to smuggle a message to them saying that the Sudanese army were going to raid the camp and rescue them. These two eventually managed to escape in July 1985 after being held for more than a year.

The other six hostages were taken from the Jonglei Canal project on 10 February 1984. They included two French technicians, a British technician, a Kenyan pilot and his pregnant German-born wife and 18-month-old son. The wife was released with her son on 12 March and was able to report that the four men had been moved to a camp in Ethiopia, where they were held for nearly a year while prolonged negotiations took place involving the Ethiopian government, who were clearly in league with the SPLA.

Eventually a settlement was reached for a ransom comprising cash, equipment and medicine to a total value of $4.4 million and the hostages were released on 28 January 1985 after 354 days in captivity. Though they had been held under harsh conditions and had lost weight, they had been reasonably well treated and were physically in good health.

At the time of writing (1986) work on both the Jonglei Canal and the Bentiu oil refinery remains in suspension.

ZIMBABWE

A rather more mysterious abduction took place in Zimbabwe on 23 July 1982. Nine tourists (six young men and three girls), with a driver, were travelling in a bus as part of an Encounter Overland tour of Africa and were abducted on the road from Victoria Falls to Bulawayo. They were ambushed by armed dissidents from **ZIPRA**, the guerrilla movement which had supported Joshua Nkomo. The tourists were told to start walking and the bus driver was sent back to the bus with a note demanding the release of two ZIPRA leaders, Dabengwa and Masuku, and the return of ZIPRA lands confiscated by the Mugabe government.

After a time, the three girls were released – apparently because they were slowing down progress through the bush; they found their way back to the bus and travelled on to Bulawayo where they reported the abduction. The Zimbabwe security forces immediately searched the area but could find no trace of the kidnappers or the hostages.

Two of the young men were Americans, two Australian and two British, so four governments (including that of Zimbabwe) and several families were involved. Investigations continued over the next two years, but were hampered by many false reports of sightings of young white men in various places. Most were probably deliberate hoaxes but all had to be followed up. ZIPRA dissidents were questioned to no avail. There were numerous unsubstantiated reports that the hostages were still alive.

Eventually, in March 1985, a dissident who had been arrested led the authorities to a grave where human bones were found and these were subsequently identified as those of the hostages. They had been killed during their first two days of captivity and presumably the false reports were designed to divert the investigations.

Since they made a specific demand, the dissidents had probably intended to keep their victims alive to bargain for it. The demand was not repeated and there is nothing to suggest that the killing was part of a preconceived plan. One theory is that a school bus travelling on the same route was the intended target and that the kidnappers ambushed the wrong bus, decided to go ahead and then panicked; but it is unlikely that the truth will ever be known.

17 Short-Term Abductions

BRIAN NORRY

On 7 March 1984, Brian Norry, wages chief for Observer Newspapers, was taken hostage by two men who burst into his flat in London and held him prisoner overnight. Next morning, they forced him to drive them in his car to his offices where he was made to open the safe and hand over the contents. They then took him back to his car and left him handcuffed to the steering wheel. They escaped with £50 000.

STUART MELVILLE

On 11 March 1984, Stuart Melville, manager of the American Express office in Dublin, was kidnapped from his home by six men, probably members of the INLA, who broke into his home and held him and his family overnight. One of the men was dressed in police uniform and the others were masked and armed. They took him to his office next morning, warning his wife not to try to leave as they had booby-trapped the doors. At the office, they tied up 14 employees and locked them in the strong room. Melville was then forced to open the safe and they escaped with travellers' cheques and cash to a total value of IR £520 000. The travellers' cheques, however, were cancelled leaving the men with only IR£20 000.

Stuart Melville was targeted a second time on 29 October 1985 when he and his wife were abducted by four armed men from their home. They were forced into their car and driven to the American Express offices. Melville was ordered to go in and collect cash from the safe and bring it on foot to a rendezvous and they warned him that if he failed to appear his wife would be shot. They then drove her off in his car. He collected about IR£117 000 from the safe and this was snatched from him as he walked towards the rendezvous. His wife was released shortly afterwards.

ALLIED IRISH BANK

On 27 January 1985, a multiple abduction was used to rob the Allied

Irish Bank in Dublin. First, a couple unconnected with the bank were taken hostage in their home by six armed men and held overnight until the following evening. The sole object of this appeared to be to secure their house, which was in secluded surroundings, for use in the rest of the operation. Four of the armed men, on the second evening, then burst into the home of the branch manager of the bank and took him and his family to the house of the couple already being held. Next morning, leaving the other hostages under guard, some of the armed men took the manager to his bank, herded the staff into a back room, and forced him to open the safe and hand over IR£40 000.

At this point one of the staff succeeded in setting off the alarm but the robbers noticed this and forced the manager to telephone the police and tell them that the alarm had been set off accidentally. Despite this the police decided to visit the bank anyway but when they arrived the manager was forced to turn them away. The robbers escaped with the money, despite having to hijack a passing car when their van failed to start.

Meanwhile the hostages at the secluded house – the owners and the bank manager's family – were released when they were told by the rest of the gang that the money had been paid. They stole the owner's car for their getaway.

RAFAEL VILLASECA

On 7 October 1984, Rafael Villaseca, the managing director of a construction company in Barcelona, was abducted from his garage at home by members of the left-wing terrorist group, GRAPO. He was driven around for three hours while his company were told of his abduction, and ordered to pay 5 million pesetas ($185 000). A company employee withdrew the money from a bank and delivered it to the extortioners, after which the managing director was released.

18 Hijacking and Hostage Sieges

The cases studied in this chapter differ from those described in previous chapters in that the location of the hostages was known, whether they were in trains, aircraft, ships or buildings. The background of negotiation and release was therefore entirely different.

TRAIN HIJACKS IN THE NETHERLANDS

When Indonesia became independent in 1949, the South Moluccan Islands, part of the colonial Dutch East Indies, were handed over with the rest to the Jakarta government. The South Moluccan Islanders, who had a record of loyalty to the Dutch, bitterly resented it; many emigrated to Holland, where they continued to try desperately to persuade the Dutch government to apply pressure on the Indonesian government to give the islands their independence.

On 2 December 1975, South Moluccan terrorists hijacked a train near Beilen, holding about 50 passengers hostage. Their aim was publicity but they also demanded a bus to take them and the hostages to an airport. When they got no response they tried to force the pace by shooting the train driver and then two more hostages, in full view of the police besieging the train at a safe distance.

The police were advised in their negotiation by a brilliant psychiatrist, Dr Richard Mulder who had successfully handled previous sieges. Eventually the hostages' spokesman, Hans Prinz, who had established a good working relationship with the hijackers, persuaded the police that they were becoming dangerously unstable and frustrated because they had no idea what was happening outside; he persuaded the police to send in a portable radio. When the hijackers found that Dutch radio programmes were dominated by their news, their whole attitude changed and a few hours later they surrendered. The siege had lasted 12 days.

On 23 May 1977, the South Moluccans hijacked another train, near Glimmen, holding 55 hostages. They demanded the release of 21 prisoners, including those convicted for the previous train hijack. The Dutch government had firmly decided that no convicted terrorists would be released. It became clear that – as in the London Iranian Embassy siege described later – this would leave no scope for a negotiated release, so they decided to put in the military rescue force of the Dutch marines. This went in at dawn on the 19th day of the siege (11 June).

The marines had managed earlier to conceal microphones along the full length of the train in darkness, so they knew very well who was sleeping in what compartments and where the terrorists were. During the night before the assault they placed a number of small explosive charges with electric detonators at various points beside the train. At dawn, when Dr Mulder had advised that the terrorist alertness and morale would be at its lowest, they suddenly and simultaneously unleashed a massive explosion of noise which seemed to come from all directions – from the charges exploding and from fighter aircraft flying low over the train. Simultaneously they poured machine-gunfire into the compartments where they knew the terrorists were. Under cover of all this the marine assault teams, using special framed charges provided by the German GSG9 who had come to help them, blasted open selected doors and stormed the train. Six terrorists were killed, one severely wounded the remainder captured. Two hostages who tried to move during the firing were killed. Five other hostages and two marines were killed. The whole operation took 22 minutes.

A hijacked train is, in fact, very similar to a hijacked building. Unlike a hijacked aircraft, it cannot be flown away at gunpoint to another country, so the hijackers hold no cards other than the threat to kill hostages – in the almost certain knowledge that they will be caught.

These train hijacks did achieve their primary aim of publicity. Most of Europe – and indeed much of the world – heard of the South Moluccans and their cause for the first time. But the fate of their islands lay with the Indonesians and there was nothing the Dutch could do about it. The following year they made what was – up to the time of writing – their final attempt. Three South Moluccan terrorists seized 72 hostages in government buildings in Assen and murdered one of them in cold blood before the marines again went in and rescued the rest. With this and the two train hijacks – and some other hostage seizures not here described – they forfeited the very considerable sympathy which many Dutch people had previously felt for them. For the mainstream of South Moluccans this was tragic, for they have nowhere else to go and the Dutch have been their best (and almost their only) friends.

HIJACK TO ENTEBBE, 1976

The hijack which ended at Entebbe in 1976 highlighted the problems arising when a government cooperates with terrorists in holding hostages, and when the parent government of the bulk of the hostages decides to rescue them by force in defiance of that government. There are some parallels with the seizure of the US Embassy in Tehran in 1979 and the hijacking of TWA Flight 847 to Beirut in June 1985, both discussed later in this chapter.

On 27 June 1976, two German and two Arab terrorists smuggled weapons in their hand-baggage when boarding an Air France airbus at an intermediate stop in Athens. Most of the 256 passengers were Israeli and other Jewish passengers flying from Tel Aviv to Paris. After take-off from Athens, the terrorists hijacked the aircraft and, after refuelling at Benghazi, it landed at Entebbe where President Idi Amin was clearly expecting it; he arranged for the passengers to be disembarked with the hijackers into the old aircraft terminal, where he personally visited them; he told them that the hijackers' demands were reasonable but that the Israeli government was resisting them. The whole procedure was guarded and controlled by the Ugandan army in cooperation with the hijackers.

The hijackers' demands were relayed to the French government by Idi Amin, notably for 53 convicted terrorists to be flown from Israel and other places to Entebbe. Meanwhile the terrorists, in conjunction with Idi Amin, decided to release the non-Jewish passengers. The two Germans, though acting on behalf of the Palestinians, were in command, Wilfrid Böse and Brigitta Kuhlmann, both known members of the Red Army Faction. It was they who sorted out Jews from non-Jews, the woman, in particular, evoking strong memories of the Nazis. The hijackers were also reinforced by three more heavily armed Arabs, who arrived in a Mercedes on the day the aircraft landed and had clearly been awaiting them as guests of Idi Amin.

The Israeli government conducted unofficial negotiations by telephone through a reserve army lieutenant-colonel, Baruch Bar-Lev, who had spent five years in Uganda as head of the Israeli army training team, with Amin initially as chief of staff and then as president, when the two had become friends. Bar-Lev dialled Amin's personal number in Kampala and began a series of long telephone conversations which were taped and later published.* Amin,

---

* There are verbatim extracts in Yehuda Ofer, *Operation Thunder* (London, Penguin, 1976).

throughout, insisted that Israel must concede to the hijackers' demands.

Since they had no intention of doing so, the Israelis decided on a bold rescue plan. They despatched their highly-trained commando force, Sayaret Maktal, in three Hercules aircraft, via Nairobi, where they established an emergency hospital close to the aircraft to treat the anticipated casualties and then continued to Entebbe. They landed unheralded on the runway in the early hours of 4 July. The commandos poured out and charged straight for the terminal building, detaching flank guards to intercept Ugandan army reinforcements and to deal with Ugandan soldiers firing from the control tower and around the building. They achieved complete surprise. They killed all the hijackers and 20 Ugandan soldiers (putting another 60 or so to flight). The commandos lost one killed – the lieutenant-colonel leading the assault – who was shot from the control tower. Three hostages were killed in the battle and a fourth – a 74-year-old lady who had been taken to hospital – was later murdered by the Ugandans. The other 108 were rescued and flown to Israel via Nairobi.

HIJACK TO MOGADISHU, 1977

The hijack to Entebbe in 1976 was led by Germans on behalf of Palestinians; the hijack to Mogadishu in 1977 was carried out by Palestinians on behalf of the German Red Army Faction. In both cases the hostages were rescued by commandos operating outside their own country – at Entebbe in defiance of the Ugandan government, at Mogadishu with permission of the Somali government.

On 13 October 1977, Dr Hanns-Martin Schleyer had for six weeks been a kidnap hostage of the Red Army Faction, who had realized that the German government was not going to release Baader, Ennslin and the other convicted RAF terrorists. How far the Palestinians acted in collusion, or whether they wanted to show solidarity, or whether they wanted to tie a separate action to what was already front-page news is uncertain; perhaps it was a mixture of all three. The four Arab hijackers boarded a Lufthansa Boeing 737 carrying 84 passengers and crew at Palma, Majorca, where security was lax, and they carried guns and explosives in their hand-baggage. They hijacked the aircraft and it landed first in Rome, then, in Cyprus, Bahrain and Dubai. They demanded the release of the same 11 German prisoners and of two Palestinians held in Turkey, and ransoms totalling about $16 million.

After two nights and a day on the ground in the heat of Dubai, the aircraft took off again and, after being refused access to Kuwait, landed at Aden. Here the hijackers shot the captain of the aircraft dead in cold blood, as they suspected him of giving information to Yemeni troops when he was permitted to leave the aircraft to check the nosewheel. The co-pilot then flew the aircraft to Mogadishu, where the captain's body was dumped on the runway.

Meanwhile the German government, while playing for time by negotiating over the control tower radio, had moved the GSG9 commando force to Dubai, where the government asked them to brief and give a crash training course to their own troops to effect a rescue. Before this rescue could be attempted, however, the aircraft took off for Mogadishu, so the GSG9 followed it. With the aircraft wired up with explosives, the German negotiator from the control tower negotiated with great skill to get the deadline postponed, saying that the German government had put the release of the prisoners in motion. Meanwhile the German government had obtained the agreement of President Barre of Somalia (who was at war with Ethiopia and needed friends) for the GSG9 to effect a rescue. At 2 a.m. on 18 October they stormed the aircraft, assisted by two members of the SAS using stun grenades (which temporarily stun and dazzle everyone, terrorists and hostages alike). Though the terrorist leader managed to throw two grenades, none of the hostages or the troopers received more than slight injuries. Three of the hijackers were killed and the fourth, a woman, severely wounded.*

When Baader and Ennslin, in their prison in Germany, heard the news on the radio that the hijack had failed they committed suicide the same day, along with another of the original gang, Jan-Carl Raspe, and a fourth, Ingrid Schubert, did likewise three weeks later.

On 19 October, the kidnappers of Dr Schleyer dumped his body in the boot of a car in Mulhouse in eastern France.

TEHRAN: SEIZURE OF THE US EMBASSY

On 4 November 1979, 3000 Iranian militants overran the US Embassy in Tehran, taking over 60 hostages. Thirteen women and blacks were released two weeks later leaving 50 still held, who were eventually

---

* There is a detailed account of this hijack and rescue in Peter Koch and Kai Hermann, *Assault at Mogadishu* (London, Corgi, 1977).

released 444 days later. Initially, President Carter assumed that the Iranian security forces would expel the attackers and certainly the Iranian prime minister, Bazargan, intended to do so but he was overruled by the Ayatollah Khomeini and resigned. This was and remains the only occasion in modern times in which a government has thrown the full weight of its security forces to protecting and sustaining the seizure of an embassy and its diplomatic staff by a mob. The probable explanation is that the mob comprised the young and fanatical Islamic fundamentalists on whose support Khomeini primarily relied, and he did not wish to damp their ardour.

Iranian assets were frozen and intensive negotiations ensued. The incident dominated the last year of Carter's presidency and removed any chance he might otherwise have had of re-election.

Immediately, contingency planning began for a rescue operation using Delta Force, a special military unit formed and commanded by Colonel Charles Beckwith, who had spent a year with the SAS in the UK and attempted to model it on similar lines. Unfortunately, the structure of the US defence services was such that all the planning was done by top-heavy committees on which generals and admirals of all three services were present in profusion, each trying to retain control of his own contribution to the force. Although there was in theory a task force with a major-general in command, he did not have full control of either the training or the tactical command of all the troops involved, which included naval ships in the Gulf, US Marine Corps helicopters, US Air Force transport aircraft and, of course, the army's Delta Force.

The failure of the rescue attempt on 24 April 1980 is too well known to need a detailed acount. It failed primarily because, of the eight helicopters assigned for the rescue, two became unserviceable and one got lost on the way to the desert airstrip in Iran to which Delta Force had been flown in transport aircraft. Colonel Beckwith considered that six serviceable helicopters was the minmium to give a reasonable chance of success and decided that he must abort the operation. There were other factors (e.g. a busload of Iranians had blundered by chance into the desert airstrip), but the decisive one was the failure of the helicopters. It transpired that, as marine helicopters, their crews and engineers had not been properly trained either in desert navigation or in desert maintenance; this, in turn, was a consequence of having a top-heavy planning and command structure with divided responsibilities.

Even if the rescue force had reached the embassy, it is by no means certain that they would have got out successfully with the hostages. Getting in, with the advantage of surprise, would have been the easiest part. Getting out, through the streets of Tehran, to where the aircraft would have been waiting to lift them out, would have been far more hazardous.

The hostages were eventually released, with the Algerians acting as honest brokers, in exchange for the unfreezing of Iranian assets in the USA, on 20 January – just after President Carter had handed over to President Reagan.

BOGOTA: SEIZURE OF THE DOMINICAN EMBASSY

The year 1980 was a peak one for the seizure of hostages in embassies; 42 embassies were seized worldwide, 20 of them in Latin America. Hundreds of hostages, including 22 ambassadors, were held and 53 people were killed, 45 of them in Latin America, mostly hostage-takers killed in police rescue operations. During the year, governments began to take a firmer attitude against this kind of seizure (an example was the siege of the Iranian Embassy in London in April 1980 which is described later in this chapter) and, as a result, this type of terrorist operation declined.

One of the most dramatic and successful was the seizure of the Dominican Embassy in Bogota on 17 February 1980. There was a large reception in progress in the embassy with many foreign diplomats present. Across the road from the embassy was a university playing-field where 25 members of the M19 terrorist movement arranged to play football. On a signal from a lookout that the people they wanted had arrived at the embassy, the 'referee' blew his whistle. The players donned their tracksuits, in which their weapons were concealed, and ran across the road in pre-planned tactical formation, produced their weapons, killed a guard (with one of their own number also killed), ran up the stairs into the reception, and seized 75 hostages including 14 ambassadors. They released non-diplomatic staff and one ambassador but held the remainder for two months. Initially they demanded the release of 300 prisoners and a ransom of $50 million. The Colombian government refused to negotiate on either demand but eventually a consortium of businessmen from the countries whose ambassadors were held, paid a ransom of $2.5 million, upon which the Colombian government agreed that the terrorists and their diplomatic hostages would be flown to Havana where the diplomats were released

– as were the terrorists with their $2.5 million. An even greater success for the operation, however, and probably its primary aim, was the publicity which accrued from the protracted negotiations, some conducted in front of television cameras between masked terrorists and priests acting as intermediaries. With 14 countries having ambassadors as hostages (not including Britain whose ambassador luckily arrived at the party too late!), the whole event was front-page news throughout the two months.

LONDON: THE IRANIAN EMBASSY SIEGE

In 1975 (the year after the 'Stockholm syndrome' bank siege), London's Metropolitan Police developed great skill in hostage negotiation in two London sieges, at Spaghetti House (criminal) and Balcombe Street (IRA). This skill was required again in April 1980, when six anti-Khomeini terrorists seized 26 hostages in the Iranian Embassy in London. During five days of patient negotiation, during which the tension was lowered due to enlightened cooperation with the police by the BBC, five sick or pregnant hostages were released. This cooperation, in which one of the hostages who was a BBC technician played a leading part, reached a climax on the fourth day when the terrorists were advised that their demands were being broadcast on BBC Radios 1 and 2 and the World Service at specific times. They listened and were overjoyed to find that their primary aim had been achieved – world publicity for their cause. It is possible that, from this point onwards, a more flexible negotiating attitude might have resulted in a peaceful surrender and the release of the hostages without the need for a rescue operation. This would have involved giving the impression that the British government might be contemplating concessions which they were not in fact prepared to make (as the German government did in the Schleyer case, see Chapter 9).

The sticking point, however, was that the government, rightly, had no intention of releasing the terrorists to a sanctuary from which they could commit further crimes – nor indeed to anywhere other than a British prison. On the sixth day the terrorists sensed that this was so, murdered one hostage and declared that they would murder another every 40 minutes until they were given safe conduct out of Britain. Taking this threat seriously, the government agreed to the police request to send in the army SAS rescue squad. During the rescue the terrorists killed one more hostage, but all the others were rescued, five of the terrorists being killed and the sixth arrested and convicted of murder.

This operation illustrated the different roles of the police and a military rescue force and the criteria on which the police take the decision to call them in. In essence, police marksmen are trained in the defensive use of firearms; the army are trained in the offensive use of firearms and the tactical use of fire and movement to close with an enemy. When the police commander on the site decides that defensive use of firearms will no longer be likely to save the lives of the hostages, he will seek approval from his chief, who will in turn refer to the responsible government minister. (If communications break down, either would no doubt feel able to act on his own judgement and justify it afterwards, if he thought that this was the only way to save the hostages.)

The roles and attitudes were highlighted by questions asked during the cross-examination at the inquest on those killed. P.C. Lock, the British policeman who had been on duty at the entrance to the embassy, initially overpowered when the first burst of fire broke the glass door and showered it in his face, succeeded in concealing his pistol under his coat throughout the siege. When he heard the SAS breaking in, P.C. Lock was beside the terrorist leader who was speaking on the negotiating telephone. He at once overpowered him, seized his submachine gun and threw it out of reach (a brave action, because there were still five more heavily-armed terrorists in the building), and drew his own pistol. Asked by counsel at the inquest whether he had considered shooting the terrorist leader he replied: 'It did cross my mind, but I had overpowered him, his gun was out of reach and I had my pistol. It would have been contrary to my training to shoot a man whom I had disarmed and arrested and who was no threat to me.' Seconds later, two SAS men burst through the door, told P.C. Lock to roll over and shot the terrorist dead and then went on to shoot the others (except one whom they mistook for a hostage) before they could shoot or pull a second weapon or a grenade from their pockets, or blow up the building as they had threatened to do.

The police and the army have different roles and are, rightly, trained to react differently.

The operation also proved the excellence of the SAS, which is due to methods of selection and training. They are recruited, not directly, but only from fully trained soldiers in other British army regiments. Having plenty of applicants, they only invite the outstanding ones for their tests, which are both physically and mentally arduous, and they select only one or two out of every ten. Once in the SAS, their squadrons alternate between service in Northern Ireland and elsewhere. The rescue squads are kept at concert pitch by intensive training with live ammunition in their 'killing house' – a series of passages and rooms, bullet-proofed and ricochet-proofed. This selection and training, coupled with the variety of their employment (an advantage which few other countries' rescue squads enjoy) probably make them the best of their kind in the world.

HIJACK TO BEIRUT, JUNE 1985

On 14 June 1985, a TWA Boeing 727 (flight 847) was hijacked after taking off from Athens airport carrying 145 passengers of whom about 100 were Americans. It was flown to Beirut where 19 women and children were released; then to Algiers, where another 22 were released. It then flew back to Beirut for a second time and as it came in to land the hijackers shot a young American, whom they had identified as an off-duty US navy man, and pushed his body out on to the runway. They then flew to Algiers once again and finally back to Beirut where the aircraft remained, with 108 people still on board. The hijackers were Shia Muslim radicals demanding the release of over 700 Shia prisoners taken by the Israelis. The Israelis said that they were in the process of releasing these prisoners in any case and would not be hurried by terrorist actions.

The US government had very few options. The Delta Force stood by in US navy ships in the Mediterranean and could therefore in theory have attempted a rescue operation in either Algiers or Beirut. Algeria, however, had for a long time had a useful working relationship with the USA (it was they who organized the release of the hostages from Tehran in 1981) and the USA would not have wished to alienate them. Beirut airport, being close to the sea, would also have been geographically suitable for attack, but was in the part of Lebanon controlled by the Shia militia under Nabih Berri's Amal movement, so, although the hijackers were from a different and more militant Shia movement under Syrian control, Berri's militia would certainly have been on the hijackers' side if Delta Force had attacked – and would not have been as incompetent as Idi Amin was in Entebbe. Whether or not the raiders could have reached the aircraft, it is virtually certain that every hostage would have ben killed before they did so.

Eventually President Reagan did a deal with the only two people who had any influence or power to make a deal stick – Nabih Berri and President Assad of Syria. The Israelis confirmed that the Shia prisoners would be released (as they were in due course) without any commitment to dates and the American hostages (including the air crew), were transferred to Damascus and flown home via Frankfurt in a US military aircraft.

HIJACK OF THE SHIP *ACHILLE LAURO*, OCTOBER 1985

Hijacking of ships, like that of trains, is very rare and seldom succeeds, for similar reasons. On 7 October 1985, four Palestinians hijacked the Italian cruiseliner *Achille Lauro* which had sailed from Alexandria with 481 passengers and crew on board. The hijack was allegedly organized by Abu Abbas, leader of a splinter group of Yassir Arafat's El Fatah, based in Tunisia. The raid appears to have been in retaliation for Israel's bombing of PLO headquarters in Tunisia on 30 September (itself a reprisal for the kidnap and murder of three Israelis in a yacht in Cyprus).

Abu Abbas did not himself board the *Achille Lauro*. The four young hijackers appear to have intended to hijack the ship in Israeli waters but to have acted prematurely when their weapons were spotted in their cabin. They then committed the almost unbelievable blunder of shooting a 69-year-old disabled passenger in a wheelchair, Leon Klinghoffer, whose body was later found in the sea with bullets traceable to their guns.

On 9 October, the four hijackers surrendered, unexpectedly, to the Egyptian authorities in Port Said, Yassir Arafat claiming the credit for negotiating it. Next day, presumably as part of the deal, they were being flown with Abu Abbas and others in an Egyptian aircraft to Yassir Arafat's headquarters in Tunis. The aircraft was, however, intercepted by US fighter aircraft and forced to land at the NATO air base at Sigonella, in Sicily. The US military staff clearly intended to arrest the men themselves, but the Italians exercised their jurisdiction over the airfield and compelled the Americans to hand them over.

The Italians then released Abu Abbas – to the fury of the Americans – on the grounds that they had no evidence against him, but they detained the four hijackers for trial in Genoa, where they had originally boarded the ship. One was tried separately in a juvenile court but the other three were convicted in July 1986 of 'carrying out a kidnap with terrorist intent, leading to the death of a hostage' and received sentences ranging from 15 to 30 years in prison. Abu Abbas and two others were tried *in absentia* and sentenced to life imprisonment.

There is no doubt that President Reagan's action in ordering the interception of the Egyptian aircraft was popular with the US public, in the light of Klinghoffer's murder and the earlier TWA hijack to Beirut, but it caused considerable friction with Egypt and Italy and (like his later bombing of Libya as a reprisal against Gadafi's support of anti-American terrorist acts) was condemned by much of world opinion.

HIJACK TO MALTA, NOVEMBER 1985

On 24 November an Egyptian aircraft carrying 98 people was hijacked by Palestinians and landed in Malta. Next day, with permission from the Maltese government, Egyptian commandos stormed the aicraft after two passengers had been murdered in cold blood. They believed, correctly, that eight people had been shot, though the other six were later shown only to have been wounded. At the time, therefore, there was some urgency about the need to rescue the remaining passengers and crew before more were killed.

Unfortunately, the rescue went badly wrong, due to its hasty planning and not to any lack of bravery by the commandos. They entered through the baggage compartment but the opening of the door in the belly of the aircraft triggered a warning buzzer and light in the cockpit. The rescuers then blasted their way through the floor into the passenger cabin, but whether it was this or a grenade thrown by the hijackers that was the cause, the aircraft caught fire and 57 of the 98 on board died, mainly from the fire. While it is easy to criticize, the murderous nature of the hijackers probably did justify the decision to go in without delay, and in those circumstances there is always a risk of casualties.

HIJACK AT KARACHI, SEPTEMBER 1986

At 4.45 a.m. on 5 September 1986, a Pan American Boeing 747 landed from Bombay at Karachi for a 90-minute intermediate stop. At 6 a.m., while joining passengers were still embarking in the open on the ramp, four hijackers dressed in the uniform of airport security men drove unchallenged on to the ramp and hijacked the aircraft, firing as they did so and killing one passenger – presumably to nip any resistance in the bud. There were by then about 400 people on board.

The captain and his flight-deck crew, acting on Pan Am standing instructions, at once escaped by lowering ropes directly from the flight-deck on to the ramp, so the aircraft was effectively grounded. Despite demands from the hijackers for a replacement crew, the control tower negotiators managed to find reasons for not providing one. Their tactics were to keep the aircraft on the ground at all costs and play for time. The first deadline set by the hijackers (7 p.m.) passed without incident and they set a second (11 p.m.).

Meanwhile, the Pakistani commandos were preparing a rescue plan and were rehearsing it on another aircraft parked out of sight. They had been told that they had at least until midnight to prepare.

The captain warned the negotiators that the aircraft generator would run out of fuel and estimated the time at which it would do so. At 9 p.m. the lights began to flicker. Soon afterwards the aircraft lights failed altogether. The control tower tried to reassure the hijackers that this was not a tactical ploy but radio contact failed with the loss of power. The chief negotiator walked out on to the ramp with a loudhailer but failed to attract the hijackers' attention. Police then approached the aircraft to try to continue negotiation but at this point the lights on the terminal building beside the ramp also went out. That, and the sound of policemen under the aircraft caused the hijackers to panic, believing that an assault was about to come in. They herded all the passengers into the centre section of the aircraft and opened fire, killing a further 17 and wounding 129. One of the passengers operated an emergency door and its shute inflated automatically. With the police firing outside and passengers struggling to escape there was a shambles. The commandos, who were still rehearsing on the other aircraft when the shooting began, did not reach the scene for 15 minutes and, having no suitable ladders, did not enter the aircraft until 25 minutes after the shooting had begun.

Three controversial questions arise:

(a) Why was the airport security so bad that the hijackers, with no authentication other than uniforms, could drive unchallenged through the gate on to the ramp? For this there can be no excuse.
(b) Should the flight deck crew have abandoned the aircraft? The passengers and cabin crew were thereby deprived of the

leadership and negotiating authority of the captain, and he could also have explained the sudden failure of the lights and perhaps averted the hijackers' panic reaction. On the other hand, his departure did keep the aircraft on the ground and if (as the interrogation later concluded) it was the hijackers' intention to blow up the aircraft in the air if their demands were not met, this may have saved lives. Alternatively, had the aircraft gone to Tripoli or Beirut, rescue might have been impossible. With hindsight, it was clearly wise to prevent the aircraft taking off but, in a friendly country like Pakistan other methods (e.g. shooting the tyres) might have been better. This would, however, present problems in some other airports, and could panic the hijackers into starting a gun battle.

(c) Was the rescue bungled? Armchair criticism is easy enough. The commandos planned to go in at or after midnight, i.e. only 18 hours after the hijack. Had they bungled the rescue by going in without proper preparation and rehearsal, criticisms would have been equally strident. The fact that the aircraft generator failed while they were still rehearsing may have been bad luck or bad management. The ideal should be for a rescue force to have an immediate plan for action in an emergency from the start, with men standing by to carry it out, while the remainder prepare and rehearse a better plan, as more information becomes available and the situation develops, to be used if time permits.

19 Extortion by Bomb Threat and Product Contamination

WOOLWORTHS, AUSTRALIA

Woolworths run a large supermarket chain in Australia. In 1979–81 they were subject to a continuous series of product and bomb extortions, which they handled with conspicuous success and developed an effective and experienced crisis management organization.

In November and December 1979 a letter detailing a number of contaminated products was received, with a warning that there were others of which particulars would only be provided on payment of A$500 000, and there was the usual threat to tell the media if the police were informed. Woolworths tested the products designated in the letter and found that the contamination was not serious; so, after consultation with the police, they withdrew them and took no other action since the public did not seem to be at risk. The extortioner wrote again and telephoned and a meeting was arranged with a view to trapping him, but he detected the police surveillance and abandoned the extortion. He then tried to get a statement into the media, but they agreed to a police request not to publish it. After one more telephone call he gave up and nothing more was heard. This was a good example of cool, responsible handling of an actual but not very expert contamination by a lone criminal, with full cooperation from the police and the media.

A year later, on 24 October 1980, a message drew the attention of a security officer in the main Sydney Town Hall branch to a suitcase in a locker which was found to contain details of contaminated products, with a warning that unless A$800 000 were paid, poisoned goods would be placed in 80 other stores and the media would be informed. Again, the police were at once brought in and on this occasion Woolworths called a press conference to announce that they had withdrawn all the nominated goods and that the shelves would be restocked with goods, which had been checked, two days later. Since the extortioner's main threat – to tell the media – had been rendered

198

useless and he knew that the police were also involved, he abandoned the extortion and nothing more was heard.

On 17 and 19 December 1980, two stores were badly damaged by fires caused by bombs exploded without warning during the night. On 22 December a letter was left on a counter claiming to have set off the bombs and warning that more would be exploded in peak shopping hours unless A$1 million was paid in cash, gold and diamonds.

On 24 December a telephone caller warned Woolworths to evacuate a store in central Sydney and a bomb exploded in the toy department 15 minutes later, shattering the plate glass windows. Woolworths offered $250 000 reward for information leading to the conviction of the bombers and issued a press release. This was followed by a number of hoax calls.

On 29 December the media revealed exact details of the extortion demand and the code name given by the extortioner in his earlier calls. This led to literally hundreds of hoax calls using this code name. Next day there was another call from the real extortioner and a new code name was agreed.

On 31 December, in answer to a further call the company pretended that they were willing to pay and, during the next 10 days, negotiations led to agreement and instructions for payment. This was made by dropping a bag containing the money from a specified wharf in Sydney harbour. The police had surrounded the area and, observing bubbles rising to the surface arrested a skindiver – Gregory Norman McHardie – in the early hours of 13 January. The same day a call from the extortioner threatened unannounced bombs if the 'courier' collecting the money were arrested. Some weeks later a second man – Larry Burton Danielson – was arrested.

Both men were put on trial in March 1982 but during the trial McHardie escaped from prison. The judge ruled that the trial could continue without him. Both men were found guilty of the 1980 bombings and of demanding money with menaces. Danielson was sentenced in April to 20 years in prison. McHardie was recaptured in June and received a 27-year sentence in July.

Handling very different threats in very different ways, Woolworths showed a sure touch. The chairman, Sir Eric McClintock, has published their experiences widely in interviews including the fact that he employed Control Risks Ltd as consultants. Woolworths still receive threats of similar kind, mainly hoax calls but, because they maintain a permanent crisis management structure in being, as described in Chapters 11 and 12, they are able to continue trading, without any diversion of management from commercial operations, and Sir Eric has strongly advised other corporations to do the same.

COLES SUPERMARKETS, AUSTRALIA

In May 1983 a man placed products on Coles Supermarket shelves (food paste and eye drops) which had been poisoned, and demanded A$500 000 to stop him placing more. In a series of further telephone calls he said that, if the company refused to pay, not only would further poisoned products be placed on the shelves, but the demand would increase to A$1 million and then A$2 million.

The company informed the police who thereafter posed as Coles executives, took the calls and negotiated a payment. The final delivery point was a remote spot on a minor road in the Blue Mountains. The police carried out the instructions and, before the delivery car got there, surrounded the area. When an armed man appeared they called out that he was under arrest; he opened fire and was shot by the police.

QANTAS AIRWAYS, AUSTRALIA

In April 1985, a man telephoned Qantas Airways claiming that there was a bomb at Sydney airport which would be detonated unless they paid him A$300 000. The police searched the airport but found no trace of a bomb and nothing further was heard.

On 30 October 1985, Qantas received a call from a man claiming that there was a bomb on a flight which had left Auckland one hour previously, set to go off at a certain altitude, and that he would give details for disarming it if a ransom of A$400 000 were paid. In three further telephone calls, the extortionist claimed that he had left a similar bomb in a hotel to show that he meant business. The police found the hotel bomb and defused it. They had meanwhile managed to trace the telephone calls and arrested the man during a further call to Qantas. He was 37-year-old Gregory Warner, who proved also to have attempted the earlier extortion in April. No bomb was found on the aircraft.

BOMB THREATS AT AN OIL INSTALLATION

The head office of a multinational oil corporation received a letter stating that ten bombs had been placed in a huge oil storage plant and demanding payment of $15 million in return for details of the locations of the bombs and instructions for disarming them. If this first demand were not met, it would be raised to $30 million and other installations would also be bombed. The corporation was required to place an advertisement in a local paper signifying assent and giving a contact telephone number.

The company had a shadow crisis management structure and had carried out contingency planning. The Crisis Management Committee (CMC) was convened at the head office, and delegated control to the CMC of the divisional headquarters in the area concerned, with an incident management team (IMT) at the plant – as described in Chapter 12. Policies were agreed for negotiation, cooperation with the police (who were at once called in), safety precautions and relations with the media. It was decided that, once the credibility of the threat had been established, the plant would be closed and remain closed so long as the threat continued; that employees would be advised of the threat and their cooperation enlisted in bomb searches and in closing down the plant; that the media would be kept out for as long as possible but a fallback plan was made for media briefings in such a way as to keep sensitive operational information secret. It was decided to proceed with the process of negotiation and delivery of a ransom, in full cooperation with the police, with a view to achieving arrests and convictions.

On the day the threat was received the bomb search began, with police cooperation, and six of the ten bombs were discovered. The plant was evacuated. Inevitably the news leaked to the media, who discovered much of the contents of the extortion letter and monitored the police radio.

By the second day, the company was beseiged by the media, whom they begged in vain not to overfly the plant and not to risk setting off radio-activated bombs by using their transmitters, especially in low-flying helicopters.

On the fourth day telephone communications were established with the extortioners and the company agreed to provide an aircraft to fly the ransom and delivery team to an agreed delivery area. The police, meanwhile, were carrying out surveillance and, on the fifth day, two extortioners were arrested while speaking on the telephone to the delivery man. Interrogation of those two gave leads which enabled the police to arrest the remaining three members of the gang.

This was a model of crisis management by the corporation and the police. Though the cost of closing down and reopening the plant was considerable, no lives were risked, no ransom was paid and the criminals – a sophisticated gang with considerable technical expertise – were all arrested.

SUPERMARKET CHAIN, UK

In May 1981, the headquarters of a supermarket chain in UK received a message saying that three jars of different products, poisoned with paraquat, had been placed on the shelves of their supermarkets in Birmingham, Merseyside and Southport. The letter demanded £500 000 ($750 000) and warned that if it were not paid other poisoned products would be placed on their shelves throughout the UK. Detailed instructions for payment were given.

They located the products, which were clearly marked, and withdrew suspect stocks for checking. The press got wind of the story and there were heavy sales losses.

Although there was a second call from the same extortioner a few days later, nothing further transpired until August, when a further letter arrived at the headquarters accompanied by a parcel of poisoned tinned food, demanding £350 000 ($475 000), with three alternatives: (a) to pay the ransom and end the matter; (b) to go along with the demand but bring in the police, in which case the press would be notified by letters with similar packages of poisoned food; or (c) to refuse to pay, in which case contaminated food would be widely distributed on the shelves of their supermarkets. The letter added that if there was no response, future tins would be poisoned with Gramoxone for which, it said, there was no antidote; it gave instructions to place an advertisement in a named newspaper signifying assent, and this was done.

A week later a further letter was received giving detailed instructions for payment and specifying by name the manager of one of the stores to deliver it. The route was to end with an exchange of specified signals between the extortioner's torch and the car's headlights. The car completed the course and made the signal but there was no reply. After a further letter a second run was made and this time the ransom (partly in real and partly in counterfeit money) was dropped and collected. There was police surveillance of both runs. Later a man was arrested and admitted the charge; he committed suicide the day before he was due to appear in court.

TOBACCO COMPANY, UK

In April 1986, Gallaghers, the tobacco company, received a letter purporting to be from a man suffering terminal cancer as a result of smoking the company's cigarettes. He threatened that cigarettes on sale would be contaminated with cyanide unless £500 000 ($750 000) were paid. The money was to be thrown from the window of an Inter-City 125 train on receipt of orders by CB radio. The firm's representatives, with CB radio, were to be on the 8.40 p.m. train from St Pancras to Leeds on 24 and 25 April.

Scotland Yard were called in and, with the aid of regional crime squads, police were positioned at all stretches of the 194-mile route at which it was thought feasible for the money to be thrown. On the first night, nothing happened. On the second night, detectives posing as Gallagher executives on the train did receive the signal and threw out the bag – containing no money but with a message regarding further negotiations. This gave the police an idea of the area in which the collection was planned.

A further letter early in May specified a third run but this, like the first, proved to be a test run, and the radio order to throw out the bag was received the following night – just after the train pulled out of Nottingham. Police officers with night-vision equipment spotted two men, who were arrested and later jailed for four years each.

A MULTINATIONAL FOOD CORPORATION

The head office of a large multinational food corporation received a letter with a poisoned sample. The poison had been expertly introduced in such a way that inspection would be unlikely to detect evidence of tampering. The poison was lethal, colourless, odourless and tasteless, and there was no known antidote. The leader of the gang turned out to be a person with scientific qualifications. The ransom demand was for $20 million and there were indications also of political motivation.

The poisoned sample proved that the threat was credible and could not be ignored, but the corporation decided that at this stage the extortioner would not have risked letting any contaminated goods reach the public since this would at once destroy any hope he had of extorting a ransom. The public were therefore not informed and this decision was endorsed by the government and the police, who had been brought in from the start. It was agreed that negotiating decisions rested with the corporation but that government and police would be consulted throughout.

The corporation had had previous experience of product extortion and had a crisis management structure in being. The decision-maker was a senior executive with legal training and he called in heads of department and delegated responsibilities to them as appropriate, e.g. public relations and marketing. The IMT was an extension of the CMC and the negotiator reported direct to the decision-maker.

It was decided to negotiate with the intention of providing time and information in order to enable detection and arrest of the criminals.

Negotiation was used shrewdly to maintain a continuous threat assessment and to test the resolve and tenacity of the extortioner. He was made to produce a second sample and was provoked into blunders both in letters and telephone calls. Various strategems were used to impose delay, e.g. a request to change the telephone, for more time to collect cash, discussion of different currencies, etc. Great care was taken to keep the extortioner's financial hopes alive.

The media were successfully kept out of the incident and such leaks as there were had no serious effect. There was, however, a contingency plan for product recall and public warning on a massive scale (there were tens of thousands of retail outlets) in case the news broke or if for any other reason it seemed likely that the extortioner might release poisoned products on to the market, but in the event this proved unnecessary.

On the seventh day, exasperated by delaying tactics, the extortioner did place a poisoned sample in a retail store, unmarked, but notified its location. The sample was found before being sold and the store manager ingeniously found a way to withdraw his entire stock of that product from his shelves without attracting attention to it.

Thereafter the credibility of the threat declined as the extortioner appeared to lose his nerve. After three weeks, the media were on the scent and approached both the government and the company, who denied that any incident had taken place. The police had 400 plain-clothes officers deployed on surveillance duties. During the fourth week the extortioner was arrested in a call box while speaking to the negotiator. Search of his rooms revealed further phials of poison and he admitted his involvement. His two accomplices were also arrested.

His arrest was the signal for massive publicity on a pre-arranged plan by both the government and the corporation. The emphasis was on the success of the police in protecting the public and arresting the criminals, and on the corporation's policy of close cooperation with the police throughout.

JAPAN: 'THE 21-FACED MONSTER'

Following an unsuccessful attempt to kidnap the president of the Ezaki Glico confectionery company, for a ransom of Y1 billion ($6 million), the company received a letter in March 1984, threatening to poison its products in retail outlets. Products were removed from 600 stores and checked. A further letter was received saying that products had been injected with potassium cyanide and placed on shelves in western Japan, with a threat to contaminate products all round Japan if the ransom was not paid. It is believed that a payment was attempted but failed. Sales fell by 43 per cent in the first month with a loss to the company of $21 million; employees were laid off, and share prices fell before the extortioners announced that their campaign was over and that all poisoned products had been destroyed.

On 12 September 1984 the Morinaga confectionery company received a similar threat with a demand for Y100 million ($600 000). A payment was set up in cooperation with the police but no one came to collect it. On 24 September letters were sent to major newspapers publishing the same threat if the demand of Y100 million was not paid. On 8 October, further letters were sent to five major newspapers saying that 20 chocolates laced with cyanide had been placed in retail outlets and that a further 30 would be placed in ten days time. The extortioner called himself 'The 21-faced monster' (after an ancient Japanese children's fable). During the next week, 20 retail chains received letters warning them that if they did not remove Morinaga products from their shelves other products in their stores would be poisoned. Morinaga meanwhile declared that they would not deal with extortioners, that they would not pay a ransom and that they would not remove stocks from the shops. A number of poisoned products were found, however, and 870 stores withdrew Morinaga's products from their shelves. During October three more food companies were targeted and in January 1985 a group using the same name said that they would continue their campaign until they had collected Y1.3 billion ($8 million). In February three more companies were attacked by extortioners using the same name, scattering sweets laced with cyanide around the streets of two towns, all marked with a warning. Analysis of tapes of telephone calls indicated that the voice of one woman extortioner was the same as that in the Ezaki Glico case, and that a recorded child's voice had also been heard on a number of occasions.

The cost to Morinaga was enormous. By 11 October, the production of chocolates had been cut by 50 per cent and 450 workers had been laid off. Sales for the first two weeks of October were down 30 per cent – $6 million – from the previous year, and in the whole of October down 60 per cent – $24 million. By the end of the financial year they declared a loss of $15 million compared with a profit of $7 million the previous year and the president had to resign as his health had broken down.

The Japanese government did its best to help. At the end of October they offered financial assistance to Morinaga, announced that Morinaga products would be sold at 4000 local public offices, and asked 4 million civil servants to help the company.

As well as confectionery companies, other food and drink companies were also attacked – reportedly a total of 30 by the end of 1985. Some of these attacks smacked of 'copycats', some using the 21-faced-monster title and others not, and the professionalism also varied. A drinks manufacturer received an extortionary letter in September 1984 accompanied by a tissue soaked in cyanide, and set up a ransom delivery using counterfeit money, in cooperation with the police; the extortioner sent a taxi to pick it up and was arrested when it was handed over. Two other cases in January 1985 ended in arrests, the extortioners in one case turning out to be boys aged 10 and 13.

The more organized and expert extortions, however, have inflicted tremendous losses on the confectionery companies. They have been unusual in that the extortioners have sometimes published details of the contamination before receiving a ransom so the motive may have been partially or even wholly malice rather than financial gain. The cases do, however, illustrate the comparative ease with which small items of food and drink, sold in mass by tens of thousands of retail outlets, can be switched on the shelves for samples bought previously and poisoned. The only requirement is that the contaminator has no inhibitions about inflicting death, injury and terror indiscriminately on other human beings especially (in this case) on children. Although the fashion, and its success, encourages copycats amongst people similarly inclined, the public reaction it engenders is likely to provoke massive police response with public cooperation which, in the end, will be the most effective answer to the crime.

SUNSILK SHAMPOO: ANIMAL LIBERATION FRONT, UK

On Saturday 21 July 1984, the *Sunday Mirror* received a letter (with a supposedly identifying code word) stating that the ALF had planted bottles of Sunsilk shampoo contaminated with bleach on the shelves of Boots chemists' shops in Leeds, Southampton and London, and that the bottles were marked. The *Sunday Mirror* at once informed Boots, who have a well-practised crisis management system which enables the entire stock of any such item to be off the shelves at every branch in the country in a very short time.

The contaminated bottles in Leeds and Southampton were found very quickly. The ALF caller, however, had not said in which of the numerous Boots branches in London the contaminated bottles had been placed.

During the weekend, Boots representatives gave many radio interviews urging anyone who had recently bought Sunsilk shampoo in any of the three cities to return it. Realizing from the broadcasts that the bottle in London had not been located, a somewhat alarmed ALF spokesman telephoned anonymously on Sunday saying precisely where it was (in the Oxford Street branch) and it was found on Monday morning.

This case illustrates the value of having a crisis management structure in being and practised; and also the fear of most contaminators of the consequences – whether political or in terms of loss of the extortionary lever – of contaminated products getting prematurely into the hands of the public. There are exceptions (as described in Japan) but it is generally a factor to be taken into account by crisis managers.

MARS BARS: ANIMAL LIBERATION FRONT, UK

On Saturday 17 November 1984, an ALF caller, using the same code word as in the Sunsilk case, telephoned the *Sunday Mirror* stating that contaminated Mars bars had been placed on the shelves of retailers and that some of these (especially those in Boots) had no marking. The reason given for the attack was that Mars had given grants to Guys Hospital for research into tooth decay using monkeys. At the same time a Mars bar injected with rat poison was delivered to the *Sunday Mirror* and another to the BBC; these were, in the event, the only bars found to have been poisoned.

However, a number of bars bought by members of the public on Saturday, before any warning had been published, were found to have been tampered with. In each case a leaflet had been put inside the wrapper claiming that this and other bars had been poisoned. Some were eaten by children. A girl of 15 in Coventry ate her bar before discovering the note. Another family (of Mr Mark Phippen, a Dorset farm worker) bought three bars in Dorchester on the Saturday and two of these had been eaten by Mrs Phippen, their 14-year-old daughter, and their dog before Mr Phippen came home, some hours later. When he opened his bar he found the ALF leaflet inside. Mrs Phippen said that her daughter was 'absolutely petrified and just standing there shaking, waiting for something terrible to happen'.

A total of 20 bars which had been tampered with in this way were located or handed in to retailers in eight cites in England stretching from Leeds in the north-east to Plymouth in the south-west. Though clearly intended to give the impression of a large, coordinated operation, this was probably not the case. Having bought 22 bars and inserted the poison or leaflets, it would only have needed about 10 cell members, if that, to slip the leafleted bars on to the shelves of retail outlets in the eight cities and deliver the poisoned ones to the BBC and the *Sunday Mirror*.

On receipt of the warning, Mars put a recall procedure into effect and withdrew 3000 tons of Mars bars. The loss of sales was reported to be £15 million ($22.5 million) and of profit £2.8 million ($4.2 million).

On Monday 19 November, Ronnie Lee, described as the ALF press officer, stated publicly that the only bars poisoned had been those delivered to the *Sunday Mirror* and the BBC. On 29 November, in a by-lined article in the magazine *Time Out*, he complained that 'the authorities took an inordinately, and no doubt deliberately, long time to act' on the warnings and 'some unintended anxiety was therefore caused to the public'. He complained that the media's 'inaccurate and frenzied reporting . . . will no doubt have turned some people away from the animal rights campaign and against the ALF'. A spokesman was later quoted as saying that, even if 98 per cent of the public were alienated this did not matter; that those 98 per cent never did anything for animals, but that the other 2 per cent will have been inspired by the action and it was from those 2 per cent that activists would be recruited.

The terror of the child who thought she had eaten a poisoned bar, however, was symptomatic of the underlying threat which product contaminators of all kinds use to achieve their ends. It must be regarded as a form of terrorism.

As a postscript to this incident, there was an attempted product extortion against Mars in April 1985. A 25-year-old technician telephoned Mars threatening to contaminate their products unless they paid a ransom of £50 000. He claimed to be an animal rights activist but in fact he was not. Mars, in full cooperation with the police (who tapped the telephone) put an advertisement in the paper, as directed, indicating readiness to pay and followed delivery instructions with a holdall supposedly containing the money. The man was arrested while picking it up, admitted the offence and was sentenced to two years' imprisonment.

TYLENOL, USA

In October 1982, seven people died in the Chicago area and the deaths were quickly traced to cyanide-injected capsules of Tylenol, the top-selling pain-killing drug in the USA, manufactured by a subsidiary of Johnson and Johnson. Although a man was later arrested and convicted for demanding $1 million with menaces linked to the crime, the police did not consider that he was responsible for the original contamination, which appears to have been malicious rather than extortionary.

The manufacturers of Tylenol at once recalled all stocks from retailers and every possible channel was used to warn the public to return them too. Tylenol was distributed through about 100 distributors to about 11 000 retailers. In the event, no contaminated samples were found outside the Chicago area. Examination proved that the poisoning had been done after the capsules had reached retail outlets, not during manufacture.

The recall of Tylenol stocks cost about $100 million and it was estimated that the loss of sales over the next year was $400 million. Johnson and Johnson considered that to discontinue manufacture of Tylenol or to change its name would give the contaminators the reward they wanted so they decided, courageously, to attempt to regain its market share. This was coupled with an improved anti-tampering package, and a major public relations campaign costing $100 million was launched to restore public confidence. In this they were helped by widespread public sympathy and admiration for the way in which they had handled the crisis. By 1984 they estimated that they had regained 90 per cent of their market share.

In February 1986 an eighth victim, 23-year-old Diane Elsroth, died from a Tylenol capsule laced with cyanide, and Johnson and Johnson reluctantly decided to withdraw all medication in capsule form for over-the-counter sales as they were too difficult to protect in that environment.

After this, the inevitable copycats got to work. In May 1986 a man died after taking a cyanide-laced Anacin capsule and two more people died in June 1986 after taking cyanide-laced Exedrin capsules.

It may be that, as in the comment quoted about animal rights activists at the end of Chapter 6, those who killed these 11 people were motivated by a hatred of human beings. Otherwise it must be assumed that, again like the animal rights activists in the Sunsilk and Mars cases, their aim was to do the maximum economic damage to the corporations which manufacture Tylenol, Anacin and Exedrin, in this case with the intent to kill members of the public indiscriminately to that end. Cases like these are different in character from the product *extortion* cases described earlier in this chapter, where the threat is of certain action or damaging publicity unless a ransom is paid. Management is faced with quite different decisions in the two types of case (see Chapter 10). Whatever the motive, however, all these cases illustrate the vulnerability of consumer products to malicious contamination in retail outlets and to the need to tighten the law to protect both corporations and the public and to facilitate the arrest and conviction of the killers – the only effective deterrent.

Part IV
Conclusions

20 Conclusions

THE THREAT

Kidnapping and extortion have grown and will go on growing, as they give a high yield at a low risk both to criminals and political terrorists; also because technological developments are making it more difficult to obtain large amounts of money by robbery than by drug trafficking, computer fraud and extortion by threats to life.

Targets have been steadily switching from government to business and especially to both expatriate and local businessmen in high-risk areas. Threats or attacks against tourists as a means of hitting the economy have also grown. So have 'anti-development abductions' of expatriate workers, mainly in African and Middle Eastern countries, for the same purpose. The highest kidnap risks are concentrated in Colombia, Italy, Guatemala, Peru and Lebanon.

Contamination or threatened contamination of consumer products is easy to do but as a medium of extortion has a poor record of success. The price of publicity to manufacturers and retailers, however, can be so high that there is a strong temptation to hush cases up, and many cases go unreported. A fashionable variant, without the extortion element, is by animal rights activists intent on doing economic damage, and they are showing a disturbing readiness to put human lives at risk. This, however, has an adverse effect on public opinion and on most of the more responsible animal welfare organizations.

Most abductions and contaminations are by criminals, ranging from loners to international criminal networks. Some, however, are carried out by political terrorists, who may use money to finance their campaigns, and also in the hope of driving multinational investment and trade out of their countries.

Hostage seizure in known locations (such as embassies) is a province of political terrorists rather than criminals (except by misadventure). Aircraft hijacking is the most spectacular form of hostage-taking but has been controlled by good security in most airports and is, in fact, a lower risk than is generally thought. Out of 10 million take-offs a year only one in 500 000 is hijacked and, in the worst year to date (1985) out of 1000 million passengers, 68 were killed in hijacks, 57 of them in a single rescue which went wrong. This is minute compared with the risks from other hazards such as road travel and other forms of crime.

THE RESPONSE

Terrorist risks, like fire risks, can be reduced or transferred. Risk management consists of assessing the risks and the cost of the damage they could do; calculating the cost of reducing them (in terms of money, inconvenience, staff morale, etc.) or transferring them (by insurance); deciding how much to spend; implementing a security plan; and preparing contingency plans for crisis management in case, despite better security, an incident does occur.

One hundred per cent protection at work, home or travelling is not practicable. Concentric rings of security, however, can each provide warning and delay and, coupled with a manifestly positive attitude, are likely to deter selection as a target – particularly if the would-be attacker perceives a high risk of getting caught.

The highest risk of abduction is when travelling, especially on the road on routine journeys (e.g. between home and work) and as a visitor to high-risk areas. Inadequate bodyguarding can do more harm than good. For most people, the best protection lies in keeping a low profile and avoiding predictable movements and programmes.

The ordeal of a hostage is a severe one, and is best endured by those who have psychologically prepared themselves for it. Three hostages who survived a prolonged ordeal, Sir Geoffrey Jackson, William Niehous and Leon Don Richardson, have written full and moving accounts of it themselves, which are listed in the bibliography.

Hostages in hijacked aircraft have little or no control over their own fate. They can best assist a satisfactory outcome and contribute to their own survival if they avoid being either aggressive or hysterical, and try to be as inconspicuous as possible.

The laws of the land can play a positive and negative role in helping people to handle kidnap and extortion. Helpful laws include control of firearms and explosives; and laws to facilitate intelligence, detection and conviction, including laws to prevent intimidation of witnesses and juries. The dilemma lies in reconciling protection with civil liberties, but 'freedom' to kill must never override the right to live.

Laws which attempt to inhibit negotiation and prevent the payment of ransoms are almost invariably counter-productive. Governments can and should refuse to be blackmailed into releasing convicted terrorists. They often also refuse to pay ransoms to criminals or terrorists, but it is unrealistic to expect corporations or families to do the same. If the law forbids a father to pay a ransom for his daughter he will settle as best he can behind the backs of the police rather than let her die. This results in the worst of all worlds – bigger ransoms paid quickly but with the police denied the necessary time and information for detection and conviction of the kidnappers. Countries like Italy or Argentina which used to ban ransoms had a low rate of conviction. Countries like the UK and the USA, where the police give first priority to helping the firm or family to negotiate and recover the hostage have achieved a high rate of conviction and recovery of the money.

Banning of kidnap and ransom insurance is equally counter-productive. The Lloyd's syndicate handling the bulk of such insurance worldwide makes its policies conditional on cooperation with the police; they also provide consultants (like fire surveyors) who advise on reducing the risk and on handling the crisis if it occurs. Banning insurance would merely drive people to place their insurance (and pay ransoms) in countries and with insurers who neither require police involvement nor offer professional risk management advice. This, like laws to ban ransoms, would again encourage settlements behind the backs of the police, resulting in quicker payments of larger ransoms and fewer convictions.

The media, like the law, can play a positive or negative role. They will often accept a request for a news blackout if they are persuaded that lives are at risk. Positive public relations are a key factor in crisis management.

CONTINGENCY PLANNING AND CRISIS MANAGEMENT

A crisis in which lives or large assets are at risk can dominate management time. The aim of contingency planning and crisis management is therefore to save lives and preserve assets with minimum disruption of commercial operations.

Contingency planning should be made by the committee or team which will handle a crisis if it occurs and the first step is to set up such teams at every level (in the case of a large and dispersed corporation). Legal, security, financial, personnel and PR departments will be represented and, in the case of a corporate headquarters, a full-time coordinator should be earmarked in readiness to prevent undue load on others should a crisis occur. Another key figure in whatever headquarters is handling the actual crisis on the ground (corporate or subsidiary) will be the negotiator who needs very special qualities.

Since a firm or family facing a kidnap or extortion crisis is usually doing so for the first time, an experienced consultant will be as valuable in planning for and handling a kidnap or extortion crisis as a good doctor or lawyer is in a medical or legal crisis.

Both in contingency planning and crisis management, cooperation with the police is essential because, without it, the extortioners will not be subjected to the pressure during negotiation which leads to successful resolution of the crisis. In countries where the police are corrupt or unreliable, contact should first be made (if necessary with the advice of the embassy) with a senior officer known to be trustworthy and, through him, with others for whom he will personally vouch. This has worked well in even the most corrupt of countries.

Legal liabilities must be borne in mind at every stage of planning and crisis management. A corporation in a kidnap or extortion crisis may later be sued by the hostage, his family, stockholders, trading partners or joint venture partners.

The importance of public relations was discussed earlier. In this and other respects, particular care and understanding will be needed in dealing with the family of a hostage, both for compassionate and practical reasons. A wife at the end of her tether can do great damage to the handling of a crisis, and kidnappers may subtly provoke or encourage her to do so.

The crisis management organization – and security plans – should regularly be practised and tested by simulation exercises.

The art of negotiation with an extortioner lies in seeing the crisis through his eyes. Above all, he should always be led to realize that there are potential financial advantages in continuing negotiation. This is usually so, because he will lose the value of his main bargaining counter if he kills his hostage, releases poisoned products on the public or blows the threat of publicising the contamination. Provided that there is cooperation with the police, their increasing pressure will unnerve him and they will have an ever-increasing chance of detecting and convicting him. A high prospect of detection and conviction is the most effective of all deterrents.

Finally, every major crime, including, kidnap, hijack, bombing or other forms of extortion, whether by criminals or political terrorists, is preceded by detailed reconnaissance and surveillance, usually lasting several weeks or months. If their surveillance reveals an alert and positive attitude to security they will usually turn away and seek a softer target.

Bibliography

Alexander, Y. and Kilmarx, R. A., *Political Terrorism and Business* (New York, Praeger, 1979).

Becker, Jillian, *Hitler's Children* (London, Granada, 1978).

Beckwith, Charlie, *et al.*, *Delta Force* (New York, Harcourt Brace Jovanovich, 1983).

Bolz, Frank, *et al.*, *Hostage Cop* (New York, Rawson Wade, 1979).

Boulton, David, *The Making of Tania Hearst* (London, New English Library, 1975).

'Chronology: Euroterrorist Actions 1984–April 1985', in *TVI Journal*, Spring 1985.

Clutterbuck, Richard, *Guerrilla and Terrorists* (Chicago and London, Ohio University Press, 1980).

Clutterbuck, Richard, *The Media and Political Violence* (London, Macmillan, 1983).

Clutterbuck, Richard, *The Future of Political Violence* (London, Macmillan, 1986).

Cline, R. S. and Alexander, Y., *State Sponsored Terrorism* (Washington DC, US government, 1985).

Cole, Richard, B., *Executive Security* (New York, John Wiley, 1980).

Congressional Committee Staff Study, *Political Kidnappings 1968–73* (Washington DC, 1973).

Cramer, Chris, and Harris, Sim, *Hostage* (London, John Clare, 1982).

Creliston, R. D., and Szabo, D., *Hostage-Taking* (Lexington, D.C. Heath, 1979).

Dobson, Christopher, and Payne, Ronald, *Terror! The West Fights Back* (London, Macmillan, 1982).

Dobson, Christopher, and Payne, Ronald, *War Without End* (London, Harrap, 1986).

Eichelman, B., *et al.*, *Terrorism* (Washington DC, American Psychiatric Association, 1983).

Evans, Alona, and Murphy, John, *Legal Aspects of International Terrorism* (Lexington, D.C. Heath, 1978).

Federal Bureau of Investigation, *Crisis Reaction Seminar – February 8–12, 1982* (Washington DC, FBI, 1982).

Francis, Dick, *The Danger* (London, Pan, 1983).

Goren, Roberta, *The Soviet Union and Terrorism* (London, Allen and Unwin, 1984).

Hamilton, Peter, *Espionage, Terrorism and Subversion in an Industrial Society* (London, Peter Heims, 1979).

Herz, Martin F. (ed.), *Diplomats and Terrorists: What Works, What Doesn't* (Washington DC, Georgetown University, 1982).

Hoffman, Bruce, *Commando Raids, 1946–83* (Santa Monica, Rand Corporation, 1985).

Hoffman, Bruce, *Terrorism in the US During 1985* (Santa Monica, Rand Corporation, 1986).

Hoffman, Bruce, *Terrorism in the US and the Potential Threat to Nuclear Facilities* (Santa Monica, Rand Corporation, 1986).

Hooper, Alan, *The Military and the Media* (Aldershot, Gower, 1982).

Jackson, Geoffrey, *People's Prison* (London, Faber 1973); also published as *Surviving the Long Night* (New York, Vanguard, 1974).

Janke, Peter, *Guerrilla and Terrorist Organizations: A World Directory and Bibliography* (Brighton, Harvester Press, 1983).

Jenkins, Brian M., *Terrorism and Beyond* (Santa Monica, Rand Corporation, 1983).

Jenkins, Brian M., (ed.) *Terrorism and Personal Protection* (Boston and London, Butterworths, 1985).

Jenkins, Brian M., Pamphlets published by the Rand Corporation, Santa Monica:

   Should Corporations be Prevented from Paying Ransoms? (1974); *Will Terrorism Go Nuclear?* (1975); *Hostage Survival: Some Preliminary Observations* (1976); *Embassies under Siege* (1981); *Diplomats on the Front Line* (1982); *Intelligence Constraints and Domestic Terrorism: Executive Summary* (1982); *Talking to Terrorists* (1982); *New Modes of Conflict* (1983); *Some Reflections on Recent Trends in Terrorism* (1983); *Subnational Conflict in the Mediterranean Region* (1983); *Combatting Terrorism becomes a War* (1984); *The Lessons of Beirut: Testimony before the Long Commission* (1984). See also titles by Hoffman and Purnell.

Knowles, Graham, *Bomb Security Guide* (Boston and London, Butterworths, 1976).

Koch, P. and Hermann, K., *Assault on Mogadishu* (London, Corgi, 1977).

Livingstone, Neil, *The War Against Terrorism* (Lexington, D.C. Heath, 1982).

Mackenzie, G. *et al.*, *The Security Handbook* (Capetown, Flesch, 1983).

Mark, Robert, *Policing a Perplexed Society* (London, Allen and Unwin, 1977).

Mark, Robert, *In the Office of Constable* (London, Collins, 1978).

Miller, Abraham, *Terrorism and Hostage Negotiations* (Boulder, Colorado, Westview, 1980).

Moore, Kenneth, *Airport, Aircraft and Airline Security* (Los Angeles, Security World, 1976).

Moorhead, Caroline, *Fortune's Hostages* (London, Hamish Hamilton, 1979), also published as *Hostages to Fortune* (New York, Atheneum, 1980).

Netanyahu, Benjamin (ed.) *International Terrorism: Challenge and Response* (Jerusalem, Jonathan Institute, 1980).

Netanyahu, Benjamin (ed.) *Terrorism: How the West Can Win* (London, Weidenfeld and Nicolson, 1986).

Niehous, William F., 'How to Survive as a Hostage', in Martin Herz (ed.) *Diplomats and Terrorists: What Works, What Doesn't* (Washington DC, Georgetown University 1982); also in Brian Jenkins (ed.) *Terrorism and Personal Protection* (Boston and London, Butterworths, 1985).

Nelson, Barry, 'Kidnapped!', in *Canadian Business*, June 1983.
Observer, The, *Siege: Six Days at the Iranian Embassy* (London, Macmillan, 1980).
Ofer, Yehudi, *Operation Thunder: The Entebbe Raid* (Harmondsworth, Penguin, 1976).
Passow, Sam, 'Terrorism and Corporate Liability', in *TVI Journal*, Fall 1984.
'Piracy', in *Navy International*, March 1986.
Pisano, Vittorfranco, *Terrorism – The Italian Case* (Gaithersburg, Maryland, International Association of Chiefs of Police, Clandestine Tactics and Technology, 1984).
Purnell, Susanna, and Wainstein, Eleanor, *The Problems of US Businesses Operating Abroad in Terrorist Environments* (Santa Monica, Rand Corporation, 1981).
Richardson, Leon D. *et al.*, 'Surviving Captivity: A Hundred Days' and 'The Richardson Negotiations', in Brian Jenkins, (ed.) *Terrorism and Personal Protection* (Boston and London, Butterworths, 1985).
Sater, William, 'Violence and the Puerto Rican Separatist Movement', in *TVI Journal*, Summer 1984.
Seymour, Gerald, *Red Fox* (London, Collins, 1979).
Simon, Jeffrey D., 'Global Perspective: The Year of the Terrorist', in *TVI Report*, Winter 1986.
Sterling, Claire, *The Terror Network* (London, Weidenfeld and Nicolson, 1981).
'Terrorism in the Year 2000', in *TVI Report*, Fall 1985.
US Department of State, *Terrorist Attacks against Diplomats* (Washington DC, 1981).
US Vice President's Task Force, *Public Report on Combatting Terrorism* (Washington DC, 1986).
Villar, R. G., *Piracy Today* (1985), cited in *Navy International*, March 1986.
Wardlaw, Grant, *Political Terrorism* (Cambridge University Press, 1982).
Wilkinson, Paul, *Terrorism and the Liberal State* (London, Macmillan, 1986).
Wolf, John B., *Fear of Fear* (New York and London, Plenum Press, 1981).
Yallop, H. J., *Protection against Terrorism* (London, Barry Rose, 1980).

Index

Where acronyms are shown in the list of abbreviations (pp. xvii–xix), the acronym rather than the full title is normally used in this index.